PENGUIN EDUCATION

PENGUIN ENGLISH POETS
GENERAL EDITOR: CHRISTOPHER RICKS

Andrew Marvell
The Complete Poems

EDITED BY ELIZABETH STORY DONNO

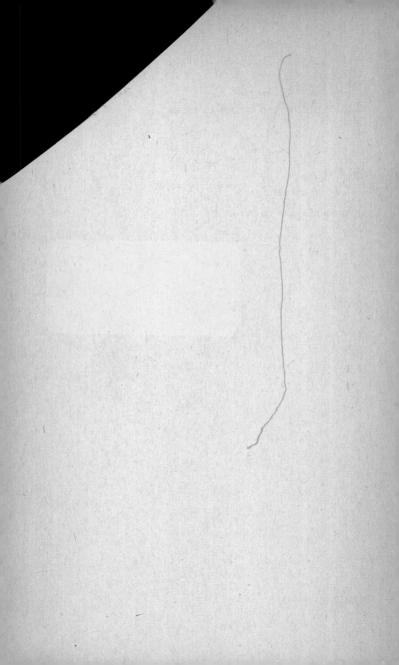

Andrew Marvell
The Complete Poems

EDITED BY ELIZABETH STORY DONNO

PENGUIN BOOKS

Penguin Books Ltd, Harmondsworth,
Middlesex, England
Penguin Books Inc, 7110 Ambassador Road,
Baltimore, Md 21207, USA.
Penguin Books Australia Ltd,
Ringwood, Victoria, Australia

First published 1972
Introduction and notes copyright © Elizabeth Story Donno, 1972

Made and printed in Great Britain by
Hazell Watson & Viney Ltd
Aylesbury, Bucks
Set in Monotype Ehrhardt

Contents

Preface

Determining the authenticity of the canon and the texts of Marvell's poetry – lyrical and satirical – offers a number of problems in that few of his poems were published during his lifetime and fewer still were acknowledged. Most of the lyrical poetry, two of the early satires, and two of the Cromwell poems were not printed until the appearance of the Folio edition in 1681. This posthumous edition, prepared from papers still in the possession of his purported wife Mary Marvell, lacks the textual authority that would have obtained had the poet arranged for its publication and seen the volume through the press. Nonetheless, it was the single means by which the bulk of Marvell's poetry was preserved though the three major Cromwell poems were cancelled from nearly all the copies.

The second important edition was that of Captain Edward Thompson which appeared in 1776 in three volumes and included both the poetry and the prose. After most of the text had been printed off, Thompson obtained a copy of a 'manuscript volume' of the poetry belonging to descendants of the poet's 'beloved' nephew William Popple. This enabled him to print the three Cromwell poems – then generally unknown and subsequently questioned – in the Addenda to volume 3. (He also printed much that was not Marvell's in the Preface to volume 1.) Long believed to have been lost, the Popple manuscript was acquired by the Bodleian Library in 1944 where it is catalogued as *Eng. poet. d. 49.* Consisting of the printed sheets of the Folio with manuscript additions, the first part of this manuscript volume not only has corrections to the printed poems in a contemporary hand, but also has copies in the same hand of the three cancelled poems on Cromwell[1]. It is thus a valuable adjunct to the Folio.

For the later poems – the post-Restoration satires – the problem

1. A comparison of the texts of the three Cromwell poems in the edition

of attribution is particularly acute since no one of them appears in the Folio. While the second part of *Eng. poet. d. 49* (128 pages) has eighteen satires in manuscript, many of these clearly are not of the poet's composition though they may indeed have been found among his papers. Two, in fact, are crossed out and ascribed to his good friend 'Mr Aylof', in a hand (perhaps Popple's) which is different from that of the copyist. Others were questioned by H. M. Margoliouth in his edition of Marvell's poems and letters (1927, 1952),[1] and still others have been questioned by later scholars. Regrettably, *Eng. poet. d. 49* does not provide conclusive evidence for the canon of Marvell's later poetry. Often the earliest printing of those satires at one time or another ascribed to him appears in one or other of the many editions of *Poems on Affairs of State*, a collection which was first published in 1689 (eleven years after the poet's death) and which continued to be issued through 1716. With the edition of 1697, the number of ascriptions was increased, the compilers apparently recognizing Marvell's appeal as satirist and patriot.

Lacking proof of his authorship for these poems and acknowledging that attributions made solely on stylistic or ideological grounds are uncertain at best and particularly uncertain in the case of the satires, I have adhered to the following rationale in attempting to determine their authenticity: firstly, the satire must have been included in *Eng. poet. d. 49* and secondly, it must have been attributed to him in one of the several parts of the *Poems on Affairs of State* appearing in 1689, that is, in one of the earliest published collections. (To some degree my inclusion of *The Loyal Scot* departs from this rationale.)

---

published by Thompson with those in *Eng. poet. d. 49* demonstrates conclusively that he derived his copy from this manuscript. (See the textual notes to these poems.) Furthermore, comments he inserted in the second part of the manuscript are signed and/or dated (e.g., 'E. Thompson. 1775.').

1. A third revision, by Pierre Legouis and E. E. Duncan-Jones, appeared while this edition was in press. M. Legouis has added to the number of textual variants, including those from *Eng. poet. d. 49*, along with spelling variants from that manuscript. He states (p. 235) that the 'conflicting impressions made by the English and the Latin corrections invite us to suspend judgement until fresh evidence turns up.' It is to be hoped that the textual notes included in this edition will make any further suspension of judgement unnecessary. References to Margoliouth in the notes are keyed to his second revision.

The poems are arranged in chronological order in so far as this can be ascertained. As a general rule the copy-text is that of the first printing. Otherwise, as in the case of the two post-Restoration satires published a good many years after Marvell's death, it is *Eng. poet. d. 49*, for the use of which I wish to acknowledge the kind permission of the Curator of Western Manuscripts.

For poems first published in the Folio, I have adopted some sixty-odd corrections in *Eng. poet. d. 49*, the overwhelming majority of them scarcely debatable since they pick up obvious errors. Nonetheless, one may question the degree of authority for these changes introduced into a copy of the Folio and for the manuscript versions of the three Cromwell poems. Since the volume belonged to Marvell's favourite nephew William Popple, we may assume that he had copies of some of his uncle's poems, and thus a number of corrections would be accounted for. But it seems unlikely that he would have had manuscripts of all of them, and thus I do not believe that we can rely on *Eng. poet. d. 49* to provide us with the *desideratum*, an authorially authorized version for every poem in the canon of Marvell's poetry, any more than we can rely on the Folio.

In the case of a poet whose works circulated in manuscript and who did not arrange for their publication, a contemporary manuscript may provide readings superior to those appearing in the published version. An instance, in my opinion, is the long poem (402 lines) on *The First Anniversary of the Government under His Highness the Lord Protector*. First published anonymously in 1655, it was then reprinted in the Folio from the original quarto and copied in *Eng. poet. d. 49* either from the quarto or from the Folio since (apart from having correct readings of the obvious errors that appear in the Folio but not in the quarto) it differs from both of them only in three instances, and these quite clearly represent slips of the copyist. There is, however, another manuscript version of the poem in the Bodleian Library which has been dated *circa* 1681. Though it gives a number of indifferent readings (e.g. *doth* for *does*), omits eight lines, and ascribes the poem to Edmund Waller, it does afford readings superior to those of the original publication in several instances. Given then the realities applying to manuscript circulation and non-authorial publication, we must acknowledge, I think, the impossibility of establishing the texts of Marvell's poetry with absolute certainty.

For the poems first published in the Folio, there are two instances in which I do not adopt the corrections of *Eng. poet. d. 49*. They are in *Eyes and Tears* (where 'teeming' in l. 35 is changed to 'seeming', a dubious reading) and in the *Dialogue between the Soul and Body* (where I retain the last four lines of the poem as printed though they have been marked for deletion there). Among the corrections adopted, those affecting *To His Coy Mistress* may well excite reaction, but I hope the evidence given in the notes, particularly as regards the famous crux in ll. 33–4, will provide justification.

Additional justification for reliance on *Eng. poet. d. 49* rests on three instances where complete lines have been substituted for the Folio readings. These appear in two of Marvell's Latin poems and in a translation from Latin, a situation strongly suggesting that they do indeed represent the poet's second thoughts rather than a corrector's attempt to 'improve' the texts. In any case, no such extensive departures from the Folio are to be found among the corrections to the English poems, though, as J. B. Leishman observed, little skill would be required to improve on some of their awkward but very typical inversions. Furthermore, if we are to accept as Marvell's the third long poem on Cromwell (*A Poem upon the Death of His Late Highness the Lord Protector*) – and the appearance of the first 148 lines in the uncancelled copy of the Folio at the British Museum surely justifies this – we must have recourse to *Eng. poet. d. 49* for the full text or rely (as Margoliouth of necessity did) on Thompson's edition of 1776, which, as Thompson stated and as my textual notes show, derived from that manuscript.

The orthography of the poems is modernized, but I have retained the punctuation of the early printing or of the manuscript whenever it did not prove misleading. For the Greek and Latin poems, the modern translations provided are those of William A. McQueen and Kiffin A. Rockwell; I wish to extend my thanks to the University of North Carolina Press for permission to reprint them; also to the Henry E. Huntington Library for a fellowship permitting me to work on Marvell and for their unbounded courtesy.

Table of Dates

1657   *May–August* writes *On the Victory Obtained by Blake*,
        anonymously published (in part) in 1674.
        September appointed Latin Secretary to the Council
        of State, with a stipend (like Milton) of £200.
        November writes *Two Songs at the Marriage of the
        Lord Fauconberg and Lady Mary Cromwell*.

1658   *September–November* writes *A Poem upon the Death of
        His Highness the Lord Protector*.

1659   *January* elected MP for Hull, a position he held for
        nearly twenty years.

1660   Attends his first parliament; exchanges blows in the
        House with Thomas Clifford.

1662–3 In Holland for eleven months.

1663–5 *July* accompanies the Earl of Carlisle on an embassy to
        Russia, Sweden, and Denmark in the capacity of
        Secretary.

1665   *January* returns to England.

1667   *August–September* writes *The Last Instructions to a
        Painter*; its earliest (extant) publication seems to have
        been 1689.

1669–70 Writes *The Loyal Scot*.

1671   After *May* writes, if it is by Marvell, the epigram in
        Latin and English on Blood's stealing the crown.

1671–2 Submits in competition Latin epigrams for an
        inscription on the Louvre.

1672   Autumn *The Rehearsal Transprosed* published
        anonymously (against Samuel Parker, Archdeacon of
        Canterbury).

1673   Winter publishes under his name *The Rehearsal
        Transposed, The Second Part*.
        Collaborates during this time with a 'Dutch Fifth
        Column' under the code name of 'Mr Thomas'.

1674   Summer writes the commendatory poem for the
        second edition of *Paradise Lost* (entered 6 July).

1676   June publishes *Mr Smirk: Or the Divine in Mode* with *A Short Historical Essay Concerning General Councils, Creeds, and Imposition in Religion* under the name Andreas Rivetus, Jr.

1677   Lodges two bankrupt relatives in a house taken in the name of his housekeeper Mary Palmer.
An Account of the Growth of Popery and Arbitrary Government published anonymously.

1678   A reward offered by the *London-Gazette* for information as to the author or printer of *An Account of the Growth of Popery*.
Remarks upon a Late Disingenuous Discourse Writ by One T.D. . . . . By a Protestant (Defence of John Howe) licensed *April*.
16 August dies of a tertian ague.

1681   *Miscellaneous Poems* – 'By Andrew Marvell, Esq; Late Member of the Honourable House of Commons. London, Printed for Robert Boulter'.

Further Reading

EDITIONS

Andrew Marvell, *Miscellaneous Poems*, London, 1681.

Thomas Cooke, *The Works of Andrew Marvell*, 2 vols., London, 1726, reissued 1772.

Edward Thompson, *The Works of Andrew Marvell*, 3 vols., London, 1776.

A. B. Grosart, *The Complete Works of Andrew Marvell*, 4 vols., privately printed, 1872–5 (the only available collection of the prose works).

H. M. Margoliouth, *The Poems and Letters of Andrew Marvell*, 2 vols., Oxford University Press, 1927; 2nd edn, 1952 (invaluable for notes on the authenticity of the later satires and for annotations), 3rd edn, 1972.

Hugh Macdonald, *The Poems of Andrew Marvell*, Routledge & Kegan Paul, 2nd edn, 1956 (excludes the post-Restoration satires).

George de F. Lord, *Poems on Affairs of State: Augustan Satirical Verse, 1660–1714*, vol. I, 1660–78, Yale University Press, 1963.

William A. McQueen and Kiffin A. Rockwell, *The Latin Poetry of Andrew Marvell*, University of North Carolina Press, 1964.

Frank Kermode, *The Selected Poetry of Marvell*, Signet Classics, 1967.

George de F. Lord, *Andrew Marvell. Complete Poetry*, Modern Library College Editions, 1968.

D. I. B. Smith, *Andrew Marvell. The Rehearsal Transpros'd and The Rehearsal Transpros'd. The Second Part*, Oxford University Press, 1971.

BIBLIOGRAPHY

W. A. Abbott, *The Writing and Speeches of Oliver Cromwell*, 4 vols., Harvard University Press, 1937.

Arthur E. Case, *A Bibliography of English Poetical Miscellanies, 1521–1750*, Oxford University Press, 1935.

M. Crum, *First-Line Index of English Poetry, 1500–1800 in Manuscripts of the Bodleian Library*, 2 vols., Oxford University Press, 1969.

Dennis G. Donovan, *Andrew Marvell 1927–1967*, Elizabethan Bibliographies Supplements, The Nether Press, 1969.

Flagellum Parliamentarium, Aungervyle Society Reprints, First Series, Edinburgh, 1881.

Ephim G. Fogel, 'The Case for Internal Evidence. Salmons in Both, or Some Caveats for Canonical Scholars', *Bulletin of the New York Public Library* LXIII (1959), 223–36, 292–308. Reprinted David Erdman and Ephim G. Fogel, *Evidence for Authorship*, Cornell University Press, 1966.

George de F. Lord, 'The Case for Internal Evidence. Two New Poems by Marvell?', *Bulletin of the New York Public Library*, LXII (1958) 551–70. Reprinted in Erdman and Fogel, *Evidence for Authorship*).

George de F. Lord, 'The Case for Internal Evidence. Comments on the Canonical Caveat', *Bulletin of the New York Public Library* LXIII (1959), 355–66. (Reprinted in Erdman and Fogel, *Evidence for Authorship*).

Hugh Macdonald, 'Andrew Marvell's *Miscellaneous Poems, 1681*' *Times Literary Supplement*, 13 July 1951, 444 (on *Bod. MS. Eng. poet. d.* 49).

M. T. Osborne, *Advice-to-a-Painter Poems, 1633–1856*, University of Texas, 1949.

Caroline Robbins, *The Diary of John Milward*, Cambridge University Press, 1938.

M. P. Tilley, *A Dictionary of the Proverbs in England*, University of Michigan Press, 1950.

STUDIES OF MARVELL

Carl E. Bain, 'The Latin Poetry of Andrew Marvell', *Philological Quarterly* XXXVIII (1959), 436–49.

Ann E. Berthoff, *The Resolved Soul*, Princeton University Press, 1970.

F. W. Bradbrook, 'The Poetry of Andrew Marvell', *From Donne to Marvell*, ed. B. Ford, The Pelican Guide to English Literature, Penguin Books, 1956, pp. 193–204.

M. C. Bradbrook and M. G. Lloyd Thomas, *Andrew Marvell*, Cambridge University Press, 1940.

John Carey, ed., *Andrew Marvell*, Critical Anthologies, Penguin Books, 1969 (selection of contemporaneous and modern criticism).

Rosalie Colie, '*My Echoing Song*', Princeton University Press, 1970.

Robert Ellrodt, *Les Poètes Métaphysiques*, Paris, 1960.

Donald M. Friedman, *Marvell's Pastoral Art*, University of California Press, 1970.

Pierre Legouis, *André Marvell, Poète, Puritain, Patriote*, Oxford University Press, 1928. Revised and abridged English version, *Andrew Marvell, Poet, Puritan, Patriot*, 1965.

J. B. Leishman, *The Art of Marvell's Poetry*, London, 1966.

Earl Miner, 'The Death of Innocence in Marvell's *Nymph Complaining for the Death of Her Faun*', *Modern Philology*, LXV (1967), 9–16.

Maren-Sofie Røstvig, *The Happy Man: Studies in the Metamorphosis of a Classical Ideal, 1600–1700*, Oxford University Press, 1954, pp. 152–91, 234–66.

Maren-Sofie Røstvig, 'Andrew Marvell and the Caroline Poets', *English Poetry and Prose 1540–1674*, Sphere History of Literature in the English Language, vol. II, ed. Christopher Ricks, 1970, pp. 206–48.

Harold E. Toliver, *Marvell's Ironic Vision*, Yale University Press, 1965.

Rosemond Tuve, *Elizabethan and Metaphysical Imagery*, Chicago University Press, 1947.

John M. Wallace, *Destiny His Choice: The Loyalism of Andrew Marvell*, Cambridge University Press, 1968.

Michael Wilding, ed., *Marvell: Modern Judgements*, Macmillan, 1969 (a collection of recent criticism).

A Dialogue between Thyrsis and Dorinda

DORINDA
When death shall part us from these kids,
And shut up our divided lids,
Tell me, Thyrsis, prithee do,
Whither thou and I must go.

THYRSIS
To the Elysium.

DORINDA
           Oh, where is't?

THYRSIS
A chaste soul can never miss't.

DORINDA
I know no way but to our home,
Is our cell Elysium?

THYRSIS
Turn thine eye to yonder sky,
There the milky way doth lie;
'Tis a sure but rugged way,
That leads to everlasting day.

DORINDA
There birds may nest, but how can I
That have no wings and cannot fly?

THYRSIS
Do not sigh, fair nymph, for fire
Hath no wings yet doth aspire
Till it hit against the Pole:
Heaven's the centre of the soul.

DORINDA
But in Elysium how do they
Pass eternity away?

THYRSIS
Oh, there's neither hope nor fear,
There's no wolf, no fox, no bear.
No need of dog to fetch our stray,
Our Lightfoot we may give away;
No oat-pipe's needful; there thy ears
May sleep with music of the spheres.

DORINDA
Oh sweet! Oh sweet! How I my future state
By silent thinking antedate:
I prithee let us spend our time to come
30 In talking of Elysium.

THYRSIS
Then I'll go on. There sheep are full
Of sweetest grass and softest wool;
There birds sing consorts, garlands grow,
Cool winds do whisper, springs do flow.
There always is a rising sun,
And day is ever but begun.
Shepherds there bear equal sway,
And every nymph's a Queen of May.

DORINDA
Ah me, ah me!

THYRSIS
                    Dorinda, why dost cry?

DORINDA
40 I'm sick, I'm sick, and fain would die.
Convince me now that this is true
By bidding with me all adieu.

THYRSIS
I cannot live without thee, I,
I'll for thee, much more with thee, die.

CHORUS
Then let us give Corillo charge o' the sheep,
And thou and I'll pick poppies, and them steep
In wine, and drink on't even till we weep,
So shall we smoothly pass away in sleep.

Clorinda and Damon

c. Damon, come drive thy flocks this way.
d. No, 'tis too late; they went astray.
c. I have a grassy scutcheon spied,
   Where Flora blazons all her pride.
   The grass I aim to feast thy sheep:
   The flowers I for thy temples keep.
d. Grass withers; and the flowers too fade.
c. Seize the short joys then, ere they vade,
   Seest thou that unfrequented cave?
d. That den?
c.   Love's Shrine.
10 d.   But virtue's grave.
c. In whose cool bosom we may lie
   Safe from the sun.
d.   Not heaven's eye.
c. Near this, a fountain's liquid bell
   Tinkles within the concave shell.
d. Might a soul bathe there and be clean,
   Or slake its drought?
c.   What is't you mean?
d. These once had been enticing things,
   Clorinda, pastures, caves, and springs.
c. And what late change?
d.   The other day
   Pan met me.
20 c   What did great Pan say?
d. Words that transcend poor shepherds' skill,
   But he e'er since my songs does fill:
   And his name swells my slender oat.

C. Sweet must Pan sound in Damon's note.
D. Clorinda's voice might make it sweet.
C. Who would not in Pan's praises meet?

CHORUS
Of Pan the flowery pastures sing,
Caves echo, and the fountains ring.
Sing then while he doth us inspire;
For all the world is our Pan's choir.

Ametas and Thestylis Making Hay-ropes

1
AMETAS
Think'st thou that this love can stand,
Whilst thou still dost say me nay?
Love unpaid does soon disband:
Love binds love as hay binds hay.

2
THESTYLIS
Think'st thou that this rope would twine
If we both should turn one way?
Where both parties so combine,
Neither love will twist nor hay.

3
AMETAS
Thus you vain excuses find,
10 Which yourselves and us delay:
And love ties a woman's mind
Looser than with ropes of hay.

4
THESTYLIS
What you cannot constant hope
Must be taken as you may.

5
AMETAS
Then let's both lay by our rope,
And go kiss within the hay.

A Dialogue, between the Resolved Soul and Created Pleasure

Courage, my Soul, now learn to wield
The weight of thine immortal shield.
Close on thy head thy helmet bright.
Balance thy sword against the fight.
See where an army, strong as fair,
With silken banners spreads the air.
Now, if thou be'st that thing divine,
In this day's combat let it shine:
And show that Nature wants an art
10 To conquer one resolvèd heart.

PLEASURE
Welcome the creation's guest,
Lord of earth, and heaven's heir.
Lay aside that warlike crest,
And of Nature's banquet share:
Where the souls of fruits and flowers
Stand prepared to heighten yours.

SOUL
I sup above, and cannot stay
To bait so long upon the way.

PLEASURE
On these downy pillows lie,
20 Whose soft plumes will thither fly:
On these roses strewed so plain
Lest one leaf thy side should strain.

SOUL
My gentler rest is on a thought,
Conscious of doing what I ought.

PLEASURE
If thou be'st with perfumes pleased,
Such as oft the gods appeased,
Thou in fragrant clouds shalt show
Like another god below.

SOUL
A soul that knows not to presume
30   Is heaven's and its own perfume.

PLEASURE
Everything does seem to vie
Which should first attract thine eye:
But since none deserves that grace,
In this crystal view *thy* face.

SOUL
When the Creator's skill is prized,
The rest is all but earth disguised.

PLEASURE
Hark how music then prepares
For thy stay these charming airs;
Which the posting winds recall,
40   And suspend the river's fall.

SOUL
Had I but any time to lose,
On this I would it all dispose.
Cease, tempter. None can chain a mind
Whom this sweet chordage cannot bind.

CHORUS
Earth cannot show so brave a sight
As when a single soul does fence
The batteries of alluring sense,
And heaven views it with delight.
    Then persevere: for still new charges sound:
50   And if thou overcom'st, thou shalt be crowned.

PLEASURE

All this fair, and soft, and sweet,
   Which scatteringly doth shine,
Shall within one beauty meet,
   And she be only thine.

SOUL

If things of sight such heavens be,
What heavens are those we cannot see?

PLEASURE

Wheresoe'er thy foot shall go
   The minted gold shall lie,
Till thou purchase all below,
60   And want new worlds to buy.

SOUL

Were't not a price, who'd value gold?
And that's worth naught that can be sold.

PLEASURE

Wilt thou all the glory have
   That war or peace commend?
Half the world shall be thy slave
   The other half thy friend.

SOUL

What friends, if to my self untrue!
What slaves, unless I captive you!

PLEASURE

Thou shalt know each hidden cause;
70   And see the future time:
Try what depth the centre draws;
   And then to heaven climb.

SOUL

None thither mounts by the degree
Of knowledge, but humility.

CHORUS
Triumph, triumph, victorious Soul;
The world has not one pleasure more:
The rest does lie beyond the Pole,
And is thine everlasting store.

Flecknoe, an English Priest at Rome

Obliged by frequent visits of this man,
Whom as priest, poet, and musician,
I for some branch of Melchizédek took
(Though he derives himself from my Lord Brooke);
I sought his lodging, which is at the sign
Of The Sad Pelican – subject divine
For poetry. There, three staircases high –
Which signifies his triple property –
I found at last a chamber, as 'twas said,
But seemed a coffin set on the stairs' head
Not higher than seven, nor larger than three feet;
Only there was nor ceiling, nor a sheet,
Save that the ingenious door did, as you come,
Turn in, and show to wainscot half the room.
Yet of his state no man could have complained,
There being no bed where he entertained:
And though within one cell so narrow pent,
He'd stanzas for a whole *apartément*.
    Straight without further information,
In hideous verse, he, in a dismal tone,
Begins to exorcise, as if I were
Possessed; and sure the Devil brought me there.
But I, who now imagined myself brought
To my last trial, in a serious thought
Calmed the disorders of my youthful breast,
And to my martyrdom preparèd rest.
Only this frail ambition did remain,
The last distemper of the sober brain,
That there had been some present to assure

30   The future ages how I did endure:
And how I, silent, turned my burning ear
Towards the verse; and when that could not hear,
Held him the other; and unchangèd yet,
Asked still for more, and prayed him to repeat:
Till the tyrant, weary to persecute,
Left off, and tried to allure me with his lute.
    Now as two instruments, to the same key
Being tuned by art, if the one touchèd be
The other opposite as soon replies,
40   Moved by the air and hidden sympathies;
So while he with his gouty fingers crawls
Over the lute, his murm'ring belly calls,
Whose hungry guts to the same straitness twined
In echo to the trembling strings repined.
    I, that perceived now what his music meant,
Asked civilly if he had eat this Lent.
He answered yes, with such and such an one.
For he has this of generous, that alone
He never feeds, save only when he tries
50   With gristly tongue to dart the passing flies.
I asked if he eat flesh. And he, that was
So hungry that, though ready to say Mass,
Would break his fast before, said he was sick,
And the ordinance was only politic.
Nor was I longer to invite him scant,
Happy at once to make him Protestant,
And silent. Nothing now our dinner stayed
But till he had himself a body made –
I mean till he were dressed: for else so thin
60   He stands, as if he only fed had been
With consecrated wafers: and the Host
Hath sure more flesh and blood than he can boast.
This *basso relievo* of a man,
Who as a camel tall, yet easily can
The needle's eye thread without any stitch,
(His only impossible is to be rich),
Lest his too subtle body, growing rare,

Should leave his soul to wander in the air,
He therefore circumscribes himself in rimes;
70 And swaddled in's own papers seven times,
Wears a close jacket of poetic buff,
With which he doth his third dimension stuff.
Thus armèd underneath, he over all
Does make a primitive *sottana* fall;
And above that yet casts an antique cloak,
Torn at the first Council of Antioch,
Which by the Jews long hid, and disesteemed,
He heard of by tradition, and redeemed.
But were he not in this black habit decked,
80 This half-transparent man would soon reflect
Each colour that he passed by, and be seen,
As the chameleon, yellow, blue, or green.
  He dressed, and ready to disfurnish now
His chamber, whose compactness did allow
No empty place for complimenting doubt,
But who came last is forced first to go out;
I meet one on the stairs who made me stand,
Stopping the passage, and did him demand.
I answered, 'He is here, Sir; but you see
90 You cannot pass to him but thorough me.'
He thought himself affronted, and replied,
'I whom the palace never has denied
Will make the way here;' I said, 'Sir, you'll do
Me a great favour, for I seek to go.'
He gathering fury still made sign to draw;
But himself there closed in a scabbard saw
As narrow as his sword's; and I, that was
Delightful, said, 'There can no body pass
Except by penetration hither, where
100 Two make a crowd; nor can three persons here
Consist but in one substance.' Then, to fit
Our peace, the priest said I too had some wit.
To prov't, I said, 'The place doth us invite
By its own narrowness, Sir, to unite.'
He asked me pardon; and to make me way

Went down, as I him followed to obey.
But the propitiatory priest had straight
Obliged us, when below, to celebrate
Together our atonement: so increased
110 Betwixt us two the dinner to a feast.
    Let it suffice that we could eat in peace;
And that both poems did and quarrels cease
During the table; though my new-made friend
Did, as he threatened, ere 'twere long intend
To be both witty and valiant: I, loath,
Said 'twas too late, he was already both.
    But now, alas, my first tormentor came,
Who satisfied with eating, but not tame,
Turns to recite; though judges most severe
120 After the assize's dinner mild appear,
And on full stomach do condemn but few,
Yet he more strict my sentence doth renew,
And draws out of the black box of his breast
Ten quire of paper in which he was dressed.
Yet that which was a greater cruelty
Than Nero's poem, he calls charity:
And so the pelican at his door hung
Picks out the tender bosom to its young.
    Of all his poems there he stands ungirt
130 Save only two foul copies for his shirt:
Yet these he promises as soon as clean.
But how I loathed to see my neighbour glean
Those papers which he peelèd from within
Like white flakes rising from a leper's skin!
More odious than those rags which the French youth
At ordinaries after dinner show'th
When they compare their chancres and poulains.
Yet he first kissed them, and after takes pains
To read; and then, because he understood
140 Not one word, thought and swore that they were good.
But all his praises could not now appease
The provoked author, whom it did displease
To hear his verses, by so just a curse,

That were ill made, condemned to be read, worse:
And how (impossible) he made yet more
Absurdities in them than were before.
For he his untuned voice did fall or raise
As a deaf man upon a viol plays,
Making the half points and the periods run
150 Confuseder than the atoms in the sun.
Thereat the poet swelled, with anger full,
And roared out, like Perillus in's own bull:
'Sir, you read false.' 'That, any one but you,
Should know the contrary.' Whereat, I, now
Made mediator, in my room, said, 'Why,
To say that you read false, Sir, is no lie.'
Thereat the waxen youth relented straight;
But saw with sad despair that 'twas too late.
For the disdainful poet was retired
160 Home, his most furious satire to have fired
Against the rebel, who, at this struck dead,
Wept bitterly as disinherited.
Who should commend his mistress now? Or who
Praise him? Both difficult indeed to do
With truth. I counselled him to go in time,
Ere the fierce poet's anger turned to rime.
    He hasted; and I, finding myself free,
As one 'scaped strangely from captivity,
Have made the chance be painted; and go now
170 To hang it in Saint Peter's for a vow.

To His Noble Friend Mr Richard Lovelace, upon His Poems

Sir,
Our times are much degenerate from those
Which your sweet muse with your fair fortune chose,
And as complexions alter with the climes,
Our wits have drawn the infection of our times.
That candid age no other way could tell

To be ingenious, but by speaking well.
Who best could praise had then the greatest praise,
'Twas more esteemed to give than wear the bays:
Modest ambition studied only then
10   To honour not herself but worthy men.
These virtues now are banished out of town,
Our Civil Wars have lost the civic crown.
He highest builds, who with most art destroys,
And against others' fame his own employs.
I see the envious caterpillar sit
On the fair blossom of each growing wit.
   The air's already tainted with the swarms
Of insects which against you rise in arms:
Word-peckers, paper-rats, book-scorpions,
20   Of wit corrupted, the unfashioned sons.
The barbèd censurers begin to look
Like the grim consistory on thy book;
And on each line cast a reforming eye,
Severer than the young presbýtery.
Till when in vain they have thee all perused,
You shall, for being faultless, be accused.
Some reading your *Lucasta* will allege
You wronged in her the House's Privilege.
Some that you under sequestration are,
30   Because you writ when going to the war,
And one the book prohibits, because Kent
Their first petition by the author sent.
   But when the beauteous ladies came to know
That their dear Lovelace was endangered so:
Lovelace that thawed the most congealèd breast –
He who loved best and them defended best,
Whose hand so rudely grasps the steely brand,
Whose hand so gently melts the lady's hand –
They all in mutiny though yet undressed
40   Sallied, and would in his defence contest.
And one, the loveliest that was yet e'er seen,
Thinking that I too of the rout had been,
Mine eyes invaded with a female spite,

(She knew what pain 'twould be to lose that sight.)
'O no, mistake not,' I replied, 'for I
In your defence, or in his cause, would die.'
But he, secure of glory and of time,
Above their envy, or mine aid, doth climb.
Him valiant'st men and fairest nymphs approve;
50   His book in them finds judgement, with you love.

An Elegy upon the Death of
My Lord Francis Villiers

'Tis true that he is dead: but yet to choose,
Methinks thou, Fame, should not have brought the news;
Thou canst discourse at will and speak at large:
But wast not in the fight nor durst thou charge;
While he transported all with valiant rage
His name eternized, but cut short his age;
On the safe battlements of Richmond's bowers
Thou wast espied, and from the gilded towers
Thy silver trumpets sounded a retreat
10   Far from the dust and battle's sulph'ry heat.
Yet what couldst thou have done? 'Tis always late
To struggle with inevitable fate.
Much rather thou, I know, expect'st to tell
How heavy Cromwell gnashed the earth and fell.
Or how slow death far from the sight of day
The long-deceivèd Fairfax bore away.
But until then, let us young Francis praise:
And plant upon his hearse the bloody bays,
Which we will water with our welling eyes.
20   Tears spring not still from spungy cowardice.
The purer fountains from the rocks more steep
Distill and stony valour best doth weep.
Besides revenge, if often quenched in tears,
Hardens like steel and daily keener wears.
    Great Buckingham, whose death doth freshly strike
Our memories, because to this so like.

Ere that in the eternal court he shone,
And here a favourite, there found a throne,
The fatal night before he hence did bleed,
30 Left to his princess this immortal seed,
As the wise Chinese in the fertile womb
Of earth doth a more precious clay entomb,
Which dying, by his will he leaves consigned:
Till by mature delay of time refined
The crystal metal fit to be released
Is taken forth to crown each royal feast:
Such was the fate by which this posthume breathed,
Who scarcely seems begotten but bequeathed.
   Never was any human plant that grew
40 More fair than this and ácceptably new.
'Tis truth that beauty doth most men dispraise:
Prudence and valour their esteem do raise.
But he that hath already these in store,
Can not be poorer sure for having more.
And his unimitable handsomeness
Made him indeed be more than man, not less.
We do but faintly God's resemblance bear
And like rough coins of careless mints appear:
But he of purpose made, did represent
50 In a rich medal every lineament.
   Lovely and admirable as he was,
Yet was his sword or armour all his glass.
Nor in his mistress' eyes that joy he took,
As in an enemy's himself to look.
I know how well he did, with what delight
Those serious imitations of fight.
Still in the trials of strong exercise
His was the first, and his the second prize.
   Bright Lady, thou that rulest from above
60 The last and greatest monarchy of love:
Fair Richmond, hold thy brother or he goes.
Try if the jasmine of thy hand or rose
Of thy red lip can keep him always here.
For he loves danger and doth never fear.

Or may thy tears prevail with him to stay?
    But he, resolved, breaks carelessly away.
Only one argument could now prolong
His stay and that most fair and so most strong:
The matchless Clora whose pure fires did warm
70 His soul and only could his passions charm.
    You might with much more reason go reprove
The amorous magnet which the North doth love.
Or preach divorce, and say it is amiss
That with tall elms the twining vines should kiss,
Than chide two such so fit, so equal fair
That in the world they have no other pair,
Whom it might seem that heaven did create
To restore man unto his first estate.
Yet she for honour's tyrannous respect
80 Her own desires did, and his neglect.
And like the modest plant at every touch
Shrunk in her leaves and feared it was too much.
    But who can paint the torments and that pain
Which he professed and now she could not feign?
He like the sun but overcast and pale:
She like a rainbow, that ere long must fail,
Whose roseal cheek where heaven itself did view
Begins to separate and dissolve to dew.
    At last he leave obtains though sad and slow,
90 First of her and then of himself to go.
How comely and how terrible he sits
At once, and war as well as love befits!
Ride where thou wilt and bold adventures find:
But all the ladies are got up behind.
Guard them, though not thyself: for in thy death
Th' eleven thousand virgins lose their breath.
    So Hector issuing from the Trojan wall
The sad Ilíads to the gods did call,
With hands displayed and with dishevelled hair,
100 That they the empire in his life would spare,
While he secure through all the field doth spy
Achilles, for Achilles only cry.

Ah, ignorant that yet ere night he must
Be drawn by him inglorious through the dust.
   Such fell young Villiers in the cheerful heat
Of youth: his locks entangled all with sweat
And those eyes which the sentinel did keep
Of love, closed up in an eternal sleep.
While Venus of Adonis thinks no more
110 Slain by the harsh tusk of the savage boar,
Hither she runs and hath him hurried far
Out of the noise and blood, and killing war:
Where in her gardens of sweet myrtle laid
She kisses him in the immortal shade.
   Yet died he not revengeless: much he did
Ere he could suffer. A whole pyramid
Of vulgar bodies he erected high:
Scorning without a sepulchre to die.
And with his steel which did whole troops divide
120 He cut his epitaph on either side.
Till finding nothing to his courage fit
He rid up last to death and conquered it.
   Such are the obsequies to Francis own:
He best the pomp of his own death hath shown.
And we hereafter to his honour will
Not write so many, but so many kill.
Till the whole army by just venegance come
To be at once his trophy and his tomb.

Mourning

1
You, that decipher out the fate
Of human offsprings from the skies,
What mean these infants which of late
Spring from the stars of Clora's eyes?

2

Her eyes confused, and doubled o'er,
With tears suspended ere they flow,
Seem bending upwards, to restore
To heaven, whence it came, their woe.

3

When, moulding of the watery spheres,
Slow drops untie themselves away,
As if she, with those precious tears,
Would strow the ground where Strephon lay.

4

Yet some affirm, pretending art,
Her eyes have so her bosom drowned,
Only to soften near her heart
A place to fix another wound.

5

And, while vain pomp does her restrain
Within her solitary bower,
She courts herself in amorous rain;
Herself both Danaë and the shower.

6

Nay, others, bolder, hence esteem
Joy now so much her master grown,
That whatsoever does but seem
Like grief, is from her windows thrown.

7

Nor that she pays, while she survives,
To her dead love this tribute due,
But casts abroad these donatives,
At the installing of a new.

8

How wide they dream! The Indian slaves
That dive for pearl through seas profound
Would find her tears yet deeper waves
And not of one the bottom sound.

9

I yet my silent judgement keep,
Disputing not what they believe:
But sure as oft as women weep,
It is to be supposed they grieve.

The Fair Singer

1

To make a final conquest of all me,
Love did compose so sweet an enemy,
In whom both beauties to my death agree,
Joining themselves in fatal harmony;
That while she with her eyes my heart does bind,
She with her voice might captivate my mind.

2

I could have fled from one but singly fair:
My disentangled soul itself might save,
Breaking the curlèd trammels of her hair;
But how should I avoid to be her slave,
Whose subtle art invisibly can wreathe
My fetters of the very air I breathe?

3

It had been easy fighting in some plain,
Where victory might hang in equal choice.
But all resistance against her is vain,
Who has the advantage both of eyes and voice,
And all my forces needs must be undone,
She having gainèd both the wind and sun.

The Gallery

1

Clora, come view my soul, and tell
Whether I have contrived it well.
Now all its several lodgings lie
Composed into one gallery;
And the great arras-hangings, made
Of various faces, by are laid;
That, for all furniture, you'll find
Only your picture in my mind.

2

Here thou are painted in the dress
10   Of an inhuman murderess;
Examining upon our hearts
Thy fertile shop of cruel arts:
Engines more keen than ever yet
Adorned a tyrant's cabinet;
Of which the most tormenting are
Black eyes, red lips, and curlèd hair.

3

But, on the other side, th'art drawn
Like to Aurora in the dawn;
When in the East she slumbering lies,
20   And stretches out her milky thighs;
While all the morning choir does sing,
And manna falls, and roses spring;
And, at thy feet, the wooing doves
Sit pérfecting their harmless loves.

4

Like an enchantress here thou show'st,
Vexing thy restless lover's ghost;
And, by a light obscure, dost rave
Over his entrails, in the cave;
Divining thence, with horrid care,
30   How long thou shalt continue fair;
And (when informed) them throw'st away,
To be the greedy vulture's prey.

5

But, against that, thou sit'st afloat
Like Venus in her pearly boat.
The halcyons, calming all that's nigh,
Betwixt the air and water fly;
Or, if some rolling wave appears,
A mass of ambergris it bears.
Nor blows more wind than what may well
40 Convoy the perfume to the smell.

6

These pictures and a thousand more
Of thee my gallery do store
In all the forms thou canst invent
Either to please me, or torment:
For thou alone to people me,
Art grown a numerous colony;
And a collection choicer far
Than or Whitehall's or Mantua's were.

7

But, of these pictures and the rest,
50 That at the entrance likes me best:
Where the same posture, and the look
Remains, with which I first was took:
A tender shepherdess, whose hair
Hangs loosely playing in the air,
Transplanting flowers from the green hill,
To crown her head, and bosom fill.

The Unfortunate Lover

1
Alas, how pleasant are their days
With whom the infant Love yet plays!
Sorted by pairs, they still are seen
By fountains cool, and shadows green.
But soon these flames do lose their light,
Like meteors of a summer's night:
Nor can they to that region climb,
To make impression upon time.

2
'Twas in a shipwreck, when the seas
10   Ruled, and the winds did what they please,
That my poor lover floating lay,
And, ere brought forth, was cast away:
Till at the last the master-wave
Upon the rock his mother drave;
And there she split against the stone,
In a Caesarean sectión.

3
The sea him lent those bitter tears
Which at his eyes he always wears;
And from the winds the sighs he bore,
20   Which through his surging breast do roar.
No day he saw but that which breaks
Through frighted clouds in forkèd streaks,
While round the rattling thunder hurled,
As at the funeral of the world.

4
While Nature to his birth presents
This masque of quarrelling elements,
A numerous fleet of cormorants black,
That sailed insulting o'er the wrack,
Received into their cruel care
30   Th' unfortunate and abject heir:
Guardians most fit to entertain
The orphan of the hurricane.

5

They fed him up with hopes and air,
Which soon digested to despair,
And as one cormorant fed him, still
Another on his heart did bill,
Thus while they famish him, and feast,
He both consumèd, and increased:
And languishèd with doubtful breath,
40   The amphibíum of life and death.

6

And now, when angry heaven would
Behold a spectacle of blood,
Fortune and he are called to play
At sharp before it all the day:
And tyrant Love his breast does ply
With all his winged artillery,
Whilst he, betwixt the flames and waves,
Like Ajax, the mad tempest braves.

7

See how he nak'd and fierce does stand,
50   Cuffing the thunder with one hand,
While with the other he does lock,
And grapple, with the stubborn rock:
From which he with each wave rebounds,
Torn into flames, and ragg'd with wounds,
And all he 'says, a lover dressed
In his own blood does relish best.

8

This is the only banneret
That ever Love created yet:
Who though, by the malignant stars,
60   Forcèd to live in storms and wars,
Yet dying leaves a perfume here,
And music within every ear:
And he in story only rules,
In a field sable a lover gules.

Daphnis and Chloe

1
Daphnis must from Chloe part:
Now is come the dismal hour
That must all his hopes devour,
All his labour, all his art.

2
Nature, her own sex's foe,
Long had taught her to be coy:
But she neither knew t'enjoy,
Nor yet let her lover go.

3
But with this sad news surprised,
Soon she let that niceness fall,
And would gladly yield to all,
So it had his stay comprised.

4
Nature so herself does use
To lay by her wonted state,
Lest the world should separate;
Sudden parting closer glues.

5
He, well-read in all the ways
By which men their siege maintain,
Knew not that the fort to gain,
Better 'twas the siege to raise.

6
But he came so full possessed
With the grief of parting thence,
That he had not so much sense
As to see he might be blessed.

7
Till Love in her language breathed
Words she never spake before,
But than legacies no more
To a dying man bequeathed.

8

For, alas, the time was spent,
30   Now the latest minute's run
When poor Daphnis is undone,
Between joy and sorrow rent.

9

At that 'Why', that 'Stay, my Dear',
His disordered locks he tare;
And with rolling eyes did glare,
And his cruel fate forswear.

10

As the soul of one scarce dead,
With the shrieks of friends aghast,
Looks distracted back in haste,
40   And then straight again is fled,

11

So did wretched Daphnis look,
Frighting her he lovèd most.
At the last, this lover's ghost
Thus his leave resolvèd took.

12

'Are my hell and heaven joined
More to torture him that dies?
Could departure not suffice,
But that you must then grow kind?

13

'Ah, my Chloe, how have I
50   Such a wretched minute found,
When thy favours should me wound
More than all thy cruelty?

14

'So to the condemnèd wight
The delicious cup we fill;
And allow him all he will,
For his last and short delight.

15

'But I will not now begin
  Such a debt unto my foe;
  Nor to my departure owe
60 What my presence could not win.

16

'Absence is too much alone:
  Better 'tis to go in peace,
  Than my losses to increase
  By a late fruition.

17

'Why should I enrich my fate?
  'Tis a vanity to wear,
  For my executioner,
  Jewels of so high a rate.

18

'Rather I away will pine
70 In a manly stubborness
  Than be fatted up express
  For the cannibal to dine.

19

'Whilst this grief does thee disarm,
  All th' enjoyment of our love
  But the ravishment would prove
  Of a body dead while warm.

20

'And I parting should appear
  Like the gourmand Hebrew dead,
  While with quails and manna fed,
80 He does through the desert err.

21

'Or the witch that midnight wakes
  For the fern, whose magic weed
  In one minute casts the seed,
  And invisible him makes.

22

'Gentler times for love are meant:
Who for parting pleasure strain
Gather roses in the rain,
Wet themselves, and spoil their scent.

23

'Farewell, therefore, all the fruit
90 Which I could from love receive:
Joy will not with sorrow weave,
Nor will I this grief pollute.

24

'Fate, I come, as dark, as sad,
As thy malice could desire;
Yet bring with me all the fire
That Love in his torches had.'

25

At these words away he broke;
As who long has praying li'n,
To his headsman makes the sign,
100 And receives the parting stroke.

26

But hence, virgins, all beware:
Last night he with Phlogis slept;
This night for Dorinda kept;
And but rid to take the air.

27

Yet he does himself excuse;
Nor indeed without a cause:
For, according to the laws,
Why did Chloe once refuse?

Upon the Death of the Lord Hastings

Go, intercept some fountain in the vein,
Whose virgin-source yet never steeped the plain.
Hastings is dead, and we must find a store

Of tears untouched, and never wept before.
Go, stand betwixt the morning and the flowers;
And, ere they fall, arrest the early showers.
Hastings is dead; and we, disconsolate,
With early tears must mourn his early fate.
    Alas, his virtues did his death presage:
10 Needs must he die, that doth out-run his age.
The phlegmatic and slow prolongs his day,
And on Time's wheel sticks like a remora.
What man is he that hath not heaven beguiled,
And is not thence mistaken for a child?
While those of growth more sudden, and more bold,
Are hurried hence, as if already old.
For, there above, they number not as here,
But weigh to man the geometric year.
    Had he but at this measure still increased,
20 And on the Tree of Life once made a feast,
As that of Knowledge; what loves had he given
To earth, and then what jealousies to heaven!
But 'tis a maxim of that state, that none,
Lest he become like them, taste more than one.
Therefore the democratic stars did rise,
And all that worth from hence did ostracize.
    Yet as some prince, that, for state-jealousy,
Secures his nearest and most loved ally;
His thought with richest triumphs entertains,
30 And in the choicest pleasures charms his pains:
So he, not banished hence, but there confined,
There better recreates his active mind.
    Before the crystal palace where he dwells,
The armèd angels hold their carousels;
And underneath, he views the tournaments
Of all these sublunary elements.
But most he doth the Eternal Book behold,
On which the happy names do stand enrolled;
And gladly there can all his kindred claim,
40 But most rejoices at his Mother's name.
    The gods themselves cannot their joy conceal,

But draw their veils, and their pure beams reveal:
Only they drooping Hymeneus note,
Who, for sad purple, tears his saffron coat;
And trails his torches through the starry hall
Reversèd at his darling's funeral.
And Aesculapius, who, ashamed and stern,
Himself at once condemneth, and Mayern
Like some sad chemist, who, prepared to reap
50   The golden harvest, sees his glasses leap.
For, how immortal must their race have stood,
Had Mayern once been mixed with Hastings' blood!
How sweet and verdant would these laurels be,
Had they been planted on that balsam tree!
    But what could he, good man, although he bruised
All herbs, and them a thousand ways infused?
All he had tried, but all in vain, he saw,
And wept, as we, without redress or law.
For man (alas) is but the heaven's sport;
60   And art indeed is long, but life is short.

The Definition of Love

1
My love is of a birth as rare
As 'tis for object strange and high:
It was begotten by Despair
Upon Impossibility.

2
Magnanimous Despair alone
Could show me so divine a thing,
Where feeble Hope could ne'er have flown
But vainly flapped its tinsel wing.

3
And yet I quickly might arrive
10   Where my extended soul is fixed,
But Fate does iron wedges drive,
And always crowds itself betwixt.

4

For Fate with jealous eye does see
Two perfect loves, nor lets them close:
Their union would her ruin be,
And her tyrannic power depose.

5

And therefore her decrees of steel
Us as the distant Poles have placed,
(Though Love's whole world on us doth wheel)
20   Not by themselves to be embraced,

6

Unless the giddy heaven fall,
And earth some new convulsion tear;
And, us to join, the world should all
Be cramped into a planisphere.

7

As lines (so loves) oblique may well
Themselves in every angle greet:
But ours so truly parallel,
Though infinite, can never meet.

8

Therefore the love which us doth bind,
30   But Fate so enviously debars,
Is the conjunction of the mind,
And opposition of the stars.

ability to come to rest in contradiction

To His Coy Mistress

Had we but world enough, and time,
This coyness, Lady, were no crime.
We would sit down, and think which way
To walk, and pass our long love's day.
Thou by the Indian Ganges' side
Shouldst rubies find: I by the tide
Of Humber would complain. I would

Love you ten years before the flood:
And you should, if you please, refuse
10   Till the conversion of the Jews.
My vegetable love should grow
Vaster than empires, and more slow.
An hundred years should go to praise
Thine eyes, and on thy forehead gaze.
Two hundred to adore each breast:
But thirty thousand to the rest.
An age at least to every part,
And the last age should show your heart:
For, Lady, you deserve this state;
20   Nor would I love at lower rate.
    But at my back I always hear
Time's wingèd chariot hurrying near:
And yonder all before us lie
Deserts of vast eternity.
Thy beauty shall no more be found;
Nor, in thy marble vault, shall sound
My echoing song: then worms shall try
That long-preserved virginity:
And your quaint honour turn to dust;
30   And into ashes all my lust.
The grave's a fine and private place,
But none, I think, do there embrace.
    Now, therefore, while the youthful glue
Sits on thy skin like morning dew,
And while thy willing soul transpires
At every pore with instant fires,
Now let us sport us while we may;
And now, like amorous birds of prey,
Rather at once our time devour,
40   Than languish in his slow-chapped power.
Let us roll all our strength, and all
Our sweetness, up into one ball:
And tear our pleasures with rough strife,
Thorough the iron grates of life.
Thus, though we cannot make our sun
Stand still, yet we will make him run.

Eyes and Tears

1

How wisely Nature did decree,
With the same eyes to weep and see!
That, having viewed the object vain,
We might be ready to complain.

2

Thus since the self-deluding sight,
In a false angle takes each height,
These tears, which better measure all,
Like watery lines and plummets fall.

3

Two tears, which Sorrow long did weigh
10 Within the scales of either eye,
And then paid out in equal poise,
Are the true price of all my joys.

4

What in the world most fair appears,
Yea, even laughter, turns to tears:
And all the jewels which we prize,
Melt in these pendants of the eyes.

5

I have through every garden been,
Amongst the red, the white, the green,
And yet, from all the flowers I saw,
20 No honey but these tears, could draw.

6

So the all-seeing sun each day
Distills the world with chemic ray,
But finds the essence only show'rs,
Which straight in pity back he pours.

7
Yet happy they whom grief doth bless,
That weep the more, and see the less:
And, to preserve their sight more true,
Bathe still their eyes in their own dew.

8
*So Magdalen, in tears more wise
30 Dissolved those captivating eyes,
Whose liquid chains could flowing meet
To fetter her Redeemer's feet.

9
Not full sails hasting loaden home,
Nor the chaste lady's pregnant womb,
Nor Cynthia teeming shows so fair,
As two eyes swoll'n with weeping are.

10
The sparkling glance that shoots desire,
Drenched in these waves does lose its fire.
Yea, oft the Thunderer pity takes
40 And here the hissing lightning slakes.

11
The incense was to heaven dear,
Not as a perfume, but a tear.
And stars show lovely in the night,
But as they seem the tears of light.

12
Ope then, mine eyes, your double sluice,
And practise so your noblest use;
For others too can see, or sleep,
But only human eyes can weep.

13
Now, like two clouds dissolving, drop,
50 And at each tear in distance stop:
Now, like two fountains, trickle down;
Now, like two floods o'erturn and drown.

* See translation overleaf.

14

Thus let your streams o'erflow your springs,
    Till eyes and tears be the same things:
    And each the other's difference bears;
    These weeping eyes, those seeing tears.

*Magdala, lascivos sic quum dimisit amantes,
    Fervidaque in castas lumina solvit aquas;
Haesit in irriguo lachrymarum compede Christus,
    Et tenuit sacros uda catena pedes.

The Coronet

When for the thorns with which I long, too long,
    With many a piercing wound,
    My Saviour's head have crowned,
I seek with garlands to redress that wrong:
    Through every garden, every mead,
I gather flowers (my fruits are only flowers),
    Dismantling all the fragrant towers
That once adorned my shepherdess's head.
And now when I have summed up all my store,
10   Thinking (so I myself deceive)
        So rich a chaplet thence to weave
As never yet the King of Glory wore:
        Alas, I find the serpent old
        That, twining in his speckled breast,
        About the flowers disguised does fold,
        With wreaths of fame and interest.
Ah, foolish man, that wouldst debase with them,
And mortal glory, Heaven's diadem!
But Thou who only couldst the serpent tame,
20 Either his slippery knots at once untie;
And disentangle all his winding snare;
Or shatter too with him my curious frame,
And let these wither, so that he may die,
Though set with skill and chosen out with care:
That they, while Thou on both their spoils dost tread,
May crown thy feet, that could not crown thy head.

An Horatian Ode upon Cromwell's Return from Ireland

The forward youth that would appear
Must now forsake his muses dear,
    Nor in the shadows sing
    His numbers languishing.
'Tis time to leave the books in dust,
And oil the unusèd armour's rust:
    Removing from the wall
    The corslet of the hall.
So restless Cromwell could not cease
10 In the inglorious arts of peace,
    But through adventurous war
    Urgèd his active star.
And, like the three-forked lightning, first
Breaking the clouds where it was nursed,
    Did thorough his own side
    His fiery way divide.
(For 'tis all one to courage high
The emulous or enemy:
    And with such to inclose
20   Is more than to oppose.)
Then burning through the air he went,
And palaces and temples rent:
    And Caesar's head at last
    Did through his laurels blast.
'Tis madness to resist or blame
The force of angry heaven's flame:
    And, if we would speak true,
    Much to the man is due,
Who, from his private gardens, where
30 He lived reservèd and austere,
    As if his highest plot
    To plant the bergamot,
Could by industrious valour climb
To ruin the great work of time,
    And cast the kingdoms old

Into another mould.
Though justice against fate complain,
And plead the ancient rights in vain:
    But those do hold or break
40   As men are strong or weak.
Nature, that hateth emptiness,
Allows of penetration less:
    And therefore must make room
    Where greater spirits come.
What field of all the Civil Wars,
Where his were not the deepest scars?
    And Hampton shows what part
    He had of wiser art,
Where, twining subtle fears with hope,
50 He wove a net of such a scope,
    That Charles himself might chase
    To Carisbrooke's narrow case:
That thence the royal actor born
The tragic scaffold might adorn:
    While round the armèd bands
    Did clap their bloody hands.
He nothing common did or mean
Upon that memorable scene:
    But with his keener eye
60   The axe's edge did try:
Nor called the gods with vulgar spite
To vindicate his helpless right,
    But bowed his comely head,
    Down, as upon a bed.
This was that memorable hour
Which first assured the forcèd power.
    So when they did design
    The Capitol's first line,
A bleeding head where they begun,
70 Did fright the architects to run;
    And yet in that the State
    Foresaw its happy fate.
And now the Irish are ashamed

To see themselves in one year tamed:
   So much one man can do,
   That does both act and know. ← *Cromwell*
They can affirm his praises best,
And have, though overcome, confessed
   How good he is, how just,
80   And fit for highest trust:
Nor yet grown stiffer with command,
But still in the Republic's hand:
   How fit he is to sway
   That can so well obey.
He to the Commons' feet presents
A kingdom, for his first year's rents:
   And, what he may, forbears
   His fame, to make it theirs:
And has his sword and spoils ungirt,
90 To lay them at the public's skirt.
   So when the falcon high
   Falls heavy from the sky,
She, having killed, no more does search
But on the next green bough to perch,
   Where, when he first does lure,
   The falc'ner has her sure.
What may not then our isle presume
While Victory his crest does plume?
   What may not others fear
100 If thus he crowns each year?
A Caesar, he, ere long to Gaul,
To Italy an Hannibal,
   And to all states not free
   Shall climactéric be.
The Pict no shelter now shall find *Scots*
Within his parti-coloured mind,
   But from this valour sad
   Shrink underneath the plaid:
Happy, if in the tufted brake
110 The English hunter him mistake,
   Nor lay his hounds in near

  The Caledonian deer.
But thou, the Wars' and Fortune's son,
March indefatigably on,
  And for the last effect
  Still keep thy sword erect:
Besides the force it has to fright
The spirits of the shady night,
  The same arts that did gain
120 A power, must it maintain.

Tom May's Death

As one put drunk into the packet-boat,
Tom May was hurried hence and did not know't.
But was amazed on the Elysian side,
And with an eye uncertain, gazing wide,
Could not determine in what place he was,
(For whence, in Stephen's Alley, trees or grass?)
Nor where The Pope's Head, nor The Mitre lay,
Signs by which still he found and lost his way.
At last while doubtfully he all compares,
10 He saw near hand, as he imagined, Ayres.
Such did he seem for corpulence and port,
But 'twas a man much of another sort;
'Twas Ben that in the dusky laurel shade
Amongst the chorus of old poets layed,
Sounding of ancient heroes, such as were
The subjects' safety, and the rebels' fear,
And how a double-headed vulture eats
Brutus and Cassius, the people's cheats.
But seeing May, he varied straight his song,
20 Gently to signify that he was wrong.
'Cups more than civil of Emathian wine,
I sing' (said he) 'and the Pharsalian Sign,
Where the historian of the commonwealth
In his own bowels sheathed the conquering health.'
By this, May to himself and them was come,

He found he was translated, and by whom,
Yet then with foot as stumbling as his tongue
Pressed for his place among the learned throng.
But Ben, who knew not neither foe nor friend,
30 Sworn enemy to all that do pretend,
Rose; more than ever he was seen severe,
Shook his gray locks, and his own bays did tear
At this intrusion. Then with laurel wand –
The awful sign of his supreme command,
At whose dread whisk Virgil himself does quake,
And Horace patiently its stroke does take –
As he crowds in, he whipped him o'er the pate
Like Pembroke at the masque, and then did rate:
    'Far from these blessed shades tread back again
40 Most servile wit, and mercenary pen,
Polydore, Lucan, Alan, Vandal, Goth,
Malignant poet and historian both,
Go seek the novice statesmen, and obtrude
On them some Roman-cast similitude,
Tell them of liberty, the stories fine,
Until you all grow consuls in your wine;
Or thou, Dictator of the glass, bestow
On him the Cato, this the Cicero,
Transferring old Rome hither in your talk,
50 As Bethlem's House did to Loreto walk.
Foul architect, that hadst not eye to see
How ill the measures of these states agree,
And who by Rome's example England lay,
Those but to Lucan do continue May.
But thee nor ignorance nor seeming good
Misled, but malice fixed and understood.
Because some one than thee more worthy wears
The sacred laurel, hence are all these tears?
Must therefore all the world be set on flame,
60 Because a gázette-writer missed his aim?
And for a tankard-bearing muse must we
As for the basket, Guelphs and Ghib'llines be?
When the sword glitters o'er the judge's head,

And fear has coward churchmen silencèd,
Then is the poet's time, 'tis then he draws,
And single fights forsaken virtue's cause.
He, when the wheel of empire whirleth back,
And though the world's disjointed axle crack,
Sings still of ancient rights and better times,
70 Seeks wretched good, arraigns successful crimes.
But thou, base man, first prostituted hast
Our spotless knowledge and the studies chaste,
Apostatizing from our arts and us,
To turn the chronicler to Spartacus.
Yet wast thou taken hence with equal fate,
Before thou couldst great Charles his death relate.
But what will deeper wound thy little mind,
Hast left surviving D'Avenant still behind,
Who laughs to see in this thy death renewed,
80 Right Roman poverty and gratitude.
Poor poet thou, and grateful senate they,
Who thy last reckoning did so largely pay,
And with the public gravity would come,
When thou hadst drunk thy last to lead thee home,
If that can be thy home where Spenser lies,
And reverend Chaucer, but their dust does rise
Against thee, and expels thee from their side,
As th' eagle's plumes from other birds divide.
Nor here thy shade must dwell. Return, return,
90 Where sulphury Phlegethon does ever burn.
Thee Cerberus with all his jaws shall gnash,
Megaera thee with all her serpents lash.
Thou riveted unto Ixion's wheel
Shalt break, and the perpetual vulture feel.
'Tis just, what torments poets e'er did feign,
Thou first historically shouldst sustain.'
      Thus, by irrevocable sentence cast,
May, only Master of these Revels, passed.
And straight he vanished in a cloud of pitch,
100 Such as unto the Sabbath bears the witch.

In Legationem Domini Oliveri St John ad Provincias Foederatas

Ingeniosa viris contingunt nomina magnis,
    Ut dubites casu vel ratione data.
Nam sors, caeca licet, tamen est praesaga futuri;
    Et sub fatidico nomine vera premit.
Et tu, cui soli voluit respublica credi,
    Foedera seu Belgis seu nova bella feras;
Haud frustra cecidit tibi compellatio fallax,
    Ast scriptum ancipiti nomine munus erat;
Scilicet hoc Martis, sed pacis nuntius illo:
10   Clavibus his Jani ferrea claustra regis.
Non opus arcanos chartis committere sensus,
    Et varia licitos condere fraude dolos.
Tu quoque si taceas tamen est legatio nomen
    Et velut in scytale publica verba refert.
Vultis Oliverum, Batavi, Sanctumve Johannem?
    Antiochus gyro non breviore stetit.

ON THE EMBASSY OF LORD OLIVER ST JOHN
TO THE UNITED PROVINCES

Such apt names befall great men
    That one doubts whether they are given by chance or
        reason.
For fortune, although blind, yet presages the future,
    And under a prophetic name covers the truth.
And you, to whom alone the republic wished to be
        entrusted,
    May bear to the Dutch either a treaty or a new war.
Not without cause did the captious meeting fall to you,
    For your office was written in your double name:
In the last, the messenger of war, but in the first, of peace.
10   With these keys you control the iron locks of Janus.
Nor is it necessary to commit secret meanings to paper
    And to hide allowed deceptions with shifting guile.
Even if you are silent, yet your name is an embassy,

And, just as in secret writing, it bears official words.
Dutchmen, do you wish Oliver or Saint John?
Antiochus stood not in a shorter circle.

To His Worthy Friend Doctor Witty upon His Translation of the 'Popular Errors'

Sit further, and make room for thine own fame,
Where just desert enrolls thy honoured name –
The good interpreter. Some in this task
Take off the cypress veil, but leave a mask,
Changing the Latin, but do more obscure
That sense in English which was bright and pure.
So of translators they are authors grown,
For ill translators make the book their own.
Others do strive with words and forcèd phrase
10 To add such lustre, and so many rays,
That, but to make the vessel shining, they
Much of the precious metal rub away.
He is translation's thief that addeth more,
As much as he that taketh from the store
Of the first author. Here he maketh blots
That mends; and added beauties are but spots.
   Celia whose English doth more richly flow
Than Tagus, purer than dissolvèd snow,
And sweet as are her lips that speak it, she
20 Now learns the tongues of France and Italy;
But she is Celia still: no other grace
But her own smiles commend that lovely face;
Her native beauty's not Italianated,
Nor her chaste mind into the French translated:
Her thoughts are English, though her sparkling wit
With other language doth them fitly fit.
   Translators learn of her. But stay, I slide
Down into error with the vulgar tide;
Women must not teach here: the Doctor doth
30 Stint them to caudles, almond-milk, and broth.

Now I reform, and surely so will all
Whose happy eyes on thy translation fall.
I see the people hasting to thy book,
Liking themselves the worse the more they look,
And so disliking, that they nothing see
Now worth the liking, but thy book and thee.
And (if I judgement have) I censure right;
For something guides my hand that I must write.
You have translation's statutes best fulfilled,
40   That, handling, neither sully nor would gild.

The Picture of Little T.C. in a Prospect of Flowers

1

See with what simplicity
This nymph begins her golden days!
In the green grass she loves to lie,
And there with her fair aspect tames
The wilder flowers, and gives them names:
But only with the roses plays;
           And them does tell
What colour best becomes them, and what smell.

2

Who can foretell for what high cause
10   This Darling of the Gods was born!
Yet this is she whose chaster laws
The wanton Love shall one day fear,
And, under her command severe,
See his bow broke and ensigns torn.
           Happy, who can
Appease this virtuous enemy of man!

3

O, then let me in time compound,
And parley with those conquering eyes;
Ere they have tried their force to wound,
20   Ere, with their glancing wheels, they drive

In triumph over hearts that strive,
And them that yield but more despise.
           Let me be laid,
Where I may see thy glories from some shade.

4

Meantime, whilst every verdant thing
Itself does at thy beauty charm,
Reform the errors of the spring;
Make that the tulips may have share
Of sweetness, seeing they are fair;
30 And roses of their thorns disarm:
           But most procure
That violets may a longer age endure.

5

But, O young beauty of the woods,
Whom Nature courts with fruits and flowers,
Gather the flowers, but spare the buds;
Lest Flora angry at thy crime,
To kill her infants in their prime,
Do quickly make the example yours;
           And, ere we see,
Nip in the blossom all our hopes and thee.

Young Love

1

Come, little infant, love me now,
  While thine unsuspected years
Clear thine agèd father's brow
  From cold jealousy and fears.

2

Pretty, surely, 'twere to see
  By young love old time beguiled,
While our sportings are as free
  As the nurse's with the child.

3

Common beauties stay fifteen;
   Such as yours should swifter move,
Whose fair blossoms are too green
   Yet for lust, but not for love.

4

Love as much the snowy lamb,
   Or the wanton kid, does prize,
As the lusty bull or ram,
   For his morning sacrifice.

5

Now then love me: time may take
   Thee before thy time away:
Of this need we'll virtue make,
   And learn love before we may.

6

So we win of doubtful fate;
   And if good she to us meant,
We that good shall antedate,
   Or, if ill, that ill prevent.

7

Thus as kingdoms, frustrating
   Other titles to their crown,
In the cradle crown their king,
   So all foreign claims to drown,

8

So, to make all rivals vain,
   Now I crown thee with my love:
Crown me with thy love again,
   And we both shall monarchs prove.

The Match

1

Nature had long a treasure made
   Of all her choicest store;
Fearing, when she should be decayed,
   To beg in vain for more.

2

Her orientest colours there,
   And essences most pure,
With sweetest perfumes hoarded were,
   All, as she thought, secure.

3

She seldom them unlocked, or used,
10   But with the nicest care;
For, with one grain of them diffused,
   She could the world repair.

4

But likeness soon together drew
   What she did sep'rate lay;
Of which one perfect beauty grew,
   And that was Celia.

5

Love wisely had of long foreseen
   That he must once grow old;
And therefore stored a magazine,
20   To save him from the cold.

6

He kept the several cells replete
   With nitre thrice refined;
The naphtha's and the sulphur's heat,
   And all that burns the mind.

7

He fortified the double gate,
   And rarely thither came;
For, with one spark of these, he straight
   All Nature could inflame.

8

Till, by vicinity so long,
30   A nearer way they sought;
And, grown magnetically strong,
   Into each other wrought.

9

Thus all his fuel did unite
   To make one fire high:
None ever burned so hot, so bright:
   And, Celia, that am I.

10

So we alone the happy rest,
   Whilst all the world is poor,
And have within ourselves possessed
40   All Love's and Nature's store.

The Nymph Complaining for the Death of Her Fawn

The wanton troopers riding by
Have shot my fawn, and it will die.
Ungentle men! They cannot thrive –
To kill thee! Thou ne'er didst alive
Them any harm: alas, nor could
Thy death yet do them any good.
I'm sure I never wished them ill;
Nor do I for all this; nor will:
But if my simple prayers may yet
10 Prevail with heaven to forget
Thy murder, I will join my tears
Rather than fail. But, O my fears!

It cannot die so. Heaven's King
Keeps register of everything:
And nothing may we use in vain.
E'en beasts must be with justice slain,
Else men are made their deodands.
Though they should wash their guilty hands
In this warm life-blood, which doth part
20   From thine, and wound me to the heart,
Yet could they not be clean: their stain
Is dyed in such a purple grain,
There is not such another in
The world, to offer for their sin.
    Unconstant Sylvio, when yet
I had not found him counterfeit,
One morning (I remember well),
Tied in this silver chain and bell
Gave it to me: nay, and I know
30   What he said then; I'm sure I do.
Said he, 'Look how your huntsman here
Hath caught a fawn to hunt his *dear*.'
But Sylvio soon had me beguiled.
This waxèd tame, while he grew wild,
And quite regardless of my smart,
Left me his fawn, but took his heart.
    Thenceforth I set myself to play
My solitary time away
With this: and very well content,
40   Could so mine idle life have spent.
For it was full of sport; and light
Of foot, and heart; and did invite
Me to its game: it seemed to bless
Itself in me. How could I less
Than love it? O I cannot be
Unkind, t'a beast that loveth me.
    Had it lived long, I do not know
Whether it too might have done so
As Sylvio did: his gifts might be
50   Perhaps as false or more than he.

But I am sure, for ought that I
Could in so short a time espy,
Thy love was far more better than
The love of false and cruel men.
   With sweetest milk, and sugar, first
I it at mine own fingers nursed.
And as it grew, so every day
It waxed more white and sweet than they.
It had so sweet a breath! And oft
60 I blushed to see its foot more soft,
And white (shall I say than my hand?)
Nay, any lady's of the land.
   It is a wondrous thing, how fleet
'Twas on those little silver feet.
With what a pretty skipping grace,
It oft would challenge me the race:
And when 't had left me far away,
'Twould stay, and run again, and stay.
For it was nimbler much than hinds;
70 And trod, as on the foúr winds.
   I have a garden of my own
But so with roses overgrown,
And lilies, that you would it guess
To be a little wilderness.
And all the springtime of the year
It only lovèd to be there.
Among the beds of lilies, I
Have sought it oft, where it should lie;
Yet could not, till itself would rise,
80 Find it, although before mine eyes.
For, in the flaxen lilies' shade,
It like a bank of lilies laid.
Upon the roses it would feed,
Until its lips e'en seemed to bleed:
And then to me 'twould boldly trip,
And print those roses on my lip.
But all its chief delight was still
On roses thus itself to fill:

And its pure virgin limbs to fold
90   In whitest sheets of lilies cold.
Had it lived long, it would have been
Lilies without, roses within.
   O help! O help! I see it faint:
And die as calmly as a saint.
See how it weeps. The tears do come
Sad, slowly dropping like a gum.
So weeps the wounded balsam: so
The holy frankincense doth flow.
The brotherless Heliades
100   Melt in such amber tears as these.
   I in a golden vial will
Keep these two crystal tears; and fill
It till it do o'erflow with mine;
Then place it in Diana's shrine.
   Now my sweet fawn is vanished to
Whither the swans and turtles go:
In fair Elysium to endure,
With milk-white lambs, and ermines pure.
O do not run too fast: for I
110   Will but bespeak thy grave, and die.
   First my unhappy statue shall
Be cut in marble; and withal,
Let it be weeping too – but there
The engraver sure his art may spare,
For I so truly thee bemoan,
That I shall weep though I be stone:
Until my tears (still dropping) wear
My breast, themselves engraving there.
There at my feet shalt thou be laid,
120   Of purest alabaster made:
For I would have thine image be
White as I can, though not as thee.

Upon the Hill and Grove at Bilbrough

TO THE LORD FAIRFAX

1
See how the archèd earth does here
Rise in a perfect hemisphere!
The stiffest compass could not strike
A line more circular and like;
Nor softest pencil draw a brow
So equal as this hill does bow.
It seems as for a model laid,
And that the world by it was made.

2
Here learn, ye mountains more unjust,
10 Which to abrupter greatness thrust,
That do with your hook-shouldered height
The earth deform and heaven fright,
For whose excrescence, ill-designed,
Nature must a new centre find,
Learn here those humble steps to tread,
Which to securer glory lead.

3
See what a soft access and wide
Lies open to its grassy side;
Nor with the rugged path deters
20 The feet of breathless travellers.
See then how courteous it ascends,
And all the way it rises bends;
Nor for itself the height does gain,
But only strives to raise the plain.

4

Yet thus it all the field commands,
And in unenvied greatness stands,
Discerning further than the cliff
Of heaven-daring Tenerife.
How glad the weary seamen haste
30   When they salute it from the mast!
By night the Northern Star their way
Directs, and this no less by day.

5

Upon its crest this mountain grave
A plump of agèd trees does wave.
No hostile hand durst ere invade
With impious steel the sacred shade.
For something always did appear
Of the great Master's terror there:
And men could hear his armour still
40   Rattling through all the grove and hill.

6

Fear of the Master, and respect
Of the great Nymph, did it protect,
Vera the Nymph that him inspired,
To whom he often here retired,
And on these oaks engraved her name;
Such wounds alone these woods became:
But ere he well the barks could part
'Twas writ already in their heart.

7

For they ('tis credible) have sense,
50   As we, of love and reverence,
And underneath the coarser rind
The genius of the house do bind.
Hence they successes seem to know,
And in their Lord's advancement grow;
But in no memory were seen,
As under this, so straight and green;

8

Yet now no further strive to shoot,
Contented if they fix their root.
Nor to the wind's uncertain gust,
60 Their prudent heads too far intrust.
Only sometimes a fluttering breeze
Discourses with the breathing trees,
Which in their modest whispers name
Those acts that swelled the cheek of fame.

9

'Much other groves', say they, 'than these
And other hills him once did please.
Through groves of pikes he thundered then,
And mountains raised of dying men.
For all the civic garlands due
70 To him, our branches are but few.
Nor are our trunks enow to bear
The trophies of one fertile year.'

10

'Tis true, ye trees, nor ever spoke
More certain oracles in oak.
But peace, (if you his favour prize):
That courage its own praises flies.
Therefore to your obscurer seats
From his own brightness he retreats:
Nor he the hills without the groves,
80 Nor height, but with retirement, loves.

*Epigramma in Duos Montes Amosclivium et
Bilboreum: Farfacio*

Cernis ut ingenti distinguant limite campum
    Montis Amosclivi Bilboreique juga!
Ille stat indomitus turritis undique saxis:
    Cingit huic laetum fraxinus alta caput.
Illi petra minax rigidis cervicibus horret:

Huic quatiunt virides lenia colla jubas.
Fulcit Atlanteo rupes ea vertice caelos:
    Collis at hic humeros subjicit Herculeos.
Hic ceu carceribus visum sylvaque coercet:
10   Ille oculos alter dum quasi meta trahit.
Ille giganteum surgit ceu Pelion Ossa:
    Hic agit ut Pindi culmine nympha choros.
Erectus, praeceps, salebrosus, et arduus ille:
    Acclivis, placidus, mollis, amoenus hic est.
Dissimilis domino coiit Natura sub uno;
    Farfaciaque tremunt sub ditione pares.
Dumque triumphanti terras perlabitur axe,
    Praeteriens aequa stringit utrumque rota.
Asper in adversos, facilis cedentibus idem;
20   Ut credas montes extimulasse suos.
Hi sunt Alcidae Borealis nempe columnae,
    Quos medio scindit vallis opaca freto.
An potius, longe sic prona cacumina nutant,
    Parnassus cupiant esse, Maria, tuus.

EPIGRAM ON TWO MOUNTAINS, ALMSCLIFF AND BILBROUGH: TO FAIRFAX

See how the heights of Almscliff
    And of Bilbrough mark the plain with huge boundary.
The former stands untamed with towering stones all
      about;
    The tall ash tree circles the pleasant summit of the other.
On the former, the jutting stone stands erect in stiffened
      ridges:
    On the latter, the soft slopes shake their green manes.
That cliff supports the heavens on its Atlantean peak:
    But this hill submits its Herculean shoulders.
This shuts off the view with its forest as by barriers,
10   While the other draws the eyes as does the turning-post.
That rises gigantic, as Pelion on Ossa:
    This as a nymph leads the dance on the top of Pindus.
That is lofty, steep, uneven, and arduous:
    This is sloping, gentle, soft, and pleasing.

Nature joined dissimilar things under one master;
    And they quake as equals under Fairfaxian sway.
And as he glides over the land in triumphant car,
    His equitable wheel, passing, draws both together.
Harsh to those opposing, yet mild to those yielding,
20   As, you might suppose, his mountains urged.
These are indeed the pillars of the Northern Hercules,
    Which the dark valley divides with its middle strait.
Or rather, thus the peaks bow from a distance,
    Desiring to be your Parnassus, Mary.

Upon Appleton House

TO MY LORD FAIRFAX

1

Within this sober frame expect
Work of no foreign architect,
That unto caves the quarries drew,
And forests did to pastures hew,
Who of his great design in pain
Did for a model vault his brain,
Whose columns should so high be raised
To arch the brows that on them gazed.

2

Why should of all things man unruled
10 Such unproportioned dwellings build?
The beasts are by their dens expressed:
And birds contrive an equal nest;
The low-roofed tortoises do dwell
In cases fit of tortoise shell:
No creature loves an empty space;
Their bodies measure out their place.

3

But he, superfluously spread,
Demands more room alive than dead;
And in his hollow palace goes
20 Where winds (as he) themselves may lose;
What need of all this marble crust
T'impark the wanton mote of dust,
That thinks by breadth the world t'unite
Though the first builders failed in height?

4

But all things are composèd here
Like Nature, orderly and near:
In which we the dimensions find
Of that more sober age and mind,
When larger-sizèd men did stoop
30 To enter at a narrow loop;
As practising, in doors so strait,
To strain themselves through heaven's gate.

5

And surely when the after age
Shall hither come in pilgrimage,
These sacred places to adore,
By Vere and Fairfax trod before,
Men will dispute how their extent
Within such dwarfish confines went:
And some will smile at this, as well
40 As Romulus his bee-like cell.

6

Humility alone designs
Those short but admirable lines,
By which, ungirt and unconstrained,
Things greater are in less contained.
Let others vainly strive t'immure
The circle in the quadrature!
These holy mathematics can
In every figure equal man.

7
Yet thus the laden house does sweat,
And scarce endures the Master great:
But where he comes the swelling hall
Stirs, and the square grows spherical,
More by his magnitude distressed,
Then he is by its straitness pressed:
And too officiously it slights
That in itself which him delights.

8
So honour better lowness bears,
Than that unwonted greatness wears:
Height with a certain grace does bend,
But low things clownishly ascend.
And yet what needs there here excuse,
Where everything does answer use?
Where neatness nothing can condemn,
Nor pride invent what to contemn?

9
A stately frontispiece of poor
Adorns without the open door:
Nor less the rooms within commends
Daily new furniture of friends.
The house was built upon the place
Only as for a mark of grace;
And for an inn to entertain
Its Lord a while, but not remain.

10
Him Bishop's Hill or Denton may,
Or Bilbrough, better hold than they:
But Nature here hath been so free
As if she said, 'Leave this to me.'
Art would more neatly have defaced
What she had laid so sweetly waste,
In fragrant gardens, shady woods,
Deep meadows, and transparent floods.

11

While with slow eyes we these survey,
And on each pleasant footstep stay,
We opportunely may relate
The progress of this house's fate.
A nunnery first gave it birth
(For virgin buildings oft brought forth);
And all that neighbour-ruin shows
The quarries whence this dwelling rose.

12

Near to this gloomy cloister's gates
90 There dwelt the blooming virgin Thwaites,
Fair beyond measure, and an heir
Which might deformity make fair.
And oft she spent the summer suns
Discoursing with the subtle nuns.
Whence in these words one to her weaved,
(As 'twere by chance) thoughts long conceived.

13

'Within this holy leisure we
Live innocently, as you see.
These walls restrain the world without,
100 But hedge our liberty about.
These bars inclose that wider den
Of those wild creatures callèd men.
The cloister outward shuts its gates,
And, from us, locks on them the grates.

14

'Here we, in shining armour white,
Like virgin Amazons do fight.
And our chaste lamps we hourly trim,
Lest the great Bridegroom find them dim.
Our orient breaths perfumèd are
110 With incense of incessant prayer.
And holy-water of our tears
Most strangely our complexion clears.

15

'Not tears of grief; but such as those
With which calm pleasure overflows;
Or pity, when we look on you
That live without this happy vow.
How should we grieve that must be seen
Each one a spouse, and each a queen,
And can in heaven hence behold
120 Our brighter robes and crowns of gold?

16

'When we have prayèd all our beads,
Someone the holy legend reads;
While all the rest with needles paint
The face and graces of the saint.
But what the linen can't receive
They in their lives do interweave.
This work the saints best represents;
That serves for altar's ornaments.

17

'But much it to our work would add
130 If here your hand, your face we had:
By it we would Our Lady touch;
Yet thus She you resembles much.
Some of your features, as we sewed,
Through every shrine should be bestowed.
And in one beauty we would take
Enough a thousand saints to make.

18

'And (for I dare not quench the fire
That me does for your good inspire)
'Twere sacrilege a man t'admit
140 To holy things, for heaven fit.
I see the angels in a crown
On you the lilies showering down:
And around about you glory breaks,
That something more than human speaks.

19

 'All beauty, when at such a height,
  Is so already consecrate.
 Fairfax I know; and long ere this
  Have marked the youth, and what he is.
 But can he such a rival seem
150 For whom you heav'n should disesteem?
  Ah, no! and 'twould more honour prove
  He your *devoto* were than love.

20

 'Here live belovèd, and obeyed:
  Each one your sister, each your maid.
 And, if our rule seem strictly penned,
  The rule itself to you shall bend.
 Our abbess too, now far in age,
  Doth your succession near presage.
 How soft the yoke on us would lie,
160 Might such fair hands as yours it tie!

21

 'Your voice, the sweetest of the choir,
  Shall draw heaven nearer, raise us higher.
 And your example, if our head,
  Will soon us to perfection lead.
 Those virtues to us all so dear,
  Will straight grow sanctity when here:
 And that, once sprung, increase so fast
  Till miracles it work at last.

22

 'Nor is our order yet so nice,
170 Delight to banish as a vice.
 Here pleasure piety doth meet;
  One pérfecting the other sweet.
 So through the mortal fruit we boil
  The sugar's uncorrupting oil:
 And that which perished while we pull,
  Is thus preservèd clear and full.

23

'For such indeed are all our arts,
    Still handling Nature's finest parts.
    Flowers dress the altars; for the clothes,
180 The sea-born amber we compose;
    Balms for the grieved we draw; and pastes
    We mold, as baits for curious tastes.
    What need is here of man? unless
    These as sweet sins we should confess.

24

'Each night among us to your side
    Appoint a fresh and virgin bride;
    Whom if Our Lord at midnight find,
    Yet neither should be left behind.
    Where you may lie as chaste in bed,
190 As pearls together billeted,
    All night embracing arm in arm
    Like crystal pure with cotton warm.

25

'But what is this to all the store
    Of joys you see, and may make more!
    Try but a while, if you be wise:
    The trial neither costs, nor ties.'
    Now, Fairfax, seek her promised faith:
    Religion that dispensèd hath,
    Which she henceforward does begin;
200 The nun's smooth tongue has sucked her in.

26

Oft, though he knew it was in vain,
    Yet would he valiantly complain.
    'Is this that sanctity so great,
    An art by which you finelier cheat?
    Hypocrite witches, hence avaunt,
    Who though in prison yet enchant!
    Death only can such thieves make fast,
    As rob though in the dungeon cast.

27

'Were there but, when this house was made,
210   One stone that a just hand had laid,
       It must have fall'n upon her head
       Who first thee from thy faith misled.
       And yet, how well soever meant,
       With them 'twould soon grow fraudulent:
       For like themselves they alter all,
       And vice infects the very wall.

28

'But sure those buildings last not long,
       Founded by folly, kept by wrong.
       I know what fruit their gardens yield,
220   When they it think by night concealed.
       Fly from their vices. 'Tis thy 'state,
       Not thee, that they would consecrate.
       Fly from their ruin. How I fear,
       Though guiltless, lest thou perish there.'

29

       What should he do? He would respect
       Religion, but not right neglect:
       For first religion taught him right,
       And dazzled not but cleared his sight.
       Sometimes resolved, his sword he draws,
230   But reverenceth then the laws:
       For justice still that courage led;
       First from a judge, then soldier bred.

30

       Small honour would be in the storm.
       The court him grants the lawful form;
       Which licensed either peace or force,
       To hinder the unjust divorce.
       Yet still the nuns his right debarred,
       Standing upon their holy guard.
       Ill-counselled women, do you know
240   Whom you resist, or what you do?

31

Is not this he whose offspring fierce ⌉
Shall fight through all the universe; ⌋
And with successive valour try
France, Poland, either Germany;
Till one, as long since prophesied,
His horse through conquered Britain ride?
Yet, against fate, his spouse they kept,
And the great race would intercept.

32

Some to the breach against their foes
250   Their wooden saints in vain oppose.
Another bolder stands at push
With their old holy-water brush.
While the disjointed abbess threads
The jingling chain-shot of her beads.
But their loudest cannon were their lungs;
And sharpest weapons were their tongues.

33

But waving these aside like flies,
Young Fairfax through the wall does rise.
Then th' unfrequented vault appeared,
260   And superstitions vainly feared.
The relics false were set to view; ⌉
Only the jewels there were true – ⌋
But truly bright and holy Thwaites
That weeping at the altar waits.

34

But the glad youth away her bears,
And to the nuns bequeaths her tears:
Who guiltily their prize bemoan,
Like gypsies that a child had stolen.
Thenceforth (as when the enchantment ends,
270   The castle vanishes or rends)
The wasting cloister with the rest
Was in one instant dispossessed.

35

At the demolishing, this seat
To Fairfax fell as by escheat.
And what both nuns and founders willed
'Tis likely better thus fulfilled.
For if the virgin proved not theirs,
The cloister yet remainèd hers.
Though many a nun there made her vow,
280   'Twas no religious house till now.

36

From that blest bed the hero came,
Whom France and Poland yet does fame:
Who, when retirèd here to peace,
His warlike studies could not cease;
But laid these gardens out in sport
In the just figure of a fort;
And with five bastions it did fence,
As aiming one for every sense.

37

When in the east the morning ray
290   Hangs out the colours of the day,
The bee through these known alleys hums,
Beating the *dian* with its drums.
Then flowers their drowsy eyelids raise,
Their silken ensigns each displays,
And dries its pan yet dank with dew,
And fills its flask with odours new.

38

These, as their Governor goes by,
In fragrant volleys they let fly;
And to salute their Governess
300   Again as great a charge they press:
None for the virgin Nymph; for she
Seems with the flowers a flower to be.
And think so still! though not compare
With breath so sweet, or cheek so fair.

39

Well shot, ye firemen! Oh how sweet,
And round your equal fires do meet,
Whose shrill report no ear can tell,
But echoes to the eye and smell.
See how the flowers, as at parade,
310 Under their colours stand displayed:
Each regiment in order grows,
That of the tulip, pink, and rose.

40

But when the vigilant patrol
Of stars walks round about the Pole,
Their leaves, that to the stalks are curled,
Seem to their staves the ensigns furled.
Then in some flower's belovèd hut
Each bee as sentinel is shut,
And sleeps so too: but, if once stirred,
320 She runs you through, nor asks the word.

41

Oh thou, that dear and happy isle
The garden of the world ere while,
Thou paradise of foúr seas,
Which heaven planted us to please,
But, to exclude the world, did guard
With watery if not flaming sword;
What luckless apple did we taste,
To make us mortal, and thee waste?

42

Unhappy! shall we never more
330 That sweet militía restore,
When gardens only had their towers,
And all the garrisons were flowers,
When roses only arms might bear,
And men did rosy garlands wear?
Tulips, in several colours barred,
Were then the Switzers of our Guard.

43

The gardener had the soldier's place,
And his more gentle forts did trace.
The nursery of all things green
340   Was then the only magazine.
The winter quarters were the stoves,
Where he the tender plants removes.
But war all this doth overgrow;
We ordnance plant and powder sow.

44

And yet there walks one on the sod
Who, had it pleasèd him and God,
Might once have made our gardens spring
Fresh as his own and flourishing.
But he preferred to the Cinque Ports
350   These five imaginary forts,
And, in those half-dry trenches, spanned
Power which the ocean might command.

45

For he did, with his utmost skill,
Ambition weed, but conscience till –
Conscience, that heaven-nursèd plant,
Which most our earthy gardens want.
A prickling leaf it bears, and such
As that which shrinks at every touch;
But flowers eternal, and divine,
360   That in the crowns of saints do shine.

46

The sight does from these bastions ply,
The invisible artillery;
And at proud Cawood Castle seems
To point the battery of its beams.
As if it quarrelled in the seat
The ambition of its prelate great.
But o'er the meads below it plays,
Or innocently seems to graze.

47

And now to the abyss I pass
Of that unfathomable grass,
Where men like grasshoppers appear,
But grasshoppers are giants there:
They, in their squeaking laugh, contemn
Us as we walk more low than them:
And, from the precipices tall
Of the green spires, to us do call.

48

To see men through this meadow dive,
We wonder how they rise alive,
As, under water, none does know
Whether he fall through it or go.
But, as the mariners that sound,
And show upon their lead the ground,
They bring up flowers so to be seen,
And prove they've at the bottom been.

49

No scene that turns with engines strange
Does oftener than these meadows change.
For when the sun the grass hath vexed,
The tawny mowers enter next;
Who seem like Israelites to be,
Walking on foot through a green sea.
To them the grassy deeps divide,
And crowd a lane to either side.

50

With whistling scythe, and elbow strong,
These massacre the grass along:
While one, unknowing, carves the rail,
Whose yet unfeathered quills her fail.
The edge all bloody from its breast
He draws, and does his stroke detest,
Fearing the flesh untimely mowed
To him a fate as black forebode.

51

But bloody Thestylis, that waits
To bring the mowing camp their cates,
Greedy as kites, has trussed it up,
And forthwith means on it to sup:
When on another quick she lights,
And cries, 'He called us Israelites;
But now, to make his saying true,
Rails rain for quails, for manna, dew.'

52

Unhappy birds! what does it boot
410 To build below the grass's root;
When lowness is unsafe as height,
And chance o'ertakes, what 'scapeth spite?
And now your orphan parents' call
Sounds your untimely funeral.
Death-trumpets creak in such a note,
And 'tis the sourdine in their throat.

53

Or sooner hatch or higher build:
The mower now commands the field,
In whose new traverse seemeth wrought
420 A camp of battle newly fought:
Where, as the meads with hay, the plain
Lies quilted o'er with bodies slain:
The women that with forks it fling,
Do represent the pillaging.

54

And now the careless victors play,
Dancing the triumphs of the hay;
Where every mower's wholesome heat
Smells like an Alexander's sweat.
Their females fragrant as the mead
430 Which they in fairy circles tread:
When at their dance's end they kiss,
Their new-made hay not sweeter is.

55

When after this 'tis piled in cocks,
Like a calm sea it shows the rocks,
We wondering in the river near
How boats among them safely steer.
Or, like the desert Memphis sand,
Short pyramids of hay do stand.
And such the Roman camps do rise   *war*
440 In hills for soldiers' obsequies.

56

This scene again withdrawing brings
A new and empty face of things,
A levelled space, as smooth and plain
As cloths for Lely stretched to stain.
The world when first created sure ⎤
Was such a table rase and pure.   ⎦
Or rather such is the *toril*
Ere the bulls enter at Madril.

57

For to this naked equal flat,
450 Which Levellers take pattern at,
The villagers in common chase
Their cattle, which it closer rase;
And what below the scythe increased
Is pinched yet nearer by the beast.
Such, in the painted world, appeared
D'Avenant with the universal herd.

58

They seem within the polished grass
A landskip drawn in looking-glass,
And shrunk in the huge pasture show
460 As spots, so shaped, on faces do –
Such fleas, ere they approach the eye,
In multiplying glasses lie.
They feed so wide, so slowly move,
As constellations do above.

59

Then, to conclude these pleasant acts,
Denton sets ope its cataracts,
And makes the meadow truly be
(What it but seemed before) a sea.
For, jealous of its Lord's long stay,
470   It tries t'invite him thus away.
The river in itself is drowned,
And isles the astonished cattle round.

60

Let others tell the paradox,
How eels now bellow in the ox;
How horses at their tails do kick,
Turned as they hang to leeches quick;
How boats can over bridges sail;
And fishes do the stables scale.
How salmons trespassing are found;
480   And pikes are taken in the pound.

61

But I, retiring from the flood,
Take sanctuary in the wood,
And, while it lasts, myself embark
In this yet green, yet growing ark,
Where the first carpenter might best
Fit timber for his keel have pressed.
And where all creatures might have shares,
Although in armies, not in pairs.

62

The double wood of ancient stocks,
490   Linked in so thick, an union locks,
It like two pedigrees appears,
On th' one hand Fairfax, th' other Vere's:
Of whom though many fell in war,
Yet more to heaven shooting are:
And, as they Nature's cradle decked,
Will in green age her hearse expect.

63

When first the eye this forest sees
It seems indeed as wood not trees:
As if their neighbourhood so old
500 To one great trunk them all did mould.
There the huge bulk takes place, as meant
To thrust up a fifth element,
And stretches still so closely wedged
As if the night within were hedged.

64

Dark all without it knits; within
It opens passable and thin;
And in as loose an order grows,
As the Corinthean porticoes.
The arching boughs unite between
510 The columns of the temple green;
And underneath the wingèd choirs
Echo about their tunèd fires.

65

The nightingale does here make choice
To sing the trials of her voice.
Low shrubs she sits in, and adorns
With music high the squatted thorns.
But highest oaks stoop down to hear,
And listening elders prick the ear.
The thorn, lest it should hurt her, draws
520 Within the skin its shrunken claws.

66

But I have for my music found
A sadder, yet more pleasing sound:
The stock-doves, whose fair necks are graced
With nuptial rings, their ensigns chaste;
Yet always, for some cause unknown,
Sad pair unto the elms they moan.
O why should such a couple mourn,
That in so equal flames do burn!

67

Then as I careless on the bed
530 Of gelid strawberries do tread,
And through the hazels thick espy
The hatching throstles shining eye,
The heron from the ash's top,
The eldest of its young lets drop,
As if it stork-like did pretend
That tribute to its Lord to send.

68

But most the hewel's wonders are,
Who here has the holtfelster's care.
He walks still upright from the root,
540 Measuring the timber with his foot,
And all the way, to keep it clean,
Doth from the bark the woodmoths glean.
He, with his beak, examines well
Which fit to stand and which to fell.

69

The good he numbers up, and hacks,
As if he marked them with the axe.
But where he, tinkling with his beak,
Does find the hollow oak to speak,
That for his building he designs,
550 And through the tainted side he mines.
Who could have thought the tallest oak
Should fall by such a feeble stroke!

70

Nor would it, had the tree not fed
A traitor-worm, within it bred,
(As first our flesh corrupt within
Tempts impotent and bashful sin).
And yet that worm triumphs not long,
But serves to feed the hewel's young,
While the oak seems to fall content,
560 Viewing the treason's punishment.

71

Thus I, easy philosopher,
Among the birds and trees confer.
And little now to make me wants
Or of the fowls, or of the plants:
Give me but wings as they, and I
Straight floating on the air shall fly:
Or turn me but, and you shall see
I was but an inverted tree.

72

Already I begin to call
570   In their most learn'd original:
And where I language want, my signs
The bird upon the bough divines;
And more attentive there doth sit
Than if she were with lime-twigs knit.
No leaf does tremble in the wind
Which I, returning, cannot find.

73

Out of these scattered sibyl's leaves
Strange prophecies my fancy weaves:
And in one history consumes,
580   Like Mexique paintings, all the plumes.
What Rome, Greece, Palestine, ere said
I in this light mosaic read.
Thrice happy he who, not mistook,
Hath read in Nature's mystic book.

74

And see how chance's better wit
Could with a mask my studies hit!
The oak leaves me embroider all,
Between which caterpillars crawl:
And ivy, with familiar trails,
590   Me licks, and clasps, and curls, and hales.
Under this antic cope I move
Like some great prelate of the grove.

75

Then, languishing with ease, I toss
On pallets swollen of velvet moss,
While the wind, cooling through the boughs,
Flatters with air my panting brows.
Thanks for my rest, ye mossy banks;
And unto you, cool zephyrs, thanks,
Who, as my hair, my thoughts too shed,
600   And winnow from the chaff my head.

76

How safe, methinks, and strong, behind
These trees have I encamped my mind;
Where beauty, aiming at the heart,
Bends in some tree its useless dart;
And where the world no certain shot
Can make, or me it toucheth not.
But I on it securely play,
And gall its horsemen all the day.

77

Bind me, ye woodbines, in your twines,
610   Curl me about, ye gadding vines,
And, oh, so close your circles lace,
That I may never leave this place:
But lest your fetters prove too weak,
Ere I your silken bondage break,
Do you, O brambles, chain me too,
And, courteous briars, nail me through.

78

Here in the morning tie my chain,
Where the two woods have made a lane,
While, like a guard on either side,
620   The trees before their Lord divide;
This, like a long and equal thread,
Betwixt two labyrinths does lead.
But where the floods did lately drown,
There at the evening stake me down.

79

For now the waves are fall'n and dried,
And now the meadows fresher dyed,
Whose grass, with moister colour dashed,
Seems as green silks but newly washed.
No serpent new nor crocodile
630 Remains behind our little Nile,
Unless itself you will mistake,
Among these meads the only snake.

80

See in what wanton harmless folds
It everywhere the meadow holds;
And its yet muddy back doth lick,
Till as a crystal mirror slick,
Where all things gaze themselves, and doubt
If they be in it or without.
And for his shade which therein shines,
640 Narcissus-like, the sun too pines.

81

Oh what a pleasure 'tis to hedge
My temples here with heavy sedge,
Abandoning my lazy side,
Stretched as a bank unto the tide,
Or to suspend my sliding foot
On th' osier's underminèd root,
And in its branches tough to hang,
While at my lines the fishes twang!

82

But now away my hooks, my quills,
650 And angles – idle utensíls.
The young Maria walks tonight:
Hide, trifling youth, thy pleasures slight.
'Twere shame that such judicious eyes
Should with such toys a man surprise;
She, that already is the law
Of all her sex, her age's awe.

83

See how loose Nature, in respect
To her, itself doth recollect;
And everything so whisht and fine,
660　Starts forthwith to its *bonne mine*.
The sun himself, of her aware,
Seems to descend with greater care;
And lest she see him go to bed,
In blushing clouds conceals his head.

84

So when the shadows laid asleep
From underneath these banks do creep,
And on the river as it flows
With eben shuts begin to close;
The modest halcyon comes in sight,
670　Flying betwixt the day and night;
And such an horror calm and dumb,
Admiring Nature does benumb.

85

The viscous air, wheres'e'er she fly,
Follows and sucks her azure dye;
The jellying stream compacts below,
If it might fix her shadow so;
The stupid fishes hang, as plain
As flies in crystal overta'en;
And men the silent scene assist,
680　Charmed with the sapphire-wingèd mist.

86

Maria such, and so doth hush
The world, and through the evening rush.
No new-born comet such a train
Draws through the sky, nor star new-slain.
For straight those giddy rockets fail,
Which from the putrid earth exhale,
But by her flames, in heaven tried,
Nature is wholly vitrified.

87

'Tis she that to these gardens gave
690   That wondrous beauty which they have;
She straightness on the woods bestows;
To her the meadow sweetness owes;
Nothing could make the river be
So crystal pure but only she;
She yet more pure, sweet, straight, and fair,
Than gardens, woods, meads, rivers are.

88

Therefore what first she on them spent,
They gratefully again present:
The meadow, carpets where to tread;
700   The garden, flowers to crown her head;
And for a glass, the limpid brook,
Where she may all her beauties look;
But, since she would not have them seen,
The wood about her draws a screen.

89

For she, to higher beauties raised,
Disdains to be for lesser praised.
She counts her beauty to converse
In all the languages as hers;
Nor yet in those herself employs
710   But for the wisdom, not the noise;
Nor yet that wisdom would affect,
But as 'tis heaven's dialect.

90

Blest Nymph! that couldst so soon prevent
Those trains by youth against thee meant:
Tears (watery shot that pierce the mind);
And sighs (Love's cannon charged with wind);
True praise (that breaks through all defence);
And feigned complying innocence;
But knowing where this ambush lay,
720   She 'scaped the safe, but roughest way.

91

This 'tis to have been from the first
In a domestic heaven nursed,
Under the discipline severe
Of Fairfax, and the starry Vere;
Where not one object can come nigh
But pure, and spotless as the eye;
And goodness doth itself entail
On females, if there want a male.

92

Go now, fond sex, that on your face
730   Do all your useless study place,
Nor once at vice your brows dare knit
Lest the smooth forehead wrinkled sit:
Yet your own face shall at you grin,
Thorough the black-bag of your skin,
When knowledge only could have filled
And virtue all those furrows tilled.

93

Hence she with graces more divine
Supplies beyond her sex the line;
And like a sprig of mistletoe
740   On the Fairfacian oak does grow;
Whence, for some universal good,
The priest shall cut the sacred bud,
While her glad parents most rejoice,
And make their destiny their choice.

94

Meantime, ye fields, springs, bushes, flowers,
Where yet she leads her studious hours,
(Till fate her worthily translates,
And find a Fairfax for our Thwaites),
Employ the means you have by her,
750   And in your kind yourselves prefer;
That, as all virgins she precedes,
So you all woods, streams, gardens, meads.

95

For you, Thessalian Tempe's seat
Shall now be scorned as obsolete;
Aranjuez, as less, disdained;
The Bel-Retiro as constrained;
But name not the Idalian grove –
For 'twas the seat of wanton love –
Much less the dead's Elysian Fields,
760   Yet nor to them your beauty yields.

96

'Tis not, what once it was, the world,
But a rude heap together hurled,
All negligently overthrown,
Gulfs, deserts, precipices, stone.
Your lesser world contains the same,
But in more decent order tame;
You, heaven's centre, Nature's lap,
And paradise's only map.

97

But now the salmon-fishers moist
770   Their leathern boats begin to hoist,
And like Antipodes in shoes,
Have shod their heads in their canoes.
How tortoise-like, but not so slow,
These rational amphibii go!
Let's in: for the dark hemisphere
Does now like one of them appear.

The Garden

1

How vainly men themselves amaze
To win the palm, the oak, or bays,
And their uncessant labours see
Crowned from some single herb or tree,
Whose short and narrow vergèd shade
Does prudently their toils upbraid,
While all flowers and all trees do close
To weave the garlands of repose.

2

Fair Quiet, have I found thee here,
And Innocence, thy sister dear!
Mistaken long, I sought you then
In busy companies of men.
Your sacred plants, if here below,
Only among the plants will grow.
Society is all but rude,
To this delicious solitude.

3

No white nor red was ever seen
So am'rous as this lovely green.
Fond lovers, cruel as their flame,
Cut in these trees their mistress' name.
Little, alas, they know, or heed,
How far these beauties hers exceed!
Fair trees! wheres'e'er your barks I wound,
No name shall but your own be found.

4

When we have run our passion's heat,
Love hither makes his best retreat.
The gods, that mortal beauty chase,
Still in a tree did end their race.
Apollo hunted Daphne so,
Only that she might laurel grow.
And Pan did after Syrinx speed,
Not as a nymph, but for a reed.

5

What wondrous life is this I lead!
Ripe apples drop about my head;
The luscious clusters of the vine
Upon my mouth do crush their wine;
The nectarene, and curious peach,
Into my hands themselves do reach;
Stumbling on melons, as I pass,
40 Ensnared with flowers, I fall on grass.

6

Meanwhile the mind, from pleasures less,
Withdraws into its happiness:
The mind, that ocean where each kind
Does straight its own resemblance find,
Yet it creates, transcending these,
Far other worlds, and other seas,
Annihilating all that's made
To a green thought in a green shade.

7

Here at the fountain's sliding foot,
50 Or at some fruit-tree's mossy root,
Casting the body's vest aside,
My soul into the boughs does glide:
There like a bird it sits, and sings,
Then whets, and combs its silver wings;
And, till prepared for longer flight,
Waves in its plumes the various light.

8

Such was that happy garden-state,
While man there walked without a mate:
After a place so pure, and sweet,
60 What other help could yet be meet!
But 'twas beyond a mortal's share
To wander solitary there:
Two paradises 'twere in one
To live in paradise alone.

9

How well the skilful gardener drew
Of flowers and herbs this dial new,
Where from above the milder sun
Does through a fragrant zodiac run;
And, as it works, the industrious bee
70 Computes its time as well as we.
How could such sweet and wholesome hours
Be reckoned but with herbs and flowers!

On a Drop of Dew

See how the orient dew,
Shed from the bosom of the morn
   Into the blowing roses,
Yet careless of its mansion new,
For the clear region where 'twas born
   Round in itself incloses:
   And in its little globe's extent,
Frames as it can its native element.
   How it the purple flower does slight,
10   Scarce touching where it lies,
   But gazing back upon the skies,
   Shines with a mournful light,
     Like its own tear,
Because so long divided from the sphere.
   Restless it rolls and unsecure,
    Trembling lest it grow impure,
   Till the warm sun pity its pain,
And to the skies exhale it back again.
    So the soul, that drop, that ray
20 Of the clear fountain of eternal day,
Could it within the human flower be seen,
   Remembering still its former height,
   Shuns the sweet leaves and blossoms green,
   And, recollecting its own light,
Does, in its pure and circling thoughts, express

    The greater heaven in an heaven less.
        In how coy a figure wound,
        Every way it turns away:
        So the world excluding round,
30   Yet receiving in the day,
        Dark beneath, but bright above,
        Here disdaining, there in love.
   How loose and easy hence to go,
   How girt and ready to ascend,
   Moving but on a point below,
    It all about does upwards bend.
Such did the manna's sacred dew distill,
White and entire, though congealèd and chill,
Congealed on earth: but does, dissolving, run
40 Into the glories of th' almighty sun.

A Dialogue between the Soul and Body

SOUL

O, who shall from this dungeon raise
A soul, enslaved so many ways,
With bolts of bones, that fettered stands
In feet, and manacled in hands.
Here blinded with an eye; and there
Deaf with the drumming of an ear,
A soul hung up, as 'twere, in chains
Of nerves, and arteries, and veins,
Tortured, besides each other part,
10 In a vain head, and double heart?

BODY

O, who shall me deliver whole,
From bonds of this tyrannic soul,
Which, stretched upright, impales me so,
That mine own precipice I go;
And warms and moves this needless frame
(A fever could but do the same),
And, wanting where its spite to try,
Has made me live to let me die,
A body that could never rest,
20   Since this ill spirit it possessed?

SOUL

What magic could me thus confine
Within another's grief to pine,
Where, whatsoever it complain,
I feel, that cannot feel, the pain,
And all my care itself employs,
That to preserve, which me destroys:
Constrained not only to endure
Diseases, but, what's worse, the cure:
And ready oft the port to gain,
30   Am shipwrecked into health again?

BODY

But physic yet could never reach
The maladies thou me dost teach:
Whom first the cramp of hope does tear,
And then the palsy shakes of fear;
The pestilence of love does heat,
Or hatred's hidden ulcer eat;
Joy's cheerful madness does perplex,
Or sorrow's other madness vex;
Which knowledge forces me to know,
40   And memory will not forgo.
What but a soul could have the wit
To build me up for sin so fit?
So architects do square and hew,
Green trees that in the forest grew.

The Mower against Gardens

Luxurious man, to bring his vice in use,
  Did after him the world seduce,
And from the fields the flowers and plants allure,
  Where nature was most plain and pure.
He first enclosed within the gardens square
  A dead and standing pool of air,
And a more luscious earth for them did knead,
  Which stupified them while it fed.
The pink grew then as double as his mind;
10 The nutriment did change the kind.
With strange perfumes he did the roses taint,
  And flowers themselves were taught to paint.
The tulip, white, did for complexion seek,
  And learned to interline its cheek:
Its onion root they then so high did hold,
  That one was for a meadow sold.
Another world was searched, through oceans new,
  To find the *Marvel of Peru*.
And yet these rarities might be allowed
20 To man, that sovereign thing and proud,
Had he not dealt between the bark and tree,
  Forbidden mixtures there to see.
No plant now knew the stock from which it came;
  He grafts upon the wild the tame:
That th' uncertain and adulterate fruit
  Might put the palate in dispute.
His green seraglio has its eunuchs too,
  Lest any tyrant him outdo.
And in the cherry he does nature vex,
30 To procreate without a sex.
'Tis all enforced, the fountain and the grot,
  While the sweet fields do lie forgot:
Where willing nature does to all dispense
  A wild and fragrant innocence:
And fauns and fairies do the meadows till,
  More by their presence than their skill.

Their statues, polished by some ancient hand,
  May to adorn the gardens stand:
But howsoe'er the figures do excel,
  The gods themselves with us do dwell.

Damon the Mower

1

Hark how the Mower Damon sung,
With love of Juliana stung!
While everything did seem to paint
The scene more fit for his complaint.
Like her fair eyes the day was fair,
But scorching like his am'rous care.
Sharp like his scythe his sorrow was,
And withered like his hopes the grass.

2

'Oh what unusual heats are here,
10 Which thus our sunburned meadows sear!
The grasshopper its pipe gives o'er;
And hamstringed frogs can dance no more.
But in the brook the green frog wades;
And grasshoppers seek out the shades.
Only the snake, that kept within,
Now glitters in its second skin.

3

'This heat the sun could never raise,
Nor Dog Star so inflame the days.
It from an higher beauty grow'th,
20 Which burns the fields and mower both:
Which mads the dog, and makes the sun
Hotter than his own Phaëton.
Not July causeth these extremes,
But Juliana's scorching beams.

4

'Tell me where I may pass the fires
Of the hot day, or hot desires.
To what cool cave shall I descend,
Or to what gelid fountain bend?
Alas! I look for ease in vain,
30 When remedies themselves complain.
No moisture but my tears do rest,
Nor cold but in her icy breast.

5

'How long wilt thou, fair shepherdess,
Esteem me, and my presents less?
To thee the harmless snake I bring,
Disarmèd of its teeth and sting;
To thee chameleons, changing hue,
And oak leaves tipped with honey dew.
Yet thou, ungrateful, hast not sought
40 Nor what they are, nor who them brought.

6

'I am the Mower Damon, known
Through all the meadows I have mown.
On me the morn her dew distills
Before her darling daffodils.
And, if at noon my toil me heat,
The sun himself licks off my sweat.
While, going home, the evening sweet
In cowslip-water bathes my feet.

7

'What, though the piping shepherd stock
50 The plains with an unnumbered flock,
This scythe of mine discovers wide
More ground than all his sheep do hide.
With this the golden fleece I shear
Of all these closes every year.
And though in wool more poor than they,
Yet am I richer far in hay.

8

'Nor am I so deformed to sight,
If in my scythe I lookèd right;
In which I see my picture done,
60 As in a crescent moon the sun.
The deathless fairies take me oft
To lead them in their dances soft:
And, when I tune myself to sing,
About me they contract their ring.

9

'How happy might I still have mowed,
Had not Love here his thistles sowed!
But now I all the day complain,
Joining my labour to my pain;
And with my scythe cut down the grass,
70 Yet still my grief is where it was:
But, when the iron blunter grows,
Sighing, I whet my scythe and woes.'

10

While thus he threw his elbow round,
Depopulating all the ground,
And, with his whistling scythe, does cut
Each stroke between the earth and root,
The edgèd steel by careless chance
Did into his own ankle glance;
And there among the grass fell down,
80 By his own scythe, the Mower mown.

11

'Alas!' said he, 'these hurts are slight
To those that die by love's despite.
With shepherd's-purse, and clown's-all-heal,
The blood I staunch, and wound I seal.
Only for him no cure is found,
Whom Juliana's eyes do wound.
'Tis death alone that this must do:
For Death thou art a Mower too.'

The Mower to the Glowworms

1
Ye living lamps, by whose dear light
The nightingale does sit so late,
And studying all the summer night,
Her matchless songs does meditate;

2
Ye country comets, that portend
No war, nor prince's funeral,
Shining unto no higher end
Than to presage the grass's fall;

3
Ye glowworms, whose officious flame
10   To wandering mowers shows the way,
That in the night have lost their aim,
And after foolish fires do stray;

4
Your courteous lights in vain you waste,
Since Juliana here is come,
For she my mind hath so displaced
That I shall never find my home.

The Mower's Song

1
My mind was once the true survey
Of all these meadows fresh and gay,
And in the greenness of the grass
Did see its hopes as in a glass;
When Juliana came, and she
What I do to the grass, does to my thoughts and me.

cruel woman

2

But these, while I with sorrow pine,
Grew more luxuriant still and fine,
That not one blade of grass you spied,
10   But had a flower on either side;
When Juliana came, and she
What I do to the grass, does to my thoughts and me.

3

Unthankful meadows, could you so
A fellowship so true forgo,
And in your gaudy May-games meet,
While I lay trodden under feet?
When Juliana came, and she
What I do to the grass, does to my thoughts and me.

4

But what you in compassion ought,
20   Shall now by my revenge be wrought:
And flowers, and grass, and I and all,
Will in one common ruin fall.
For Juliana comes, and she
What I do to the grass, does to my thoughts and me.

5

And thus, ye meadows, which have been
Companions of my thoughts more green,
Shall now the heraldry become
With which I will adorn my tomb;
For Juliana comes, and she
30   What I do to the grass, does to my thoughts and me.

Music's Empire

1

First was the world as one great cymbal made,
Where jarring winds to infant Nature played.
All music was a solitary sound,
To hollow rocks and murmuring fountains bound.

2

Jubal first made the wilder notes agree;
And Jubal tuned music's first jubilee:
He called the echoes from their sullen cell,
And built the organ's city where they dwell.

3

Each sought a consort in that lovely place;
10   And virgin trebles wed the manly base.
From whence the progeny of numbers new
Into harmonious colonies withdrew.

4

Some to the lute, some to the viol went,
And others chose the cornet eloquent,
These practising the wind, and those the wire,
To sing men's triumphs, or in heaven's choir.

5

Then music, the mosaic of the air,
Did of all these a solemn noise prepare:
With which she gained the empire of the ear,
20   Including all between the earth and sphere.

6

Victorious sounds! Yet here your homage do
Unto a gentler conqueror than you:
Who though he flies the music of his praise,
Would with you heaven's hallelujahs raise.

The Character of Holland

Holland, that scarce deserves the name of land,
As but the off-scouring of the British sand;
And so much earth as was contributed
By English pilots when they heaved the lead;
Or what by th' ocean's slow alluvion fell
Of shipwrecked cockle and the mussel shell;
This indigested vomit of the sea
Fell to the Dutch by just propriety.
   Glad then, as miners that have found the ore,
10 They with mad labour fished the land to shore,
And dived as desperately for each piece
Of earth, as if't had been of ambergris,
Collecting anxiously small loads of clay,
Less than what building swallows bear away,
Or than those pills which sordid beetles roll,
Transfusing into them their dunghill soul.
   How did they rivet, with gigantic piles,
Thorough the centre their new-catchèd miles,
And to the stake a struggling country bound,
20 Where barking waves still bait the forcèd ground,
Building their watery Babel far more high
To reach the sea, than those to scale the sky.
   Yet still his claim the injured ocean laid,
And oft at leap-frog o'er their steeples played:
As if on purpose it on land had come
To show them what's their *Mare Liberum*.
A daily deluge over them does boil;
The earth and water play at level-coil;
The fish ofttimes the burger dispossessed,
30 And sat not as a meat but as a guest.
And oft the tritons and the sea nymphs saw
Whole shoals of Dutch served up for cabillau;
Or as they over the new level ranged
For pickled herring, pickled *Heeren* changed.
Nature, it seemed, ashamed of her mistake,
Would throw their land away at duck and drake.

    Therefore necessity, that first made kings,
Something like government among them brings.
For as with pygmies, who best kills the crane,
40   Among the hungry, he that treasures grain,
Among the blind, the one-eyed blinkard reigns,
So rules among the drownèd, he that drains.
Not who first sees the rising sun commands,
But who could first discern the rising lands.
Who best could know to pump an earth so leak
Him they their Lord and country's Father speak.
To make a bank was a great plot of state;
Invent a shovel, and be magistrate.
Hence some small dyke-grave unperceived invades
50   The power, and grows, as 'twere, a King of Spades.
But for less envy some joint states endures,
Who look like a Commission of the Sewers.
For these Half-anders, half wet, and half dry,
Nor bear strict service, nor pure liberty.
    'Tis probable religion after this
Came next in order, which they could not miss.
How could the Dutch but be converted, when
The Apostles were so many fishermen?
Besides, the waters of themselves did rise,
60   And, as their land, so them did re-baptize,
Though herring for their god few voices missed,
And Poor-John to have been the Evangelist.
Faith, that could never twins conceive before,
Never so fertile, spawned upon this shore,
More pregnant than their Margaret, that laid down
For *Hans-in-Kelder* of a whole Hans-town.
    Sure when religion did itself embark,
And from the East would Westward steer its ark,
It struck, and splitting on this unknown ground,
70   Each one thence pillaged the first piece he found:
Hence Amsterdam, Turk-Christian-Pagan-Jew,
Staple of sects and mint of schism grew,
That bank of conscience, where not one so strange
Opinion but finds credit, and exchange.

In vain for Catholics ourselves we bear;
The Universal Church is only there.
   Nor can civility there want for tillage,
Where wisely for their court they chose a village.
How fit a title clothes their governors,
80 Themselves the *Hogs*, as all their subjects *Bores*!
   Let it suffice to give their country fame
That it had one Civilis called by name,
Some fifteen hundred and more years ago;
But surely never any that *was* so.
   See but their mermaids with their tails of fish,
Reeking at church over the chafing-dish:
A vestal turf enshrined in earthen ware
Fumes through the loopholes of a wooden square.
Each to the temple with these altars tend
90 (But still does place it at her western end),
While the fat steam of female sacrifice
Fills the priest's nostrils and puts out his eyes.
   Or what a spectacle the skipper gross,
A water-Hercules butter-coloss,
Tunned up with all their several towns of *Beer*;
When staggering upon some land, snick and sneer,
They try, like statuaries, if they can
Cut out each other's Athos to a man:
And carve in their large bodies, where they please,
100 The arms of the United Provinces.
   But when such amity at home is showed,
What then are their confederacies abroad?
Let this one court'sy witness all the rest:
When their whole navy they together pressed –
Not Christian captives to redeem from bands,
Or intercept the Western golden sands –
No, but all ancient rights and leagues must vail,
Rather than to the English strike their sail;
To whom their weather-beaten province owes
110 Itself – when as some greater vessel tows
A cockboat tossed with the same wind and fate –
We buoyed so often up their sinking state.

Was this *Jus Belli & Pacis*? Could this be
Cause why their burgomaster of the sea
Rammed with gun powder, flaming with brand wine,
Should raging hold his linstock to the mine,
While, with feigned treaties, they invade by stealth
Our sore new circumcisèd Commonwealth?
    Yet of his vain attempt no more he sees
120 Than of case-butter shot and bullet-cheese.
And the torn navy staggered with him home,
While the sea laughed itself into a foam.
'Tis true since that (as fortune kindly sports),
A wholesome danger drove us to our ports,
While half their banished keels the tempest tossed,
Half, bound at home in prison to the frost:
That ours meantime at leisure might careen,
In a calm winter, under skies serene,
As the obsequious air and waters rest,
130 Till the dear halcyon hatch out all its nest.
The Commonwealth doth by its losses grow;
And, like its own seas, only ebbs to flow.
Besides, that very agitation laves,
And purges out the corruptible waves.
    And now again our armèd *Bucentore*
Doth yearly their sea nuptials restore.
And now their hydra of seven provinces
Is strangled by our infant Hercules.
Their tortoise wants its vainly stretchèd neck;
140 Their navy all our conquest or our wreck;
Or, what is left, their Carthage overcome
Would render fain unto our better Rome,
Unless our Senate, lest their youth disuse
The war, (but who would?) peace, if begged, refuse.
    For now of nothing may our state despair,
Darling of heaven, and of men the care;
Provided that they be what they have been,
Watchful abroad, and honest still within.
For while our Neptune doth a trident shake,
150 Steeled with those piercing heads – Deane, Monck, and
    Blake –

And while Jove governs in the highest sphere,
Vainly in Hell let Pluto domineer.

Bermudas

Where the remote Bermudas ride
In the ocean's bosom unespied,
From a small boat, that rowed along,
The listening winds received this song.
   'What should we do but sing his praise
That led us through the watery maze,
Unto an isle so long unknown,
And yet far kinder than our own?
Where he the huge sea-monsters wracks,
10   That lift the deep upon their backs,
He lands us on a grassy stage,
Safe from the storms, and prelate's rage.
He gave us this eternal spring,
Which here enamels everything,
And sends the fowl to us in care,
On daily visits through the air.
He hangs in shades the orange bright,
Like golden lamps in a green night,
And does in the pom'granates close
20   Jewels more rich than Ormus shows.
He makes the figs our mouths to meet,
And throws the melons at our feet,
But apples plants of such a price,
No tree could ever bear them twice.
With cedars, chosen by his hand,
From Lebanon, he stores the land,
And makes the hollow seas, that roar,
Proclaim the ambergris on shore.
He cast (of which we rather boast)
30   The gospel's pearl upon our coast,
And in these rocks for us did frame
A temple, where to sound his name.

Oh let our voice his praise exalt,
Till it arrive at heaven's vault:
Which thence (perhaps) rebounding, may
Echo beyond the Mexique Bay.'
    Thus sung they, in the English boat,
An holy and a cheerful note,
And all the way, to guide their chime,
With falling oars they kept the time.

A Letter to Doctor Ingelo
(THEN WITH MY LORD WHITLOCKE, AMBASSADOR
FROM THE PROTECTOR TO THE QUEEN OF SWEDEN)

Quid facis arctoi charissime transfuga caeli,
    Ingele, proh sero cognite, rapte cito?
Num satis hybernum defendis pellibus astrum,
    Qui modo tam mollis nec bene firmus eras?
Quae gentes hominum, quae sit natura locorum,
    Sint homines, potius dic ibi sintne loca?
Num gravis horrisono polus obruit omnia lapsu,
    Jungitur et praeceps mundus utraque nive?
An melius canis horrescit campus aristis,
10   Annuus agricolis et redit orbe labor?
Incolit, ut fertur, saevam gens mitior oram,
    Pace vigil, bello strenua, justa foro.
Quin ibi sunt urbes, atque alta palatia regum,
    Musarumque domus, et sua templa Deo.
Nam regit imperio populum Christina ferocem,
    Et dare jura potest regia virgo viris.
Utque trahit rigidum magnes aquilone metallum,
    Gaudet eam soboles ferrea sponte sequi.
Dic quantum licat fallaci credere famae,
20   Invida num taceat plura, sonetve loquax.
At, si vera fides, mundi melioris ab ortu,
    Saecula Christinae nulla tulere parem.
Ipsa licet redeat (nostri decus orbis) Eliza,
    Qualis nostra tamen quantaque Eliza fuit.

Vidimus effigiem, mistasque coloribus umbras:
    Sic quoque sceptripotens, sic quoque visa dea.
Augustam decorant (raro concordia) frontem
    Majestas et Amor, Forma Pudorque simul.
Ingens virgineo spirat Gustavus in ore:
30   Agnoscas animos, fulmineumque patrem.
Nulla suo nituit tam lucida stella sub axe;
    Non ea quae meruit crimine nympha polum.
Ah quoties pavidum demisit conscia lumen,
    Utque suae timuit Parrhasis ora deae!
Et, simulet falsa ni pictor imagine vultus,
    Delia tam similis nec fuit ipsa sibi.
Ni quod inornati Triviae sint forte capilli,
    Sollicita sed huic distribuantur acu.
Scilicet ut nemo est illa reverentior aequi;
40   Haud ipsas igitur fert sine lege comas.
Gloria sylvarum pariter communis utrique
    Est, et perpetuae virginitatis honos.
Sic quoque nympharum supereminet agmina collo,
    Fertque choros Cynthi per juga, perque nives.
Haud aliter pariles ciliorum contrahit arcus
    Acribus ast oculis tela subesse putes.
Luminibus dubites an straverit illa sagittis
    Quae fovet exuviis ardua colla feram.
Alcides humeros coopertus pelle Nemaea
50   Haud ita labentis sustulit orbis onus.
Heu quae cervices subnectunt pectora tales,
    Frigidiora gelu, candidiora nive.
Caetera non licuit, sed vix ea tota, videre;
    Nam clausi rigido stant adamante sinus.
Seu chlamys artifici nimium succurrerit auso,
    Sicque imperfectum fugerit impar opus:
Sive tribus spernat victrix certare deabus,
    Et pretium formae nec spoliata ferat.
Junonis properans et clara trophaea Minervae;
60   Mollia nam Veneris praemia nosse piget.
Hinc neque consuluit fugitivae prodiga formae,
    Nec timuit seris invigilasse libris.

Insomnem quoties nymphae monuere sequaces
    Decedet roseis heu color ille genis.
Jamque vigil leni cessit Philomela sopori,
    Omnibus et sylvis conticuere ferae.
Acrior illa tamen pergit, curasque fatigat:
    Tanti est doctorum volvere scripta virum.
Et liciti quae sint moderamina discere regni,
70   Quid fuerit, quid sit, noscere quicquid erit.
Sic quod in ingenuas Gothus peccaverit artes
    Vindicat, et studiis expiat una suis.
Exemplum dociles imitantur nobile gentes,
    Et geminis infans imbuit ora sonis.
Transpositos Suecis credas migrasse Latinos,
    Carmine Romuleo sic strepit omne nemus.
Upsala nec priscis impar memoratur Athenis,
    Aegidaque et currus hic sua Pallas habet.
Illinc O quales liceat sperasse liquores,
80   Quum dea praesideat fontibus ipsa sacris!
Illic lacte ruant illic et flumina melle,
    Fulvaque inauratam tingat arena Salam.
Upsalides Musae nunc et majora canemus,
    Quaeque mihi Famae non levis aura tulit.
Creditur haud ulli Christus signasse suorum
    Occultam gemma de meliore notam.
Quemque tenet charo descriptum, nomine semper,
    Non minus exculptum pectore fida refert.
Sola haec virgineas depascit flamma medullas,
90   Et licito pergit solvere corda foco.
Tu quoque Sanctorum fastos Christina sacrabis,
    Unica nec virgo Volsiniensis erit.
Discite nunc reges (majestas proxima caelo)
    Discite proh magnos hinc coluisse deos.
Ah pudeat tantos puerilia fingere coepta,
    Nugas nescio quas, et male quaerere opes.
Acer equo cunctos dum praeterit ille Britanno
    Et pecoris spolium nescit inerme sequi.
Ast aquilam poscit Germano pellere nido,
100   Deque Palatino monte fugare lupam.

Vos etiam latos in praedam jungite campos,
   Impiaque arctatis cingite lustra plagis.
Victor Oliverus nudum caput exerit armis,
   Ducere sive sequi nobile laetus iter.
Qualis jam senior Solymae Godfredus ad arces,
   Spina cui canis floruit alba comis.
Et Lappos Christina potest et solvere Finnos,
   Ultima quos Boreae carcere claustra premunt.
Aeoliis quales venti fremuere sub antris,
110   Et tentant montis corripuisse moras.
Hanc dea si summa demiserit arce procellam
   Quam gravis Austriacis Hesperiisque cadat!
Omnia sed rediens olim narraveris ipse;
   Nec reditus spero tempora longa petit.
Non ibi lenta pigro stringuntur frigore verba,
   Solibus, et tandem vere liquanda novo.
Sed radiis hyemem regina potentior urit;
   Haeque magis solvit, quam ligat illa polum.
Dicitur et nostros moerens audisse labores,
120   Fortis et ingenuam gentis amasse fidem.
Oblatae Batavam nec paci commodat aurem;
   Nec versat Danos insidiosa dolos.
Sed pia festinat mutatis foedera rebus,
   Et libertatem quae dominatur amat.
Digna cui Salomon meritos retulisset honores,
   Et Saba concretum thure cremasset iter.
Hanc tua, sed melius, celebraverit, Ingele, musa;
   Et labor est vestrae debitus ille lyrae.
Nos sine te frustra Thamisis saliceta subimus,
130   Sparsaque per steriles turba vagamur agros.
Et male tentanti querulum respondet avena:
   Quin et Rogerio dissiluere fides.
Haec tamen absenti memores dictamus amico,
   Grataque speramus qualiacumque fore.

What are you doing, dear Ingelo, a deserter to the
    northern zone,
   Oh lately known, and so swiftly taken away?

Are you warding off the wintry star with sufficient furs,
   You who were already in poor health?
What kinds of men are there, what is the nature of the
      place?
   Are men there? Tell me rather, is there such a place?
Does the heavy Pole overwhelm all with the awful sound
      of its motion,
   And does the precipitous earth blend one winter's snow
      with the next?
Or does the field ripen fairer with the spikes of grain
10   And is the farmer's seasonal toil better repaid?
A milder race, it is said, inhabits the harsh region,
   Vigilant in peace, vigorous in war, just in trade.
Indeed, there are cities there, and a high palace of kings,
   A home of the muses, and temples for God.
For it is Christina who rules this rugged people,
   A royal virgin who gives laws to men.
As a magnet swings the stubborn metal to the north,
   That iron race delights to follow her.
Tell me how much one may trust in deceptive rumour,
20   Which, envious, sometimes omits many things and
      sometimes babbles too loquaciously.
But if the report is true, since a better world began
   No age has borne the equal of Christina.
Though Eliza herself (the glory of our world) should
      return,
   Yet our Eliza was just such as she and as great.
We have seen her picture, shadows mixed with colours:
   She seemed both queen and goddess.
Majesty and Love, Beauty and Modesty together,
   Rarely in concord, adorn her royal brow.
Great Gustavus lives again in her virginal features:
30   You may recognize the spirit, and the lightning of her
      father.
No star under heaven ever shone so clear;
   Not that nymph who became a star for her crime.
(Ah, how often, conscious of her guilt, Parrhasis lowered
   her bashful gaze,

And how she feared the face of her goddess!)
And, unless the painter represented her features with a
　false image,
　Delia herself was not so similar to her.
Except perhaps that Trivia's hair blows free,
　While hers is carefully arranged.
It is evident that no one is more respectful of justice than
　she;
40　She doesn't move her very hairs without a law.
Equally the glory of the woods and of the state
　She is, and the ornament of perpetual virginity.
Thus, too, she towers over her trains of nymphs by a
　head,
　And leads the dance along the peaks of Cynthus and
　through the snows.
She does not contract the equal bows of her eyelids,
　But you think that darts are underneath in her fierce
　eyes.
You would doubt whether she killed with arrows or with
　a glance
　The beast whose fur warms her straight neck.
Hercules, having covered his shoulders with a Nemean
　skin,
50　Did not bear the burden of the tottering world so
　gracefully.
Oh, such a neck, which joins a breast
　Colder than frost, whiter than snow.
It was not permitted to see the rest, but scarcely all this;
　For her breasts are encased in rigid steel.
I am doubtful whether the chlamys came to the aid of the
　overly daring artist,
　And so he, unequal to the effort, avoided the unfinished
　task,
Or whether she scorns to compete with three goddesses,
　And, without undressing, carries away the prize for
　beauty,
Bearing off the shining trophies of Juno and Minerva –
60　For to have known the soft rewards of Venus is
　shameful.

Hence, she, prodigal, has not given a thought to fleeting
    beauty,
    Nor feared to wake late hours with books.
How often the attendant maidens have warned her,
    sleepless,
    That colour, alas, will depart from rosy cheeks.
And now wakeful Philomel has yielded to gentle sleep,
    And in all the woods the beasts have hushed.
Yet she continues, more vigorous, and wears out her cares:
    That is the price of perusing the writings of many
    learned men,
    And learning what acts of kings are lawful,
70   Of knowing what has been, what is, and whatever will
    be.
Thus, whatever sins the Goth may have committed against
    the liberal arts,
    She, alone, vindicates and expiates with her studies.
The people, eager to be taught, follow her noble example,
    And the infant fills his mouth with double sounds.
You would think the Latins, transposed, to have changed
    to Swedes,
    So does every grove resound with Roman song.
Upsala is thought not unequal to ancient Athens,
    Here Pallas has both her aegis and chariot.
O what streams one might expect from there,
80   Since the goddess herself presides over the sacred
    fountains!
There the rivers may run with milk and honey,
    And golden sand dyes golden Sala.
And now Upsalian Muses, let us sing greater things,
    Everything that the solemn breath of Fame has borne
    to me.
Christ is believed to have signed for none of his chosen
    The secret mark with a better seal.
And He whom she holds always described in her dear
    name,
    Not less faithful, she bears carved in her heart.
This flame alone consumes her virginal marrow,

90   And she proceeds to release her inner feelings at this
         lawful hearth.
      You too will consecrate the calendar of saints, Christina,
         The virgin of Bolsena shall not be alone.
      Learn now, kings (majesty nearest to heaven),
         Ah, learn from this source to worship the great gods.
      Ah, may it be shameful to form so many childish
            undertakings,
         I know not what trifles, and to seek wealth excessively,
      While one man, zealous, surpasses all with the British
            horse,
         And scorns to seek an undefended prize.
      But he desires to drive the eagle from its German nest,
100   And to rout the she-wolf from the Palatine.
      You two should join your broad fields in hope of booty,
         And surround the dens of iniquity with tightened nets.
      Victorious Oliver exposes his bare head in battle,
         Glad to lead or to follow a noble course,
      Just as once to the citadel of Jerusalem went Godfrey, the
            Elder,
         On whose gray hairs flowered the white thorn.
      Christina can loose both the Lapps and the Finns,
         Whom the distant barriers of Boreas hold in prison,
      Just as the winds roared in Aeolian caves,
110   And tried to sweep away the mountain barriers.
      If the goddess should send this tempest down from her
            high citadel,
         How heavy it would fall on the Austrians and the
            Spanish!
      But, returning, you yourself shall tell everything:
         Nor, I hope, is your return far off.
      Slow words are not bound there with sluggish cold,
         Finally to be melted by the sun and the new spring.
      For the queen, more potent, scorches winter with her
            beams,
         And thaws more than winter binds the Pole.
      She is said, lamenting, to have heard of our travails,
120   And to have loved the free-born faith of a brave people.

Nor does she please the Dutch ear with offered peace,
Or, deceitful, consider Danish tricks.
But she hastens honest treaties as affairs change,
And she who has dominion loves liberty.
Solomon would have paid her deserved praise,
And Sheba's queen would have burned the frozen way
with incense.
But your muse might proclaim her better, Ingelo,
And that labour is owed to your lyre.
Without you, we go in vain under the willows of the
Thames;
130   A scattered band, we wander through barren fields,
And the pipe responds mournfully to those attemping it
unskilfully.
And, indeed, Rogers' strings have burst asunder.
Nevertheless, we write these remembrances to an absent
friend,
And we hope that, whatever their merit, they will be
pleasing.

In Effigiem Oliveri Cromwell

Haec est quae toties inimicos umbra fugavit,
At sub qua cives otia lenta terunt.

ON A PORTRAIT OF OLIVER CROMWELL

This is an image which put enemies to flight,
But under which citizens enjoy quiet leisure.

In Eandem [Effigiem Oliveri Cromwell]
Reginae Sueciae Transmissam

Bellipotens virgo, septem regina trionum.
Christina, arctoi lucida stella poli;
Cernis quas merui dura sub casside rugas;

Sicque senex armis impiger ora fero;
Invia fatorum dum per vestigia nitor,
    Exequor et populi fortia jussa manu.
At tibi submittit frontem reverentior umbra,
    Nec sunt hi vultus regibus usque truces.

TO CHRISTINA, QUEEN OF SWEDEN

Bright Martial Maid, Queen of the frozen zone,
    The northern pole supports thy shining throne.
Behold what furrows age and steel can plough;
    The helmet's weight oppressed this wrinkled brow.
Through fate's untrodden paths I move; my hands
    Still act my free-born people's bold commands;
Yet this stern shade, to you submits his frowns,
    Nor are these looks always severe to crowns.

*The First Anniversary of the Government
under His Highness the Lord Protector, 1655*

Like the vain curlings of the watery maze,
Which in smooth streams a sinking weight does raise,
So Man, declining always, disappears
In the weak circles of increasing years;
And his short tumults of themselves compose,
While flowing Time above his head does close.
    Cromwell alone with greater vigour runs,
(Sun-like) the stages of succeeding suns:
And still the day which he doth next restore,
Is the just wonder of the day before.
Cromwell alone doth with new lustre spring,
And shines the jewel of the yearly ring.
    'Tis he the force of scattered time contracts,
And in one year the work of ages acts:
While heavy monarchs make a wide return,
Longer, and more malignant than Saturn:

And though they all Platonic years should reign,
In the same posture would be found again.
Their earthy projects under ground they lay,
20 More slow and brittle than the China clay:
Well may they strive to leave them to their son,
For one thing never was by one king done.
Yet some more active for a frontier town,
Taken by proxy, beg a false renown;
Another triumphs at the public cost,
And will have won, if he no more have lost;
They fight by others, but in person wrong,
And only are against their subjects strong;
Their other wars seem but a feigned contést,
30 This common enemy is still oppressed;
If conquerors, on them they turn their might;
If conquered, on them they wreak their spite:
They neither build the temple in their days,
Nor matter for succeeding founders raise;
Nor sacred prophecies consult within,
Much less themself to pérfect them begin;
No other care they bear of things above,
But with astrologers divine of Jove
To know how long their planet yet reprieves
40 From the deservèd fate their guilty lives:
Thus (image-like) an useless time they tell,
And with vain sceptre strike the hourly bell,
Nor more contribute to the state of things,
Than wooden heads unto the viol's strings.
    While indefatigable Cromwell hies,
And cuts his way still nearer to the skies,
Learning a music in the region clear,
To tune this lower to that higher sphere.
    So when Amphion did the lute command,
50 Which the god gave him, with his gentle hand,
The rougher stones, unto his measures hewed,
Danced up in order from the quarries rude;
This took a lower, that an higher place,
As he the treble altered, or the bass:

No note he struck, but a new stone was laid,
And the great work ascended while he played.

The listening structures he with wonder eyed,
And still new stops to various time applied:
Now through the strings a martial rage he throws,
60 And joining straight the Theban tower arose;
Then as he strokes them with a touch more sweet,
The flocking marbles in a palace meet;
But for he most the graver notes did try,
Therefore the temples reared their columns high:
Thus, ere he ceased, his sacred lute creates
Th' harmonious city of the seven gates.

Such was that wondrous order and consent,
When Cromwell tuned the ruling Instrument,
While tedious statesmen many years did hack,
70 Framing a liberty that still went back,
Whose numerous gorge could swallow in an hour
That island, which the sea cannot devour:
Then our Amphion issues out and sings,
And once he struck, and twice, the powerful strings.

The Commonwealth then first together came,
And each one entered in the willing frame;
All other matter yields, and may be ruled;
But who the minds of stubborn men can build?
No quarry bears a stone so hardly wrought,
80 Nor with such labour from its centre brought;
None to be sunk in the foundation bends,
Each in the house the highest place contends,
And each the hand that lays him will direct,
And some fall back upon the architect;
Yet all composed by his attractive song,
Into the animated city throng.

The Commonwealth does through their centres all
Draw the circumference of the public wall;
The crossest spirits here do take their part,
90 Fastening the contignation which they thwart;
And they, whose nature leads them to divide,
Uphold this one, and that the other side;

But the most equal still sustain the height,
And they as pillars keep the work upright,
While the resistance of opposèd minds,
The fabric (as with arches) stronger binds,
Which on the basis of a senate free,
Knit by the roof's protecting weight, agree.
    When for his foot he thus a place had found,
100 He hurls e'er since the world about him round,
And in his several aspects, like a star,
Here shines in peace, and thither shoots in war,
While by his beams observing princes steer,
And wisely court the influence they fear.
O would they rather by his pattern won
Kiss the approaching, not yet angry Son;
And in their numbered footsteps humbly tread
The path where holy oracles do lead;
How might they under such a captain raise
110 The great designs kept for the latter days!
But mad with reason (so miscalled) of state
They know them not, and what they know not, hate.
Hence still they sing hosanna to the whore,
And her, whom they should massacre, adore:
But Indians, whom they should convert, subdue;
Nor teach, but traffic with, or burn the Jew.
    Unhappy princes, ignorantly bred,
By malice some, by error more misled,
If gracious heaven to my life give length,
120 Leisure to time, and to my weakness strength,
Then shall I once with graver accents shake
Your regal sloth, and your long slumbers wake:
Like the shrill huntsman that prevents the east,
Winding his horn to kings that chase the beast.
    Till then my muse shall hollo far behind
Angelic Cromwell who outwings the wind,
And in dark nights, and in cold days alone
Pursues the monster thorough every throne:
Which shrinking to her Roman den impure,
130 Gnashes her gory teeth; nor there secure.

  Hence oft I think if in some happy hour
High grace should meet in one with highest power,
And then a seasonable people still
Should bend to his, as he to heaven's will,
What we might hope, what wonderful effect
From such a wished conjuncture might reflect.
Sure, the mysterious work, where none withstand,
Would forthwith finish under such a hand:
Foreshortened time its useless course would stay,
140 And soon precipitate the latest day.
But a thick cloud about that morning lies,
And intercepts the beams of mortal eyes,
That 'tis the most which we determine can,
If these the times, then this must be the man.
And well he therefore does, and well has guessed,
Who in his age has always forward pressed:
And knowing not where heaven's choice may light,
Girds yet his sword, and ready stands to fight;
But men, alas, as if they nothing cared,
150 Look on, all unconcerned, or unprepared;
And stars still fall, and still the dragon's tail
Swinges the volumes of its horrid flail.
For the great justice that did first suspend
The world by sin, does by the same extend.
Hence that blest day still counterpoisèd wastes,
The ill delaying what the elected hastes;
Hence landing nature to new seas is tossed,
And good designs still with their authors lost.
  And thou, great Cromwell, for whose happy birth
160 A mould was chosen out of better earth;
Whose saint-like mother we did lately see
Live out an age, long as a pedigree;
That she might seem (could we the Fall dispute),
T'have smelled the blossom, and not eat the fruit;
Though none does of more lasting parents grow,
Yet never any did them honour so,
Though thou thine heart from evil still unstained,
And always hast thy tongue from fraud refrained;

Thou, who so oft through storms of thundering lead
170 Hast born securely thine undaunted head,
Thy breast through poniarding conspiracies,
Drawn from the sheath of lying prophecies;
Thee proof beyond all other force or skill,
Our sins endanger, and shall one day kill.
     How near they failed, and in thy sudden fall
At once assayed to overturn us all.
Our brutish fury struggling to be free,
Hurried thy horses while they hurried thee,
When thou hadst almost quit thy mortal cares,
180 And soiled in dust thy crown of silver hairs.
     Let this one sorrow interweave among
The other glories of our yearly song.
Like skilful looms, which through the costly thread
Of purling ore, a shining wave do shed:
So shall the tears we on past grief employ,
Still as they trickle, glitter in our joy.
So with more modesty we may be true,
And speak, as of the dead, the praises due:
While impious men deceived with pleasure short,
190 On their own hopes shall find the fall retort.
     But the poor beasts, wanting their noble guide,
(What could they more?) shrunk guiltily aside.
First wingèd fear transports them far away,
And leaden sorrow then their flight did stay.
See how they each his towering crest abate,
And the green grass, and their known mangers hate,
Nor through wide nostrils snuff the wanton air,
Nor their round hoofs, or curlèd manes compare;
With wandering eyes, and restless ears they stood,
200 And with shrill neighings asked him of the wood.
     Thou, Cromwell, falling, not a stupid tree,
Or rock so savage, but it mourned for thee:
And all about was heard a panic groan,
As if that Nature's self were overthrown.
It seemed the earth did from the centre tear;
It seemed the sun was fall'n out of the sphere:

Justice obstructed lay, and reason fooled;
Courage disheartened, and religion cooled.
A dismal silence through the palace went,
210 And then loud shrieks the vaulted marbles rent,
Such as the dying chorus sings by turns,
And to deaf seas, and ruthless tempests mourns,
When now they sink, and now the plundering streams
Break up each deck, and rip the oaken seams.
  But thee triumphant hence the fiery car,
And fiery steeds had borne out of the war,
From the low world, and thankless men above,
Unto the kingdom blest of peace and love:
We only mourned ourselves, in thine ascent,
220 Whom thou hadst left beneath with mantle rent.
  For all delight of life thou then didst lose,
When to command, thou didst thyself depose;
Resigning up thy privacy so dear,
To turn the headstrong people's charioteer;
For to be Cromwell was a greater thing,
Then ought below, or yet above a king:
Therefore thou rather didst thyself depress,
Yielding to rule, because it made thee less.
  For neither didst thou from the first apply
230 Thy sober spirit unto things too high,
But in thine own fields exercised'st long,
An healthful mind within a body strong;
Till at the seventh time thou in the skies,
As a small cloud, like a man's hand, didst rise;
Then did thick mists and winds the air deform,
And down at last thou poured'st the fertile storm,
Which to the thirsty land did plenty bring,
But, though forewarned, o'ertook and wet the King.
  What since he did, an higher force him pushed
240 Still from behind, and yet before him rushed,
Though undiscerned among the tumult blind,
Who think those high decrees by man designed.
'Twas heaven would not that his power should cease,
But walk still middle betwixt war and peace:

Choosing each stone, and poising every weight,
Trying the measures of the breadth and height;
Here pulling down, and there erecting new,
Founding a firm state by proportions true.
When Gideon so did from the war retreat,
250 Yet by the conquest of two kings grown great,
He on the peace extends a warlike power,
And Israel silent saw him raze the tower;
And how he Succoth's Elders durst suppress,
With thorns and briars of the wilderness.
No king might ever such a force have done;
Yet would not he be Lord, nor yet his son.
Thou with the same strength, and an heart as plain,
Didst (like thine olive) still refuse to reign,
Though why should others all thy labour spoil,
260 And brambles be anointed with thine oil,
Whose climbing flame, without a timely stop,
Had quickly levelled every cedar's top?
Therefore first growing to thyself a law,
Th' ambitious shrubs thou in just time didst awe.
So have I seen at sea, when whirling winds,
Hurry the bark, but more the seamen's minds,
Who with mistaken course salute the sand,
And threatening rocks misapprehend for land,
While baleful Tritons to the shipwreck guide,
270 And corposants along the tackling slide,
The passengers all wearied out before,
Giddy, and wishing for the fatal shore,
Some lusty mate, who with more careful eye
Counted the hours, and every star did spy,
The helm does from the artless steersman strain,
And doubles back unto the safer main.
What though a while they grumble discontent,
Saving himself, he does their loss prevent.
'Tis not a freedom, that where all command;
280 Nor tyranny, where one does them withstand:
But who of both the bounders knows to lay
Him as their father must the state obey.

Thou, and thine house (like Noah's eight) did rest,
Left by the wars' flood on the mountains' crest:
And the large vale lay subject to thy will,
Which thou but as an husbandman wouldst till:
And only didst for others plant the vine
Of liberty, not drunken with its wine.
That sober liberty which men may have,
290 That they enjoy, but more they vainly crave:
And such as to their parents' tents do press,
May show their own, not see his nakedness.
Yet such a Chammish issue still does rage,
The shame and plague both of the land and age,
Who watched thy halting, and thy fall deride,
Rejoicing when thy foot had slipped aside,
That their new king might the fifth sceptre shake,
And make the world, by his example, quake:
Whose frantic army should they want for men
300 Might muster heresies, so one were ten.
What thy misfortune, they the spirit call,
And their religion only is to fall.
Oh Mahomet! now couldst thou rise again,
Thy falling-sickness should have made thee reign,
While Feake and Simpson would in many a tome,
Have writ the comments of thy sacred foam:
For soon thou mightst have passed among their rant
Were't but for thine unmovèd tulipant;
As thou must needs have owned them of thy band
310 For prophecies fit to be *Alcoraned.*.
Accursèd locusts, whom your king does spit
Out of the centre of the unbottomed pit;
Wanderers, adulterers, liars, Munster's rest,
Sorcerers, atheists, jesuits possessed;
You who the scriptures and the laws deface
With the same liberty as points and lace;
Oh race most hypocritically strict!
Bent to reduce us to the ancient Pict;
Well may you act the Adam and the Eve;
320 Ay, and the serpent too that did deceive.

But the great captain, now the danger's o'er,
Makes you for his sake tremble one fit more;
And, to your spite, returning yet alive
Does with himself all that is good revive.
So when first man did through the morning new
See the bright sun his shining race pursue,
All day he followed with unwearied sight,
Pleased with that other world of moving light;
But thought him when he missed his setting beams,
330 Sunk in the hills, or plunged below the streams.
While dismal blacks hung round the universe,
And stars (like tapers) burned upon his hearse:
And owls and ravens with their screeching noise
Did make the funerals sadder by their joys.
His weeping eyes the doleful vigils keep,
Not knowing yet the night was made for sleep:
Still to the west, where he him lost, he turned,
And with such accents as despairing mourned:
'Why did mine eyes once see so bright a ray;
340 Or why day last no longer than a day?'
When straight the sun behind him he descried,
Smiling serenely from the further side.
So while our star that gives us light and heat,
Seemed now a long and gloomy night to threat,
Up from the other world his flame he darts,
And princes (shining through their windows) starts,
Who their suspected counsellors refuse,
And credulous ambassadors accuse.
'Is this', saith one, 'the nation that we read
350 Spent with both wars, under a captain dead,
Yet rig a navy while we dress us late,
And ere we dine, raze and rebuild their state?
What oaken forests, and what golden mines!
What mints of men, what union of designs!
(Unless their ships, do, as their fowl proceed
Of shedding leaves, that with their ocean breed).
Theirs are not ships, but rather arks of war
And beakèd promontories sailed from far;

Of floating islands a new hatchèd nest;
360   A fleet of worlds, of other worlds in quest;
An hideous shoal of wood-leviathans,
Armed with three tier of brazen hurricanes,
That through the centre shoot their thundering side
And sink the earth that does at anchor ride.
What refuge to escape them can be found,
Whose watery leaguers all the world surround?
Needs must we all their tributaries be,
Whose navies hold the sluices of the sea.
The ocean is the fountain of command,
370   But that once took, we captives are on land.
And those that have the waters for their share,
Can quickly leave us neither earth nor air.
Yet if through these our fears could find a pass,
Through double oak, and lined with treble brass,
That one man still, although but named, alarms
More than all men, all navies, and all arms.
Him, in the day, him, in late night I dread,
And still his sword seems hanging o'er my head.
The nation had been ours, but his one soul
380   Moves the great bulk, and animates the whole.
He secrecy with number hath enchased,
Courage with age, maturity with haste:
The valiant's terror, riddle of the wise,
And still his falchion all our knots unties.
Where did he learn those arts that cost us dear?
Where below earth, or where above the sphere?
He seems a king by long succession born,
And yet the same to be a king does scorn.
Abroad a king he seems, and something more,
390   At home a subject on the equal floor.
O could I once him with our title see,
So should I hope that he might die as we.
But let them write his praise that love him best,
It grieves me sore to have thus much confessed.'
    Pardon, great Prince, if thus their fear or spite
More than our love and duty do thee right.

I yield, nor further will the prize contend,
So that we both alike may miss our end:
While thou thy venerable head dost raise
400 As far above their malice as my praise,
And as the Angel of our commonweal,
Troubling the waters, yearly mak'st them heal.

Upon an Eunuch: a Poet

Nec sterilem te crede; licet, mulieribus exul,
Falcem virginae nequeas immitere messi,
Et nostro peccare modo. Tibi Fama perenne
Praegnabit; rapiesque novem de monte sorores;
Et pariet modulos Echo repetita nepotes.

Don't believe yourself sterile, although, an exile from
    women,
You cannot thrust a sickle at the virgin harvest,
And sin in our fashion. Fame will be continually pregnant
    by you,
And you will snatch the nine sisters from the mountain;
10 Echo too, often struck, will bring forth musical offspring.

The Second Chorus from Seneca's Tragedy 'Thyestes'

Stet quicunque volet potens
Aulae culmine lubrico etc.

Climb at court for me that will
Giddy favour's slippery hill;
All I seek is to lie still.
Settled in some secret nest,
In calm leisure let me rest,
And far off the public stage
Pass away my silent age.
Thus when without noise, unknown,

I have lived out all my span,
10   I shall die, without a groan,
An old honest countryman,
Who exposed to others' eyes,
Into his own heart ne'er pries.
Death to him's a strange surprise.

In the French Translation of Lucan by Monsieur De Brebeuf Are These Verses: Lib 3 [395–98]

C'est de luy que nous vient cet art ingenieux
De peindre la parole, et de parler aux yeux;
Et, par les traits divers des figures tracées,
Donner de la couleur et du corps aux pensées.

TRANSLATED

Facundis dedit ille notis, interprete pluma
Insinuare sonos oculis, et pingere voces,
Conspicuamque levi mentem transmittere charta.

He that ingenious art did first descry
Of painting words, and speaking to the eye,
10   And by the several shapes of figures wrought,
Gave colour and a body to a thought.

The former [the Phoenician] gave with eloquent characters,
    a quill serving as translator,
The art of suggesting sounds to the eyes and of painting
    words,
[Transferring visible thought to smooth paper.]

An Epitaph upon —

Enough: and leave the rest to fame.
'Tis to commend her but to name.
Courtship, which living she declined,
When dead to offer were unkind.
Where never any could speak ill,
Who would officious praises spill?
Nor can the truest wit or friend,
Without detracting, her commend.
To say she lived a virgin chaste,
10 In this age loose and all unlaced;
Nor was, when vice is so allowed,
Of virtue or ashamed, or proud;
That her soul was on heav'n so bent
No minute but it came and went;
That ready her last debt to pay
She summed her life up every day;
Modest as morn; as midday bright;
Gentle as evening; cool as night;
'Tis true: but all so weakly said,
20 'Twere more significant, *she's dead.*

On the Victory Obtained by Blake over the Spaniards in the Bay of Santa Cruz, in the Island of Tenerife, 1657

Now does Spain's fleet her spacious wings unfold,
Leaves the New World and hastens for the old:
But though the wind was fair, they slowly swum
Freighted with acted guilt, and guilt to come:
For this rich load, of which so proud they are,
Was raised by tyranny, and raised for war;
Every capacious gallion's womb was filled,
With what the womb of wealthy kingdoms yield,
The New World's wounded entrails they had tore,
10 For wealth wherewith to wound the Old once more:

Wealth which all others' avarice might cloy,
But yet in them caused as much fear as joy.
For now upon the main, themselves they saw –
That boundless empire, where you give the law –
Of winds' and waters' rage, they fearful be,
But much more fearful are your flags to see.
Day, that to those who sail upon the deep,
More wished for, and more welcome is than sleep,
They dreaded to behold, lest the sun's light,
20 With English streamers, should salute their sight:
In thickest darkness they would choose to steer,
So that such darkness might suppress their fear;
At length theirs vanishes, and fortune smiles;
For they behold the sweet Canary Isles;
One of which doubtless is by Nature blessed
Above both Worlds, since 'tis above the rest.
For lest some gloominess might stain her sky,
Trees there the duty of the clouds supply;
O noble trust which heav'n on this isle pours,
30 Fertile to be, yet never need her showers.
A happy people, which at once do gain
The benefits without the ills of rain.
Both health and profit fate cannot deny;
Where still the earth is moist, the air still dry;
The jarring elements no discord know,
Fuel and rain together kindly grow;
And coolness there, with heat doth never fight,
This only rules by day, and that by night.
    Your worth to all these isles, a just right brings,
40 The best of lands should have the best of kings.
And these want nothing heaven can afford,
Unless it be – the having you their Lord;
But this great want will not a long one prove,
Your conquering sword will soon that want remove.
For Spain had better – she'll ere long confess –
Have broken all her swords, than this one peace,
Casting that league off, which she held so long,
She cast off that which only made her strong.

Forces and art, she soon will feel, are vain,
50 Peace, against you, was the sole strength of Spain.
By that alone those islands she secures,
Peace made them hers, but war will make them yours.
There the indulgent soil that rich grape breeds,
Which of the gods the fancied drink exceeds;
They still do yield, such is their precious mould,
All that is good, and are not cursed with gold –
With fatal gold, for still where that does grow,
Neither the soil, nor people, quiet know.
Which troubles men to raise it when 'tis ore,
60 And when 'tis raised, does trouble them much more.
Ah, why was thither brought that cause of war,
Kind Nature had from thence removed so far?
In vain doth she those islands free from ill,
If fortune can make guilty what she will.
But whilst I draw that scene, where you ere long,
Shall conquests act, your present are unsung.

For Santa Cruz the glad fleet takes her way,
And safely there casts anchor in the bay.
Never so many with one joyful cry,
70 That place saluted, where they all must die.
Deluded men! Fate with you did but sport,
You 'scaped the sea, to perish in your port.
'Twas more for England's fame you should die there,
Where you had most of strength, and least of fear.

The Peak's proud height the Spaniards all admire,
Yet in their breasts carry a pride much higher.
Only to this vast hill a power is given,
At once both to inhabit earth and heaven.
But this stupendous prospect did not near,
80 Make them admire, so much as they did fear.

For here they met with news, which did produce,
A grief, above the cure of grapes' best juice.
They learned with terror that nor summer's heat,
Nor winter's storms, had made your fleet retreat.
To fight against such foes was vain, they knew,
Which did the rage of elements subdue,

Who on the ocean that does horror give,
To all besides, triumphantly do live.
   With haste they therefore all their gallions moor,
90 And flank with cannon from the neighbouring shore.
Forts, lines, and sconces all the bay along,
They build and act all that can make them strong.
   Fond men who know not whilst such works they raise,
They only labour to exalt your praise.
Yet they by restless toil became at length,
So proud and confident of their made strength,
That they with joy their boasting general heard,
Wish then for that assault he lately feared.
His wish he has, for now undaunted Blake,
100 With wingèd speed, for Santa Cruz does make.
For your renown, his conquering fleet does ride,
O'er seas as vast as is the Spaniards' pride.
Whose fleet and trenches viewed, he soon did say,
'We to their strength are more obliged than they.
Were't not for that, they from their fate would run,
And a third world seek out, our arms to shun.
Those forts, which there so high and strong appear,
Do not so much suppress, as show their fear.
Of speedy victory let no man doubt,
110 Our worst work's past, now we have found them out.
Behold their navy does at anchor lie,
And they are ours, for now they cannot fly.'
   This said, the whole fleet gave it their applause,
And all assumes your courage, in your cause.
That bay they enter, which unto them owes,
The noblest wreaths, that victory bestows.
Bold Stayner leads: this fleet's designed by fate,
To give him laurel, as the last did plate.
   The thundering cannon now begins the fight,
120 And though it be at noon creates a night.
The air was soon after the fight begun,
Far more enflamed by it than by the sun.
Never so burning was that climate known,
War turned the temperate to the torrid zone.

    Fate these two fleets between both worlds had brought,
Who fight, as if for both those worlds they fought.
Thousands of ways thousands of men there die,
Some ships are sunk, some blown up in the sky.
Nature ne'er made cedars so high aspire,
130   As oaks did then, urged by the active fire,
Which by quick powder's force, so high was sent,
That it returned to its own element.
Torn limbs some leagues into the island fly,
Whilst others lower in the sea do lie.
Scarce souls from bodies severed are so far
By death, as bodies there were by the war.
The all-seeing sun, ne'er gazed on such a sight,
Two dreadful navies there at anchor fight.
And neither have or power or will to fly,
140   There one must conquer, or there both must die.
Far different motives yet engaged them thus,
Necessity did them, but Choice did us.

    A choice which did the highest worth express,
And was attended by as high success.
For your resistless genius there did reign,
By which we laurels reaped e'en on the main.
So prosperous stars, though absent to the sense,
Bless those they shine for, by their influence.

    Our cannon now tears every ship and sconce,
150   And o'er two elements triumphs at once.
Their gallions sunk, their wealth the sea does fill –
The only place where it can cause no ill.

    Ah, would those treasures which both Indies have,
Were buried in as large, and deep a grave,
Wars' chief support with them would buried be,
And the land owe her peace unto the sea.
Ages to come your conquering arms will bless,
There they destroy what had destroyed their peace.
And in one war the present age may boast
160   The certain seeds of many wars are lost.

    All the foe's ships destroyed, by sea or fire,
Victorious Blake, does from the bay retire,

His siege of Spain he then again pursues,
And there first brings of his success the news:
The saddest news that e'er to Spain was brought,
Their rich fleet sunk, and ours with laurel fraught,
Whilst fame in every place her trumpet blows,
And tells the world how much to you it owes.

Two Songs at the Marriage of the Lord Fauconberg and the Lady Mary Cromwell

FIRST SONG

Chorus Endymion Luna

CHORUS
The astrologers' own eyes are set,
And even wolves the sheep forget;
Only this shepherd, late and soon,
Upon this hill outwakes the moon.
Hark how he sings, with sad delight,
Thorough the clear and silent night.

ENDYMION
Cynthia, O Cynthia, turn thine ear,
Nor scorn Endymion's plaints to hear.
As we our flocks, so you command
10   The fleecy clouds with silver wand.

CYNTHIA
If thou a mortal, rather sleep;
Or if a shepherd, watch thy sheep.

ENDYMION
The shepherd, since he saw thine eyes,
And sheep are both thy sacrifice.
Nor merits he a mortal's name,
That burns with an immortal flame.

CYNTHIA
I have enough for me to do,
Ruling the waves that ebb and flow.

ENDYMION
Since thou disdain'st not then to share
20   On sublunáry things thy care;
Rather restrain these double seas,
Mine eyes' uncessant deluges.

CYNTHIA
My wakeful lamp all night must move,
Securing their repose above.

ENDYMION
If therefore thy resplendent ray
Can make a night more bright than day,
Shine thorough this obscurer breast,
With shades of deep despair oppressed.

CHORUS
Courage, Endymion, boldly woo;
30   Anchises was a shepherd too:
Yet is her younger sister laid
Sporting with him in Ida's shade:
    And Cynthia, though the strongest,
Seeks but the honour to have held out longest.

ENDYMION
Here unto Latmus' top I climb:
How far below thine orb sublime?
O why, as well as eyes to see,
Have I not arms that reach to thee?

CYNTHIA
'Tis needless then that I refuse,
40   Would you but your own reason use.

ENDYMION
Though I so high may not pretend,
It is the same so you descend.

CYNTHIA
These stars would say I do them wrong,
Rivals each one for thee too strong.

ENDYMION
The stars are fixed unto their sphere,
And cannot, though they would, come near.
Less loves set off each other's praise,
While stars eclipse by mixing rays.

CYNTHIA
That cave is dark.

ENDYMION
50   Then none can spy:
Or shine thou there and 'tis the sky.

CHORUS
       Joy to Endymion,
For he has Cynthia's favour won.
       And Jove himself approves
With his serenest influence their loves.
  For he did never love to pair
  His progeny above the air;
  But to be honest, valiant, wise,
Makes mortals matches fit for deities.

SECOND SONG

Hobbinol Phyllis Tomalin

HOBBINOL
Phyllis, Tomalin, away:
Never such a merry day.
For the Northern shepherd's son
Has Menalca's daughter won.

PHYLLIS
Stay till I some flowers ha' tied
In a garland for the bride.

TOMALIN

If thou wouldst a garland bring,
Phyllis, you may wait the spring:
They ha' chosen such an hour
10   When *she* is the only flower.

PHYLLIS

Let's not then at least be seen
Without each a sprig of green.

HOBBINOL

Fear not; at Menalca's hall
There is bays enough for all.
He, when young, as we did graze,
But when old, he planted bays.

TOMALIN

Here *she* comes; but with a look
Far more catching than my hook.
'Twas those eyes, I now dare swear,
20   Led our lambs we knew not where.

HOBBINOL

Not our lambs' own fleeces are
Curled so lovely as her hair:
Nor our sheep new washed can be
Half so white or sweet as *she*.

PHYLLIS

He so looks as fit to keep
Somewhat else than silly sheep.

HOBBINOL

Come, let's in some carol new
Pay to love and them their due.

ALL

   Joy to that happy pair,
30   Whose hopes united banish our despair.
      What shepherd could for love pretend,
Whilst all the nymphs on Damon's choice attend?

What shepherdess could hope to wed
Before Marina's turn were sped?
Now lesser beauties may take place,
And meaner virtues come in play;
    While they,
    Looking from high,
    Shall grace
40 Our flocks and us with a propitious eye.
    But what is most, the gentle swain
    No more shall need of love complain;
    But virtue shall be beauty's hire,
And those be equal that have equal fire.
    Marina yields. Who dares be coy?
Or who despair, now Damon does enjoy?
    Joy to that happy pair,
Whose hopes united banish our despair.

A Poem upon the Death of His Late Highness the Lord Protector

That Providence which had so long the care
Of Cromwell's head, and numbered every hair,
Now in itself (the glass where all appears)
Had seen the period of his golden years:
And thenceforth only did attend to trace
What death might least so fair a life deface.
    The people, which what most they fear esteem,
Death when more horrid, so more noble deem,
And blame the last act, like spectators vain,
10 Unless the prince whom they applaud be slain.
Nor fate indeed can well refuse that right
To those that lived in war, to die in fight.
    But long his valour none had left that could
Endanger him, or clemency that would.
And he whom Nature all for peace had made,
But angry heaven unto war had swayed,
And so less useful where he most desired,

For what he least affected was admired,
Deservèd yet an end whose every part,
20 Should speak the wondrous softness of his heart.
    To Love and Grief the fatal writ was 'signed;
(Those nobler weaknesses of human kind,
From which those powers that issued the decree,
Although immortal, found they were not free),
That they, to whom his breast still open lies,
In gentle passions should his death disguise:
And leave succeeding ages cause to mourn,
As long as Grief shall weep, or Love shall burn.
    Straight does a slow and languishing disease
30 Eliza, Nature's and his darling, seize.
Her when an infant, taken with her charms,
He oft would flourish in his mighty arms,
And, lest their force the tender burden wrong,
Slacken the vigour of his muscles strong;
Then to the Mother's breast her softly move,
Which while she drained of milk, she filled with love.
But as with riper years her virtue grew,
And every minute adds a lustre new,
When with meridian height her beauty shined,
40 And thorough that sparkled her fairer mind,
When she with smiles serene in words discreet
His hidden soul at every turn could meet;
Then might y'ha' daily his affection spied,
Doubling that knot which destiny had tied,
While they by sense, not knowing, comprehend
How on each other both their fates depend.
With her each day the pleasing hours he shares,
And at her aspect calms his growing cares;
Or with a grandsire's joy her children sees
50 Hanging about her neck or at his knees.
Hold fast, dear infants, hold them both or none;
This will not stay when once the other's gone.
    A silent fire now wastes those limbs of wax,
And him within his tortured image racks.
So the flower withering which the garden crowned,

The sad root pines in secret under ground.
Each groan he doubled and each sigh he sighed,
Repeated over to the restless night.
No trembling string composed to numbers new,
60 Answers the touch in notes more sad, more true.
She, lest he grieve, hides what she can her pains,
And he to lessen hers his sorrow feigns:
Yet both perceived, yet both concealed their skills,
And so diminishing increased their ills:
That whether by each other's grief they fell,
Or on their own redoubled, none can tell.
   And now Eliza's purple locks were shorn,
Where she so long her Father's fate had worn:
And frequent lightning to her soul that flies,
70 Divides the air, and opens all the skies:
And now his life, suspended by her breath,
Ran out impetuously to hasting death.
Like polished mirrors, so his steely breast
Had every figure of her woes expressed,
And with the damp of her last gasp obscured,
Had drawn such stains as were not to be cured.
Fate could not either reach with single stroke,
But the dear image fled, the mirror broke.
   Who now shall tell us more of mournful swans,
80 Of halcyons kind, or bleeding pelicans?
No downy breast did e're so gently beat,
Or fan with airy plumes so soft an heat.
For he no duty by his height excused,
Nor, though a prince, to be a man refused:
But rather than in his Eliza's pain
Not love, not grieve, would neither live nor reign:
And in himself so oft immortal tried,
Yet in compassion of another died.
   So have I seen a vine, whose lasting age
90 Of many a winter hath survived the rage,
Under whose shady tent men every year
At its rich blood's expense their sorrows cheer,
If some dear branch where it extends its life

Chance to be pruned by an untimely knife,
The parent-tree unto the grief succeeds,
And through the wound its vital humour bleeds,
Trickling in watery drops, whose flowing shape
Weeps that it falls ere fixed into a grape.
So the dry stock, no more that spreading vine,
100   Frustrates the autumn and the hopes of wine.
    A secret cause does sure those signs ordain
Foreboding princes' falls, and seldom vain.
Whether some kinder powers that wish us well,
What they above cannot prevent foretell;
Or the great world do by consent presage,
As hollow seas with future tempests rage;
Or rather heaven, which us so long foresees,
Their funerals celebrates while it decrees.
But never yet was any human fate
110   By Nature solemnized with so much state.
He unconcerned the dreadful passage crossed;
But, oh, what pangs that death did Nature cost!
    First the great thunder was shot off, and sent
The signal from the starry battlement.
The winds receive it, and its force outdo,
As practising how they could thunder too;
Out of the binder's hand the sheaves they tore,
And thrashed the harvest in the airy floor;
Or of huge trees, whose growth with his did rise,
120   The deep foundations opened to the skies.
Then heavy showers the wingèd tempests lead,
And pour the deluge o'er the chaos' head.
The race of warlike horses at his tomb
Offer themselves in many a hecatomb;
With pensive head towards the ground they fall,
And helpless languish at the tainted stall.
Numbers of men decrease with pains unknown,
And hasten, not to see his death, their own.
Such tortures all the elements unfixed,
130   Troubled to part where so exactly mixed.
And as through air his wasting spirits flowed,

The universe laboured beneath their load.
    Nature, it seemed with him would Nature vie;
He with Eliza. It with him would die,
    He without noise still travelled to his end,
As silent suns to meet the night descend.
The stars that for him fought had only power
Left to determine now his fatal hour,
Which, since they might not hinder, yet they cast
140 To choose it worthy of his glories past.
    No part of time but bare his mark away
Of honour; all the year was Cromwell's day:
But this, of all the most auspicious found,
Twice had in open field him victor crowned:
When up the armèd mountains of Dunbar
He marched, and through deep Severn ending war.
What day should him eternize but the same
That had before immortalized his name?
That so who ere would at his death have joyed,
150 In their own griefs might find themselves employed;
But those that sadly his departure grieved,
Yet joyed, remembering what he once achieved.
And the last minute his victorious ghost
Gave chase to Ligny on the Belgic coast.
Here ended all his mortal toils: he laid
And slept in peace under the laurel shade.

    O Cromwell, Heaven's Favourite! To none
Have such high honours from above been shown:
For whom the elements we mourners see,
160 And heaven itself would the great herald be,
Which with more care set forth his obsequies
Than those of Moses hid from human eyes,
As jealous only here lest all be less,
That we could to his memory express.
    Then let us to our course of mourning keep:
Where heaven leads, 'tis piety to weep.
Stand back, ye seas, and shrunk beneath the veil
Of your abyss, with covered head bewail
Your Monarch: we demand not your supplies

170   To compass in our isle; our tears suffice:
      Since him away the dismal tempest rent,
      Who once more joined us to the continent;
      Who planted England on the Flandric shore,
      And stretched our frontier to the Indian ore;
      Whose greater truths obscure the fables old,
      Whether of British saints or Worthies told;
      And in a valour lessening Arthur's deeds,
      For holiness the Confessor exceeds.
        He first put arms into Religion's hand,
180 And timorous Conscience unto Courage manned:
      The soldier taught that inward mail to wear,
      And fearing God how they should nothing fear.
      'Those strokes', he said, 'will pierce through all below
      Where those that strike from heaven fetch their blow.'
      Astonished armies did their flight prepare,
      And cities strong were stormèd by his prayer;
      Of that, forever Preston's field shall tell
      The story, and impregnable Clonmel.
      And where the sandy mountain Fenwick scaled,
190 The sea between, yet hence his prayer prevailed.
      What man was ever so in heaven obeyed
      Since the commanded sun o'er Gibeon stayed?
      In all his wars needs must he triumph when
      He conquered God still ere he fought with men:
        Hence, though in battle none so brave or fierce,
      Yet him the adverse steel could never pierce.
      Pity it seemed to hurt him more that felt
      Each wound himself which he to others dealt;
      Danger itself refusing to offend
200 So loose an enemy, so fast a friend.
        Friendship, that sacred virtue, long does claim
      The first foundation of his house and name:
      But within one its narrow limits fall,
      His tenderness extended unto all.
      And that deep soul through every channel flows,
      Where kindly nature loves itself to lose.
      More strong affections never reason served,

Yet still affected most what best deserved.
If he Eliza loved to that degree,
(Though who more worthy to be loved than she?)
If so indulgent to his own, how dear
To him the children of the highest were?
For her he once did nature's tribute pay:
For these his life adventured every day:
And 'twould be found, could we his thoughts have cast,
Their griefs struck deepest, if Eliza's last.
   What prudence more than human did he need
To keep so dear, so differing minds agreed?
The worser sort, as conscious of their ill,
Lie weak and easy to the ruler's will;
But to the good (too many or too few)
All law is useless, all reward is due.
Oh ill-advised, if not for love, for shame,
Spare yet your own, if you neglect his fame;
Lest others dare to think your zeal a mask,
And you to govern, only *heaven's* task.
   Valour, religion, friendship, prudence died
At once with him, and all that's good beside;
And we death's refuse, nature's dregs, confined
To loathsome life, alas! are left behind.
Where we (so once we used) shall now no more
To fetch day, press about his chamber door –
From which he issued with that awful state,
It seemed Mars broke through Janus' double gate,
Yet always tempered with an air so mild,
No April suns that e'er so gently smiled –
No more shall hear that powerful language charm,
Whose force oft spared the labour of his arm:
No more shall follow where he spent the days
In war, in counsel, or in prayer and praise,
Whose meanest acts he would himself advance,
As ungirt David to the ark did dance.
All, all is gone of ours or his delight
In horses fierce, wild deer, or armour bright;
Francisca fair can nothing now but weep,

Nor with soft notes shall sing his cares asleep.
I saw him dead. A leaden slumber lies
And mortal sleep over those wakeful eyes:
Those gentle rays under the lids were fled,
250 Which through his looks that piercing sweetness shed;
That port which so majestic was and strong,
Loose and deprived of vigour, stretched along:
All withered, all discoloured, pale and wan –
How much another thing, nor more that man?
Oh human glory vain, oh death, oh wings,
Oh worthless world, oh transitory things!

Yet dwelt that greatness in his shape decayed,
That still though dead, greater than death he laid;
And in his altered face you something feign
260 That threatens death he yet will live again.

Not much unlike the sacred oak which shoots
To heaven its branches and through earth its roots,
Whose spacious boughs are hung with trophies round,
And honoured wreaths have oft the victor crowned.
When angry Jove darts lightning through the air,
At mortals' sins, nor his own plant will spare,
(It groans, and bruises all below, that stood
So many years the shelter of the wood.)
The tree erewhile foreshortened to our view,
270 When fall'n shows taller yet than as it grew:

So shall his praise to after times increase,
When truth shall be allowed, and faction cease,
And his own shadows with him fall. The eye
Detracts from objects than itself more high:
But when death takes them from that envied seat,
Seeing how little, we confess how great.

Thee, many ages hence in martial verse
Shall the English soldier, ere he charge, rehearse,
Singing of thee, inflame themselves to fight,
280 And with the name of *Cromwell*, armies fright.
As long as rivers to the seas shall run,
As long as Cynthia shall relieve the sun,
While stags shall fly unto the forests thick,

While sheep delight the grassy downs to pick,
As long as future times succeeds the past,
Always thy honour, praise, and name shall last.
    Thou in a pitch how far beyond the sphere
Of human glory tower'st, and reigning there
Despoiled of mortal robes, in seas of bliss,
290 Plunging dost bathe, and tread the bright abyss:
There thy great soul yet once a world does see,
Spacious enough, and pure enough for thee.
How soon thou Moses hast, and Joshua found,
And David for the sword and harp renowned?
How straight canst to each happy mansion go?
(Far better known above than here below)
And in those joys dost spend the endless day,
Which in expressing we ourselves betray.
    For we, since thou art gone, with heavy doom,
300 Wander like ghosts about thy lovèd tomb;
And lost in tears, have neither sight nor mind
To guide us upward through this region blind.
Since thou art gone, who best that way couldst teach,
Only our sighs, perhaps, may thither reach.
    And Richard yet, where his great parent led,
Beats on the rugged track: he, virtue dead,
Revives, and by his milder beams assures;
And yet how much of them his grief obscures?
    He, as his father, long was kept from sight
310 In private, to be viewed by better light;
But opened once, what splendour does he throw?
A Cromwell in an hour a prince will grow.
How he becomes that seat, how strongly strains,
How gently winds at once the ruling reins?
Heaven to this choice prepared a diadem,
Richer than any Eastern silk or gem;
A pearly rainbow, where the sun enchased
His brows, like an imperial jewel graced.
    We find already what those omens mean,
320 Earth ne'er more glad, nor heaven more serene.
Cease now our griefs, calm peace succeeds a war,

Rainbows to storms, Richard to Oliver.
Tempt not his clemency to try his power,
He threats no deluge, yet foretells a shower.

The Last Instructions to a Painter

London, 4 September 1667

After two sittings, now our Lady State
To end her picture does the third time wait.
But ere thou fall'st to work, first, Painter, see
If 't ben't too slight grown or too hard for thee.
Canst thou paint without colors? Then 'tis right:
For so we too without a fleet can fight.
Or canst thou daub a signpost, and that ill?
'Twill suit our great debauch and little skill.
Or hast thou marked how antic masters limn
10   The aly-roof with snuff of candle dim,
Sketching in shady smoke prodigious tools?
'Twill serve this race of drunkards, pimps, and fools.
But if to match our crimes thy skill presumes,
As th' Indians, draw our luxury in plumes.
Or if to score out our compendious fame,
With Hooke, then, through the microscope take aim,
Where, like the new *Comptroller*, all men laugh
To see a tall louse brandish the white staff.
Else shalt thou oft thy guiltless pencil curse,
20   Stamp on thy palette, nor perhaps the worse.
The painter so, long having vexed his cloth –
Of his hound's mouth to feign the raging froth –
His desperate pencil at the work did dart:
His anger reached that rage which passed his art;
Chance finished that which art could but begin,
And he sat smiling how his dog did grin.
So mayst thou pérfect by a lucky blow
What all thy softest touches cannot do.
      Paint then *St Albans* full of soup and gold,
30   The new court's pattern, stallion of the old.

Him neither wit nor courage did exalt,
But Fortune chose him for her pleasure salt.
Paint him with drayman's shoulders, butcher's mien,
Membered like mules, with elephantine chine.
Well he the title of St Albans bore,
For Bacon never studied nature more.
But age, allaying now that youthful heat,
Fits him in France to play at cards and treat.
40   Draw no commission lest the court should lie,
That, disavowing treaty, asks supply.
He needs no seal but to St James's lease,
Whose breeches wear the instrument of peace;
Who, if the French dispute his power, from thence
Can straight produce them a plenipotence.
Nor fears he the *Most Christian* should trepan
Two saints at once, St Germain, St Alban,
But thought the Golden Age was now restored,
When men and women took each other's word.

   Paint then again *Her Highness* to the life,
50   Philosopher beyond *Newcastle's wife*.
She, nak'd, can Archimedes self put down,
For an experiment upon the crown.
She perfected that engine, oft assayed,
How after childbirth to renew a maid,
And found how royal heirs might be matured
In fewer months than mothers once endured.
Hence *Crowther* made the rare inventress free
Of's Highness's Royal Society –
Happiest of women, if she were but able
60   To make her glassen Dukes once malleáble!
Paint her with oyster lip and breath of fame,
Wide mouth that 'sparagus may well proclaim;
With Chancellor's belly and so large a rump,
There – not behind the coach – her pages jump.
Express her studying now if China clay
Can, without breaking, venomed juice convey,
Or how a mortal poison she may draw
Out of the cordial meal of the cacao.

Witness, ye stars of night, and thou the pale
70 Moon, that o'ercome with the sick steam didst fail;
Ye neighboring elms, that your green leaves did shed,
And fawns that from the womb abortive fled;
Not unprovoked, she tries forbidden arts,
But in her soft breast love's hid cancer smarts,
While she revolves, at once, Sidney's disgrace
And her self scorned for emulous *Denham's* face,
And nightly hears the hated guards, away
Galloping with the Duke to other prey.
    Paint *Castlemaine* in colours that will hold
80 (Her, not her picture, for she now grows old):
She through her lackey's drawers, as he ran,
Discerned love's cause and a new flame began.
Her wonted joys thenceforth and court she shuns,
And still within her mind the footman runs:
His brazen calves, his brawny thighs – the face
She slights – his feet shaped for a smoother race.
Poring within her glass she readjusts
Her looks, and oft-tried beauty now distrusts,
Fears lest he scorn a woman once assayed,
90 And now first wished she e'er had been a maid.
Great Love, how dost thou triumph and how reign,
That to a groom couldst humble her disdain!
Stripped to her skin, see how she stooping stands,
Nor scorns to rub him down with those fair hands,
And washing (lest the scent her crime disclose)
His sweaty hooves, tickles him 'twixt the toes.
But envious Fame, too soon, began to note
More gold in's fob, more lace upon his coat;
And he, unwary, and of tongue too fleet,
100 No longer could conceal his fortune sweet.
Justly the rogue was whipped in porter's den,
And *Jermyn* straight has leave to come again.
Ah, Painter, now could Alexander live,
And this Campaspe thee, Apelles, give!
    Draw next a pair of tables opening, then
The *House of Commons* clattering like the men.

Describe the Court and Country, both set right
On opp'site points, the black against the white.
Those having lost the nation at tric-trac,
110   These now adventuring how to win it back.
The dice betwixt them must the fate divide
(As chance doth still in multitudes decide).
But here the Court does its advantage know,
For the cheat *Turner* for them both must throw.
As some from boxes, he so from the chair
Can strike the die and still with them goes share.
      Here, Painter, rest a little, and survey
With what small arts the public game they play.
For so too Rubens, with affairs of state,
120   His labouring pencil oft would recreate.
      The close *Cabal* marked how the Navy eats,
And thought all lost that goes not to the cheats,
So therefore secretly for peace decrees,
Yet as for war the Parliament should squeeze,
And fix to the revénue such a sum
Should *Goodrick* silence and strike *Paston* dumb,
Should pay land armies, should dissolve the vain
Commons, and ever such a court maintain;
Hyde's avarice, *Bennet's* luxury should suffice,
130   And what can these defray but the Excise?
Excise a monster worse than e'er before
Frighted the midwife and the mother tore.
A thousand hands she has and thousand eyes,
Breaks into shops and into cellars pries,
With hundred rows of teeth the shark exceeds,
And on all trade like cassowar she feeds:
Chops off the piece wheres'e'er she close the jaw,
Else swallows all down her indented maw.
She stalks all day in streets concealed from sight
140   And flies, like bats with leathern wings, by night;
She wastes the country and on cities preys.
Her, of a female harpy, in dog days,
Black Birch, of all the earth-born race most hot
And most rapacious, like himself, begot,

And, of his brat enamoured, as't increased,
Buggered in incest with the mongrel beast.
    Say, Muse, for nothing can escape thy sight
(And, Painter, wanting other, draw this fight),
Who, in an English senate, fierce debate
150 Could raise so long for this new whore of state.
    Of early wittols first the troop marched in –
For diligence renowned and discipline –
In loyal haste they left young wives in bed,
And Denham these by one consent did head.
Of the old courtiers, next a squadron came,
That sold their master, led by *Ashburnham*.
To them succeeds a despicable rout,
But know the word and well could face about;
Expectants pale, with hopes of spoil allured,
160 Though yet but pioneers, and led by *Stew'rd*.
Then damning cowards ranged the vocal plain,
Wood these commands, Knight of the Horn and Cane.
Still his hook-shoulder seems the blow to dread,
And under's ampit he defends his head.
The posture strange men laughed at of his poll,
Hid with his elbow like the spice he stole.
Headless St Denys so his head does bear,
And both of them alike French martyrs were.
Court officers, as used, the next place took,
170 And followed *Fox*, but with disdainful look.
His birth, his youth, his brokage all dispraise
In vain, for always he commands that pays.
Then the procurers under *Progers* filed –
Gentlest of men – and his lieutenant mild,
Brouncker – Love's squire – through all the field arrayed,
No troop was better clad, nor so well paid.
Then marched the troop of *Clarendon*, all full
Haters of fowl, to *teal* preferring *bull*:
Gross bodies, grosser minds, and grossest cheats,
180 And bloated *Wren* conducts them to their seats.
Charlton advances next, whose coif does awe
The Mitre troop, and with his looks gives law.

He marched with beaver cocked of bishop's brim,
And hid much fraud under an aspect grim.
Next the lawyers' mercenary band appear:
Finch in the front, and *Thurland* in the rear.
The troop of privilege, a rabble bare
Of debtors deep, fell to *Trelawney's* care.
Their fortune's error they supplied in rage,
190 Nor any further would than these engage.
Then marched the troop, whose valiant acts before
(Their public acts) obliged them still to more.
For chimney's sake they all *Sir Pool* obeyed,
Or in his absence him that first it laid.
Then comes the thrifty troop of privateers,
Whose horses each with other interferes.
Before them *Higgons* rides with brow compact,
Mourning his Countess, anxious for his Act.
Sir Frederick and *Sir Solomon* draw lots
200 For the command of politics or sots,
Thence fell to words, but quarrel to adjourn;
Their friends agreed they should command by turn.
Carteret the rich did the accountants guide
And in ill English all the world defied.
The Papists – but of these the House had none
Else *Talbot* offered to have led them on.
Bold *Duncombe* next, of the projectors chief,
And old *Fitz-harding* of the Eaters Beef.
Late and disordered out the drinkers drew,
210 Scarce them their leaders, they their leaders knew.
Before them entered, equal in command,
Apsley and *Brod'rick*, marching hand in hand.
Last then but one, *Powell* that could not ride,
Led the French standard, weltering in his stride.
He, to excuse his slowness, truth confessed
That 'twas so long before he could be dressed.
The Lord's sons, last, all these did reinforce:
Cornb'ry before them managed hobby-horse.
    Never before nor since, an host so steeled
220 Trooped on to muster in the Tothill Field:

Not the first cock-horse that with cork were shod
To rescue *Albermarle* from the sea-cod,
Nor the late feather-men, whom *Tomkins* fierce
Shall with one breath, like thistledown disperse.
All the two *Coventrys* their generals chose
For one had much, the other nought to lose;
Nor better choice all accidents could hit,
While *Hector Harry* steers by *Will the Wit*.
They both accept the charge with merry glee,
230   To fight a battle, from all gunshot free.
Pleased with their numbers, yet in valour wise,
They feign a parley, better to surprise;
They that ere long shall the rude Dutch upbraid,
Who in a time of treaty durst invade.
    Thick was the morning, and the House was thin,
The Speaker early, when they all fell in.
Propitious heavens, had not you them crossed,
Excise had got the day, and all been lost.
For the other side all in loose quarters lay,
240   Without intelligence, command, or pay:
A scattered body, which the foe ne'er tried,
But oftener did among themselves divide.
And some ran o'er each night, while others sleep,
And undescried returned ere morning peep.
But *Strangeways*, that all night still walked the round
(For vigilance and courage both renowned)
First spied the enemy and gave the 'larm,
Fighting it single till the rest might arm.
Such Roman Cocles strid before the foe,
250   The falling bridge behind, the stream below.
    Each ran, as chance him guides to several post,
And all to pattern his example boast.
Their former trophies they recall to mind
And to new edge their angry courage grind.
First entered forward *Temple*, conqueror
Of Irish cattle and Solicitor;
Then daring *Seymour*, that with spear and shield,
Had stretched the Monster Patent on the field;

Keen *Whorwood* next, in aid of damsel frail,
260 That pierced the giant *Mordaunt* through his mail;
And surly *Williams*, the accountants' bane;
And *Lovelace* young, of chimney-men the cane.
Old *Waller*, trumpet-general, swore he'd write
This combat truer than the naval fight.
How'rd on's birth, wit, strength, courage much presumes
And in his breast wears many Montezumes.
These and some more with single valour stay
The adverse troops, and hold them all at bay.
Each thinks his person represents the whole,
270 And with that thought does multiply his soul,
Believes himself an army, theirs, one man
As easily conquered, and believing can,
With heart of bees so full, and head of mites,
That each, though duelling, a battle fights.
Such once Orlando, famous in romance,
Broached whole brigades like larks upon his lance.
  But strength at last still under number bows,
And the faint sweat trickled down Temple's brows.
E'en iron Strangeways, chafing, yet gave back,
280 Spent with fatigue, to breathe a while to back.
When, marching in, a seasonable recruit
Of citizens and merchants held dispute;
And, charging all their pikes, a sullen band
Of Presbyterian Switzers made a stand.
  Nor could all these the field have long maintained
But for th' unknown reserve that still remained:
A gross of English gentry, nobly born,
Of clear estates, and to no faction sworn,
Dear lovers of their king, and death to meet
290 For country's cause, that glorious think and sweet;
To speak not forward, but in action brave,
In giving generous, but in counsel grave;
Candidly credulous for once, nay twice,
But sure the Devil cannot cheat them thrice.
The van and battle, though retiring, falls
Without disorder in their intervals.

Then, closing all in equal front, fall on,
Led by great *Garway* and great *Littleton*.
Lee, ready to obey or to command,
300 Adjutant-general, was still at hand.
The martial standard, *Sandys* displaying, shows
St Dunstan in it, tweaking Satan's nose.
See sudden chance of war! To paint or write
Is longer work and harder than to fight.
At the first charge the enemy give out,
And the Excise receives a total rout.

   Broken in courage, yet the men the same
Resolve henceforth upon their other game:
Where force had failed, with stratagem to play,
310 And what haste lost, recover by delay.
St Albans straight is sent to, to forbear,
Lest the sure peace, forsooth, too soon appear.
The seamen's clamour to three ends they use:
To cheat their pay, feign want, the House accuse.
Each day they bring the tale, and that too true,
How strong the Dutch their equipage renew.
Meantime through all the yards their orders run
To lay the ships up, cease the keels begun.
The timber rots, and useless axe doth rust,
320 Th' unpracticed saw lies buried in its dust,
The busy hammer sleeps, the ropes untwine,
The stores and wages all are mine and thine.
Along the coast and harbours they take care
That money lack, nor forts be in repair.
Long thus they could against the House conspire,
Load them with envy, and with sitting tire.
And the loved King, and never yet denied,
Is brought to beg in public and to chide;
But when this failed, and months enow were spent,
330 They with the first day's proffer seem content,
And to Land-Tax from the Excise turn round,
Bought off with *eighteen-hundred-thousand pound*.
Thus like fair thieves, the Commons' purse they share,
But all the members' lives, consulting, spare.

Blither than hare that hath escaped the hounds,
The House prorogued, the Chancellor rebounds.
Not so decrepit Aeson, hashed and stewed,
With bitter herbs, rose from the pot renewed,
And with fresh age felt his glad limbs unite;
340 His gout (yet still he cursed) had left him quite.
What frosts to fruit, what arsenic to the rat,
What to fair Denham, mortal chocolate,
What an account to Carteret, that, and more,
A Parliament is to the Chancellor.
So the Sad-tree shrinks from the morning's eye,
But blooms all night and shoots its branches high.
So, at the sun's recess, again returns
The comet dread, and earth and heaven burns.
  Now Mordaunt may, within his castle tower,
350 Imprison parents, and the child deflower.
The Irish herd is now let loose and comes
By millions over, not by hecatombs;
And now, now the Canary Patent may
Be broached again for the great holiday.
  See how he reigns in his new palace culminant,
And sits in state divine like Jove the fulminant!
First *Buckingham*, that durst to him rebel,
Blasted with lightning, struck with thunder, fell.
Next the twelve Commons are condemned to groan
360 And roll in vain at Sisyphus's stone.
But still he cared, while in revenge he braved
That peace secured and money might be saved:
Gain and revenge, revenge and gain are sweet
United most, else when by turns they meet.
France had St Albans promised (so they sing),
St Albans promised him, and he the King:
The Count forthwith is ordered all to close,
To play for Flanders and the stake to lose,
While, chained together, two ambassadors
370 Like slaves shall beg for peace at Holland's doors.
This done, among his Cyclops he retires
To forge new thunder and inspect their fires.

The court as once of war, now fond of peace,
All to new sports their wanton fears release.
From Greenwich (where intelligence they hold)
Comes news of pastime martíal and old,
A punishment invented first to awe
Masculine wives transgressing Nature's law,
Where, when the brawny female disobeys
380   And beats the husband till for peace he prays,
No concerned jury for him damage finds,
Nor partial justice her behaviour binds,
But the just street does the next house invade,
Mounting the neighbour couple on lean jade,
The distaff knocks, the grains from kettle fly,
And boys and girls in troops run hooting by:
Prudent antiquity, that knew by shame,
Better than law, domestic crimes to tame,
And taught youth by spectácle innocent!
390   So thou and I, dear Painter, represent
In quick effígy, others' faults, and feign
By making them ridiculous, to restrain.
With homely sight they chose thus to relax
The joys of state, for the new Peace and Tax.
So Holland with us had the mastery tried,
And our next neighbours, France and Flanders, ride.
But a fresh news the great designment nips,
Of, at the Isle of Candy, Dutch and ships!
Bab May and Arlington did wisely scoff
400   And thought all safe, if they were so far off.
Modern geographers, 'twas there, they thought,
Where Venice twenty years the Turk had fought,
While the first year our navy is but shown,
The next divided, and the third we've none.
They, by the name, mistook it for that isle
Where *Pilgrim Palmer* travelled in exile
With the bull's horn to measure his own head
And on Pasiphaë's tomb to drop a bead.
But *Morice* learn'd demónstrates, by the post,
410   This Isle of Candy was on Essex' coast.

Fresh messengers still the sad news assure;
More timorous now we are than first secure.
False terrors our believing fears devise,
And the French army one from Calais spies.
Bennet and May and those of shorter reach
Change all for guineas, and a crown for each,
But wiser men and well foreseen in chance
In Holland theirs had lodged before, and France.
Whitehall's unsafe; the court all meditates
420   To fly to Windsor and mure up the gates.
Each does the other blame, and all distrust;
(That Mordaunt, new obliged, would sure be just.)
Not such a fatal stupefaction reigned
At London's flame, nor so the court complained.
The *Bloodworth-Chancellor* gives, then does recall
Orders; amazed, at last gives none at all.
      St Alban's writ to, that he may bewail
To *Master Louis*, and tell coward tale
How yet the Hollanders do make a noise,
430   Threaten to beat us, and are naughty boys.
Now *Dolman's* disobedient, and they still
Uncivil; his unkindness would us kill.
Tell him our ships unrigged, our forts unmanned,
Our money spent; else 'twere at his command.
Summon him therefore of his word and prove
To move him out of pity, if not love;
Pray him to make *De Witt* and *Ruyter* cease,
And whip the Dutch unless they'll hold their peace.
But Louis was of memory but dull
440   And to St Albans too undutiful,
Nor word nor near relation did revere,
But asked him bluntly for his character.
The gravelled Count did with the answer faint –
His character was that which thou didst paint –
And so enforced, like enemy or spy,
Trusses his baggage and the camp does fly.
Yet Louis writes and, lest our heart should break,
Consoles us morally out of Seneque.

    Two letters next unto Breda are sent:
450 In cipher one to Harry Excellent;
    The first instructs our (verse the name abhors)
    Plenipotentiary ambassadors
    To prove by Scripture *treaty* does imply
    Cessation, as the look adultery,
    And that, by law of arms, in martial strife,
    Who yields his sword has title to his life.
    Presbyter Holles the first point should clear,
    The second Coventry the Cavalier;
    But, would they not be argued back from sea,
460 Then to return home straight, *infecta re*.
    But Harry's ordered, if they won't recall
    Their fleet, to threaten – we will grant them all.
    The Dutch are then in proclamation shent
    For sin against th' eleventh commandment.
    Hyde's flippant style there pleasantly curvets,
    Still his sharp wit on states and princes whets
    (So Spain could not escape his laughter's spleen:
    None but himself must choose the King a Queen),
    But when he came the odious clause to pen
470 That summons up the Parliament again,
    His writing master many a time he banned
    And wished himself the gout to seize his hand.
    Never old lecher more repugnance felt,
    Consenting, for his rupture, to be gelt;
    But still then hope him solaced, ere they come,
    To work the peace and so to send them home,
    Or in their hasty call to find a flaw,
    Their acts to vitiate, and them overawe;
    But most relied upon this Dutch pretence
480 To raise a two-edged army for's defence.
    First then he marched our whole militia's force
    (As if indeed we ships or Dutch had horse);
    Then from the usual commonplace, he blames
    These, and in standing army's praise declaims;
    And the wise court that always loved it dear,
    Now thinks all but too little for their fear.

Hyde stamps, and straight upon the ground the swarms
Of current Myrmidons appear in arms,
And for their pay he writes, as from the King –
490   With that cursed quill plucked from a vulture's wing –
Of the whole nation now to ask a loan
(The eighteen-hundred-thousand pound was gone).
    This done, he pens a proclamation stout,
In rescue of the *banquiers banquerout*,
His minion imps that, in his secret part,
Lie nuzzling at the sacramental wart,
Horse-leeches circling at the hem'rrhoid vein:
He sucks the King, they him, he them again.
The kingdom's farm he lets to them bid least
500   (Greater the bribe, and that's at interest).
Here men, induced by safety, gain, and ease,
Their money lodge; confiscate when he please.
These can at need, at instant, with a scrip
(This liked him best) his cash beyond sea whip.
When Dutch invade, when Parliament prepare,
How can he engines so convenient spare?
Let no man touch them or demand his own,
Pain of displeasure of great Clarendon.
    The state affairs thus marshalled, for the rest
510   Monck in his shirt against the Dutch is pressed.
Often, dear Painter, have I sat and mused
Why he should still be 'n all adventures used,
If they for nothing ill, like ashen wood,
Or think him, like Herb John, for nothing good;
Whether his valour they so much admire,
Or that for cowardice they all retire,
As heaven in storms, they call in gusts of state
On Monck and Parliament, yet both do hate.
All causes sure concur, but most they think
520   Under Hercúlean labours he may sink.
Soon then the independent troops would close,
And Hyde's last project would his place dispose.
    Ruyter the while, that had our ocean curbed,
Sailed now among our rivers undisturbed,

Surveyed their crystal streams and banks so green
And beauties ere this never naked seen.
Through the vain sedge, the bashful nymphs he eyed:
Bosoms, and all which from themselves they hide.
The sun much brighter, and the skies more clear,
530   He finds the air and all things sweeter here.
The sudden change, and such a tempting sight
Swells his old veins with fresh blood, fresh delight.
Like am'rous victors he begins to shave,
And his new face looks in the English wave.
His sporting navy all about him swim
And witness their complacence in their trim.
Their streaming silks play through the weather fair
And with inveigling colours court the air,
While the red flags breathe on their topmasts high
540   Terror and war, but want an enemy.
Among the shrouds the seamen sit and sing,
And wanton boys on every rope do cling.
Old Neptune springs the tides and water lent
(The gods themselves do help the provident),
And where the deep keel on the shallow cleaves,
With trident's lever, and great shoulder heaves.
Aeolus their sails inspires with eastern wind,
Puffs them along, and breathes upon them kind.
With pearly shell the Tritons all the while
550   Sound the sea-march and guide to Sheppey Isle.
    So have I seen in April's bud arise
A fleet of clouds, sailing along the skies;
The liquid region with their squadrons filled,
Their airy sterns the sun behind does gild;
And gentle gales them steer, and heaven drives,
When, all on sudden, their calm bosom rives
With thunder and lightning from each armèd cloud;
Shepherds themselves in vain in bushes shroud.
Such up the stream the Belgic navy glides
560   And at Sheerness unloads its stormy sides.
    Spragge there, though practised in the sea command,
With panting heart lay like a fish on land

And quickly judged the fort was not tenáble –
Which, if a house, yet were not tenantáble –
No man can sit there safe: the cannon pours
Thorough the walls untight and bullet showers,
The neighbourhood ill, and an unwholesome seat,
So at the first salute resolves retreat,
And swore that he would never more dwell there
570   Until the city put it in repair.
So he in front, his garrison in rear,
March straight to Chatham to increase the fear.
    There our sick ships unrigged in summer lay
Like moulting fowl, a weak and easy prey,
For whose strong bulk earth scarce could timber find,
The ocean water, or the heavens wind –
Those oaken giants of the ancient race,
That ruled all seas and did our Channel grace.
The conscious stag so, once the forest's dread,
580   Flies to the wood and hides his armless head.
Ruyter forthwith a squadron does untack;
They sail securely through the river's track.
An English pilot too (O shame, O sin!)
Cheated of pay, was he that showed them in.
Our wretched ships within their fate attend,
And all our hopes now on frail chain depend:
(Engine so slight to guard us from the sea,
It fitter seemed to captivate a flea).
A skipper rude shocks it without respect,
590   Filling his sails more force to re-collect.
Th' English from shore the iron deaf invoke
For its last aid: 'Hold chain, or we are broke.'
But with her sailing weight, the Holland keel,
Snapping the brittle links, does thorough reel,
And to the rest the opened passage show;
Monck from the bank the dismal sight does view.
Our feathered gallants, which came down that day
To be spectators safe of the new play,
Leave him alone when first they hear the gun
600   (Cornb'ry the fleetest) and to London run.

Our seamen, whom no danger's shape could fright,
Unpaid, refuse to mount our ships for spite,
Or to their fellows swim on board the Dutch,
Which show the tempting metal in their clutch.
Oft had he sent of Duncombe and of *Legge*
Cannon and powder, but in vain, to beg;
And Upnor Castle's ill-deserted wall,
Now needful, does for ammunition call.
He finds, wheres'e'er he succor might expect,
610   Confusion, folly, treach'ry, fear, neglect.
But when the *Royal Charles* (what rage, what grief)
He saw seized, and could give her no relief!
That sacred keel which had, as he, restored
His exiled sovereign on its happy board,
And thence the British Admiral became,
Crowned, for that merit, with their master's name;
That pleasure-boat of war, in whose dear side
Secure so oft he had this foe defied,
Now a cheap spoil, and the mean victor's slave,
620   Taught the Dutch colours from its top to wave;
Of former glories the reproachful thought,
With present shame compared, his mind distraught.
Such from Euphrates' bank, a tigress fell
After the robber for her whelps doth yell;
But sees enraged the river flow between,
Frustrate revenge and love, by loss more keen,
At her own breast her useless claws does arm:
She tears herself, since him she cannot harm.
   The guards, placed for the chain's and fleet's defence,
630   Long since were fled on many a feigned pretence.
Daniel had there adventured, man of might,
Sweet Painter, draw his picture while I write.
Paint him of person tall, and big of bone,
Large limbs like ox, not to be killed but shown.
Scarce can burnt ivory feign an hair so black,
Or face so red, thine ochre and thy lac.
Mix a vain terror in his martial look,
And all those lines by which men are mistook;

But when, by shame constrained to go on board,
640 He heard how the wild cannon nearer roared,
And saw himself confined like sheep in pen,
Daniel then thought he was in lion's den.
And when the frightful fireships he saw,
Pregnant with sulphur, to him nearer draw,
Captain, lieutenant, ensign, all make haste
Ere in the fiery furnace they be cast –
Three children tall, unsinged, away they row,
Like Shadrack, Meschack, and Abednego.
   Not so brave *Douglas*, on whose lovely chin
650 The early down but newly did begin,
And modest beauty yet his sex did veil,
While envious virgins hope he is a male.
His yellow locks curl back themselves to seek,
Nor other courtship knew but to his cheek.
Oft, as he in chill Esk or Seine by night
Hardened and cooled his limbs, so soft, so white,
Among the reeds, to be espied by him,
The nymphs would rustle; he would forward swim.
They sighed and said, 'Fond boy, why so untame
660 That fliest love's fires, reserved for other flame?'
Fixed on his ship, he faced that horrid day
And wondered much at those that run away.
Nor other fear himself could comprehend
Then, lest heaven fall ere thither he ascend,
But entertains the while his time too short
With birding at the Dutch, as if in sport,
Or waves his sword, and could he them conjúre
Within its circle, knows himself secure.
The fatal bark him boards with grappling fire,
670 And safely through its port the Dutch retire.
That precious life he yet disdains to save
Or with known art to try the gentle wave.
Much him the honours of his ancient race
Inspire, nor would he his own deeds deface,
And secret joy in his calm soul does rise
That Monck looks on to see how Douglas dies.

Like a glad lover, the fierce flames he meets,
And tries his first embraces in their sheets.
His shape exact, which the bright flames enfold,
680 Like the sun's statue stands of burnished gold.
Round the transparent fire about him glows,
As the clear amber on the bee does close,
And, as on angels' heads their glories shine,
His burning locks adorn his face divine.
But when in his immortal mind he felt
His altering form and soldered limbs to melt,
Down on the deck he laid himself and died,
With his dear sword reposing by his side,
And on the flaming plank, so rests his head
690 As one that's warmed himself and gone to bed.
His ship burns down, and with his relics sinks,
And the sad stream beneath his ashes drinks.
Fortunate boy, if either pencil's fame,
Or if my verse can propagate thy name,
When Oeta and Alcides are forgot,
Our English youth shall sing the valiant Scot.
    Each doleful day still with fresh loss returns:
The *Loyal London* now a third time burns,
And the true *Royal Oak* and *Royal James*,
700 Allied in fate, increase, with theirs, her flames.
Of all our navy none should now survive,
But that the ships themselves were taught to dive,
And the kind river in its creek them hides,
Fraughting their piercèd keels with oozy tides.
    Up to the bridge contagious terror struck:
The Tower itself with the near danger shook,
And were not Ruyter's maw with ravage cloyed,
E'en London's ashes had been then destroyed.
Officious fear, however, to prevent
710 Our loss does so much more our loss augment:
The Dutch had robbed those jewels of the crown;
Our merchantmen, lest they be burned, we drown.
So when the fire did not enough devour,
The houses were demolished near the Tower.

Those ships that yearly from their teeming hole
Unloaded here the birth of either Pole –
Furs from the north and silver from the west,
Wines from the south, and spices from the east;
From Gambo gold, and from the Ganges gems –
720 Take a short voyage underneath the Thames,
Once a deep river, now with timber floored,
And shrunk, least navigable, to a ford.
     Now (nothing more at Chatham left to burn),
The Holland squadron leisurely return,
And spite of Ruperts and of Albemarles,
To Ruyter's triumph lead the captive *Charles*.
The pleasing sight he often does prolong:
Her masts erect, tough cordage, timbers strong,
Her moving shapes, all these he does survey,
730 And all admires, but most his easy prey.
The seamen search her all within, without:
Viewing her strength, they yet their conquest doubt;
Then with rude shouts, secure, the air they vex,
With gamesome joy insulting on her decks.
Such the feared Hebrew, captive, blinded, shorn,
Was led about in sport, the public scorn.
     Black day accursed! On thee let no man hale
Out of the port, or dare to hoist a sail,
Nor row a boat in thy unlucky hour.
740 Thee, the year's monster, let thy dam devour,
And constant time, to keep his course yet right,
Fill up thy space with a redoubled night.
When agèd Thames was bound with fetters base,
And Medway chaste ravished before his face,
And their dear offspring murdered in their sight,
Thou and thy fellows held'st the odious light.
Sad change since first that happy pair was wed,
When all the rivers graced their nuptial bed,
And Father Neptune promised to resign
750 His empire old to their immortal line!
Now with vain grief their vainer hopes they rue,
Themselves dishonoured, and the gods untrue,

And to each other, helpless couple, moan,
As the sad tortoise for the sea does groan.
But most they for their darling *Charles* complain,
And were it burnt, yet less would be their pain.
To see that fatal pledge of sea command
Now in the ravisher De Ruyter's hand,
The Thames roared, swooning Medway turned her tide,
760 And were they mortal, both for grief had died.
    The court in farthing yet itself does please,
(And female Stuart there rules the four seas),
But fate does still accumulate our woes,
And Richmond her commands, as Ruyter those.
    After this loss, to relish discontent,
Someone must be accused by punishment.
All our miscarriages on *Pett* must fall:
His name alone seems fit to answer all.
Whose counsel first did this mad war beget?
770 Who all commands sold through the navy? *Pett*.
Who would not follow when the Dutch were beat?
Who treated out the time at Bergen? *Pett*.
Who the Dutch fleet with storms disabled met,
And rifling prizes, them neglected? *Pett*.
Who with false news prevented the Gazette,
The fleet divided, writ for Rupert? *Pett*.
Who all our seamen cheated of their debt,
And all our prizes who did swallow? *Pett*.
Who did advise no navy out to set,
780 And who the forts left unrepairèd? *Pett*.
Who to supply with powder did forget
Languard, Sheerness, Gravesend and Upnor? *Pett*.
Who all our ships exposed in Chatham's net?
Who should it be but the *Fanatic Pett*?
Pett, the sea-architect, in making ships
Was the first cause of all these naval slips:
Had he not built, none of these faults had been;
If no creation, there had been no sin.
But his great crime, one boat away he sent,
790 That lost our fleet and did our flight prevent.

  Then (that reward might in its turn take place,
And march with punishment in equal pace),
Southampton dead, much of the Treasure's care
And place in council fell to Duncombe's share.
All men admired he to that pitch could fly:
Powder ne'er blew man up so soon so high,
But sure his late good husbandry in petre
Showed him to manage the Exchequer meeter;
And who the forts would not vouchsafe a corn,
800 To lavish the King's money more would scorn.
Who hath no chimneys, to give all is best,
And ablest Speaker, who of law has least;
Who less estate, for Treasurer most fit,
And for a couns'llor, he that has least wit.
But the true cause was that, in's brother May,
The Exchequer might the Privy Purse obey.
  But now draws near the Parliament's return;
Hyde and the court again begin to mourn:
Frequent in council, earnest in debate,
810 All arts they try how to prolong its date.
Grave *Primate Sheldon* (much in preaching there)
Blames the last session and this more does fear:
With *Boynton* or with *Middleton* 'twere sweet,
But with a Parliament abhors to meet,
And thinks 'twill ne'er be well within this nation,
Till it be governed by a Convocation.
But in the Thames' mouth still De Ruyter laid;
The peace not sure, new army must be paid.
Hyde saith he hourly waits for a dispatch;
820 Harry came post just as he showed his watch,
All to agree the articles were clear –
The Holland fleet and Parliament so near –
Yet Harry must job back, and all mature,
Binding, ere the Houses meet, the treaty sure,
And 'twixt necessity and spite, till then,
Let them come up so to go down again.
  Up ambles country justice on his pad,
And vest bespeaks to be more seemly clad.

Plain gentlemen in stagecoach are o'erthrown
830   And deputy-lieutenants in their own.
The portly burgess through the weather hot
Does for his corporation sweat and trot;
And all with sun and choler come adust
And threaten Hyde to raise a greater dust.
But fresh as from the Mint, the courtiers fine
Salute them, smiling at their vain design,
And Turner gay up to his perch does march
With face new bleached, smoothened and stiff with starch;
Tells them he at Whitehall had took a turn
840   And for three days thence moves them to adjourn.
'Not so!' quoth Tomkins, and straight drew his tongue,
Trusty as steel that always ready hung,
And so, proceeding in his motion warm,
The army soon raised, he doth as soon disarm.
True Trojan! While this town can girls afford,
And long as cider lasts in Hereford,
The girls shall always kiss thee, though grown old,
And in eternal healths thy name be trolled.
Meanwhile the certain news of peace arrives
850   At court, and so reprieves their guilty lives.
Hyde orders Turner that he should come late,
Lest some new Tomkins spring a fresh debate.
The King that day raised early from his rest,
Expects (as at a play) till Turner's dressed.
At last together *Ayton* come and he:
No dial more could with the sun agree.
The Speaker, summoned, to the Lords repairs,
Nor gave the Commons leave to say their prayers,
But like his prisoners to the bar them led,
860   Where mute they stand to hear their sentence read.
Trembling with joy and fear, Hyde them prorogues,
And had almost mistook and called them rogues.
Dear Painter, draw this Speaker to the foot;
Where pencil cannot, there my pen shall do't:
That may his body, this his mind explain.
Paint him in golden gown, with mace's brain,

Bright hair, fair face, obscure and dull of head,
Like knife with ivory haft and edge of lead.
At prayers his eyes turn up the pious white,
870   But all the while his private bill's in sight.
In chair, he smoking sits like master cook,
And a poll bill does like his apron look.
Well was he skilled to season any question
And made a sauce, fit for Whitehall's digestion,
Whence every day, the palate more to tickle,
Court-mushrumps ready are, sent in in pickle.
When grievance urged, he swells like squatted toad,
Frisks like a frog, to croak a tax's load;
His patient piss he could hold longer than
880   An urinal, and sit like any hen;
At table jolly as a country host
And soaks his sack with *Norfolk*, like a toast;
At night, than Chanticleer more brisk and hot,
And Sergeant's wife serves him for Pertelotte.
       Paint last the *King*, and a dead shade of night
Only dispersed by a weak taper's light,
And those bright gleams that dart along and glare
From his clear eyes, yet these too dark with care.
There, as in the calm horror all alone
890   He wakes, and muses of th' uneasy throne;
Raise up a sudden shape with virgin's face,
(Though ill agree her posture, hour, or place),
Naked as born, and her round arms behind
With her own tresses, interwove and twined;
Her mouth locked up, a blind before her eyes,
Yet from beneath the veil her blushes rise,
And silent tears her secret anguish speak;
Her heart throbs and with very shame would break.
The object strange in him no terror moved:
900   He wondered first, then pitied, then he loved,
And with kind hand does the coy vision press
(Whose beauty greater seemed by her distress),
But soon shrunk back, chilled with her touch so cold,
And th' airy picture vanished from his hold.

In his deep thoughts the wonder did increase,
And he divined 'twas England or the Peace.
    Express him startling next with listening ear,
As one that some unusual noise does hear.
With cannon, trumpets, drums, his door surround –
910 But let some other painter draw the sound.
Thrice did he rise, thrice the vain tumult fled,
But again thunders, when he lies in bed.
His mind secure does the known stroke repeat
And finds the drums Louis's march did beat.
    Shake then the room, and all his curtains tear
And with blue streaks infect the taper clear,
While the pale ghosts his eye does fixed admire
Of grandsire *Harry* and of *Charles* his sire.
Harry sits down, and in his open side
920 The grisly wound reveals of which he died,
And ghastly Charles, turning his collar low,
The purple thread about his neck does show,
Then whispering to his son in words unheard,
Through the locked door both of them disappeared.
The wondrous night the pensive King revolves,
And rising straight on Hyde's disgrace resolves.
    At his first step, he Castlemaine does find,
Bennet, and Coventry, as 't were designed;
And they, not knowing, the same thing propose
930 Which his hid mind did in its depths enclose.
Through their feigned speech their secret hearts he knew:
To her own husband, Castlemaine untrue;
False to his master Bristol, Arlington;
And Coventry, falser than anyone,
Who to the brother, brother would betray,
Nor therefore trusts himself to such as they.
His father's ghost, too, whispered him one note,
That who does cut his purse will cut his throat,
But in wise anger he their crimes forbears,
940 As thieves reprieved for executioners;
While Hyde provoked, his foaming tusk does whet,
To prove them traitors and himself the *Pett*.

Painter, adieu! How well our arts agree,
Poetic picture, painted poetry;
But this great work is for our Monarch fit,
And henceforth Charles only to Charles shall sit.
His master-hand the ancients shall outdo,
Himself the painter and the poet too.

To the King

So his bold tube, man to the sun applied
950 And spots unknown to the bright star descried,
Showed they obscure him, while too near they please
And seem his courtiers, are but his disease.
Through optic trunk the planet seemed to hear,
And hurls them off e'er since in his career.
  And you, Great Sir, that with him empire share,
Sun of our world, as he the Charles is there,
Blame not the Muse that brought those spots to sight,
Which in your splendour hid, corrode your light:
(Kings in the country oft have gone astray
960 Nor of a peasant scorned to learn the way).
Would she the unattended throne reduce,
Banishing love, trust, ornament, and use,
Better it were to live in cloister's lock,
Or in fair fields to rule the easy flock.
She blames them only who the court restrain
And where all England serves, themselves would reign.
  Bold and accursed are they that all this while
Have strove to isle our Monarch from his isle,
And to improve themselves, on false pretence,
970 About the Common-Prince have raised a fence;
The kingdom from the crown distinct would see
And peel the bark to burn at last the tree.
(But Ceres corn, and Flora is the spring,
Bacchus is wine, the country is the King.)
  Not so does rust insinuating wear,
Nor powder so the vaulted bastion tear,
Nor earthquake so an hollow isle o'erwhelm,
As scratching courtiers undermine a realm,

And through the palace's foundations bore,
980   Burrowing themselves to hoard their guilty store.
The smallest vermin make the greatest waste,
And a poor warren once a city rased.
    But they, whom born to virtue and to wealth,
Nor guilt to flattery binds, nor want to stealth;
Whose generous conscience and whose courage high
Does with clear counsels their large souls supply;
That serve the King with their estates and care,
And, as in love, on Parliaments can stare,
(Where few the number, choice is there less hard):
990   Give us this court, and rule without a guard.

The Loyal Scot

UPON OCCASION OF THE DEATH OF CAPTAIN
DOUGLAS BURNED IN ONE OF HIS MAJESTY'S SHIPS
AT CHATHAM

By Cleveland's Ghost

    Of the old heroes when the warlike shades
Saw Douglas marching on the Elysian glades,
They straight consulting, gathered in a ring,
Which of their poets should his welcome sing,
And, as a favourable penance, chose
Cleveland, on whom that task they would impose.
He understood, but willingly addressed
His ready muse to court their noble guest.
Much had he cured the tumour of his vein,
10   He judged more clearly now, and saw more plain;
For those soft airs had tempered every thought,
And of wise Lethe he had took a draught,
Abruptly he began, to hide his art,
As of his satire this had been a part.
    Not so brave Douglas, on whose lovely chin
The early down but newly did begin;
And modest beauty yet his sex did veil,
While envious virgins hope he is a male.

His shady locks curl back themselves to seek:
20 Nor other courtship knew but to his cheek.
Oft as he in chill Eske or Seine by night
Hardened and cooled those limbs so soft, so white,
Among the reeds, to be espied by him,
The nymphs would rustle; he would forward swim.
They sighed and said, 'Fond boy, why so untame
That fliest Love's fires, reserved for other flame?'
    Fixed on his ship he faced the horrid day,
And wondered much at those that run away:
Nor other fear himself could comprehend
30 Then, lest heaven fall ere thither he ascend,
But entertains the while his time too short
With birding at the Dutch, as if in sport,
Or waves his sword, and could he them conjúre
Within its circle, knows himself secure.
    The fatal bark him boards with grappling fire,
And safely through its port the Dutch retire.
That precious life he yet disdains to save,
Or with known art to try the gentle wave.
Much him the honours of his ancient race
40 Inspire, nor would he his own deeds deface:
And secret joy in his calm soul does rise,
That Monck looks on to see how Douglas dies.
    Like a glad lover the fierce flames he meets,
And tries his first embraces in their sheets.
His shape exact, which the bright flames enfold,
Like the sun's statue stands of burnished gold.
Round the transparent fire about him glows,
As the clear amber on the bee does close.
And as on angels' heads their glories shine,
50 His burning locks adorn his face divine.
    But when in his immortal mind he felt
His altering form and soldered limbs to melt,
Down on the deck he laid himself and died,
With his dear sword reposing by his side:
And on the flaming plank so rests his head
As one that hugs himself in a warm bed.

The ship burns down and with his relics sinks,
And the sad stream beneath his ashes drinks.
    Fortunate boy, if e'er my verse may claim
60 That matchless grace to propagate thy name,
When Oeta and Alcides are forgot
Our English youth shall sing the valiant Scot.
    Skip-saddles Pegasus, thou needst not brag,
Sometimes the Gall'way proves the better nag.
Shall not a death so generous now when told
Unite the distance, fill the breaches old?
Such in the Roman Forum, Curtius brave
Galloping down closed up the gaping cave.
No more discourse of Scotch or English race,
70 Nor chant the fabulous hunt of Chevy Chase.
Mixed in Corinthian metal, at thy flame
Our nations melting, thy colossus frame.
    Prick down the point (whoever has the art),
Where Nature Scotland does from England part.
Anatomists may sooner fix the cells
Where life resides, or understanding dwells:
But this we know, though that exceeds our skill,
That whosoever sep'rates them does kill.
    Will you the Tweed that sudden bounder call
80 Of soil, of wit, of manners, and of all?
Why draw we not as well the thrifty line
From Thames, Trent, Humber, or at least the Tyne?
So may we the state corpulence redress,
And little England, when we please, make less.
    What ethic river is this wondrous Tweed,
Whose one bank vertue, other vice does breed?
Or what new perpendicular does rise
Up from her stream, continued to the skies,
That between us the common air should bar
90 And split the influence of every star?
But who considers right will find indeed
'Tis Holy Island parts us, not the Tweed.
    Nothing but clergy could us two seclude,
No Scotch was ever like a bishop's feud.

All litanies in this have wanted faith.
There's no *Deliver us* from the bishop's wrath.
Never shall Calvin pardoned be for Sales,
For Becket's sake Kent always shall have tails.
Who sermons e'er can pacify and prayers?
100 Or to the joined stools reconcile the chairs?
Though kingdoms join, yet church will kirk oppose,
The mitre still divides, the crown does close.
As in Rogation-Week they whip us round,
To keep in mind the Scotch and English bound.
What th' ocean binds is by the bishop rent,
Their sees make islands in our continent.
Nature in vain us in one land compiles,
If the cathedral still will have its aisles.
　　Nothing, not bogs, not sands, not seas, not alps,
110 Sep'rates the world, so as the bishops' scalps.
Stretch for the line, their surcingle alone,
'Twill make a more unhabitable zone.
The friendly loadstone has not more combined,
Than bishops cramped the commerce of mankind.
A bishop will like Mah'met tear the moon,
And slip one half into his sleeve as soon.
The juggling prelate on his Hocus calls,
Shows you first one, then makes that one two balls.
Instead of all the plagues, had bishops come,
120 Pharaoh at first would have sent Israel home.
From church they need not censure men away,
A bishop's self is an anathema:
Where foxes dung, their earths the badgers yield,
At bishops' musk, even foxes quit the field.
Their rank ambition all this hate has stirred,
A bishop's runnet makes the strongest curd.
　　What rev'rend things (Lord) are lawn sleeves and ease!
How a clean laundress, and no sermons please!
They wanted zeal and learning, so forsook
130 Bible and grammar for the service book.
Religion has too long the world depraved,
A shorter way to be by clergy saved.

Believe, but only as the church believes,
And learn to pin your souls upon their sleeves.
(Ah, like Lot's wife they still look back and halt,
And, surpliced, show like pillars too of salt.)
Who that is wise would pulpit-toil endure?
A bishopric is a great *Sine-cure*.
Enough for them, God knows, to count their wealth,
140 To excommunicate, and study health.
An higher work is to their call annexed;
The nations they divide, their curates, text.
No bishop? Rather than it should be so,
No church, no trade, no king, no people, no.
All mischief's moulded by these state divines;
Aaron cast calves, but Moses them calcines.
     The legion-devil did but one man possess;
One bishop-fiend spirits a whole diocese.
That power alone can loose this spell that ties:
150 And none but kings can bishops exorcise.
     Will you be treated princes, here fall too:
Fish and flesh bishops are your ambigue.
How'er insipid, yet the sauce will mend 'em,
Bishops are very good when *in commendam*.
If wealth or vice can whet your appetites,
These Templar Lords exceed the Templar Knights.
And in the baron-prelate you have both
Leviathan served up and behemóth.
     How can you bear such miscreants should live,
160 And holy ordure holy orders give?
None knows what god our flamen now adores:
One mitre fits the heads of foúr Moors.
No wonder if the orthodox do bleed,
While Arius stands at th' Athanasian Creed.
What so obdúrate pagan-heretic
But will transform for an archbishopric.
     In faith erroneous and in life profane
These hypocrites their silks and linen stain.
Seth's pillars are no antique brick or stone;
170 But of the choicest modern flesh and bone.

Who views but Gilbert's tiles will reason find
Neither before to trust him nor behind.
How oft hath age his hallowing hands misled,
Confirming breasts and armpits for the head!
Abbot missed bucks, but Sheldon ne'er missed doe:
Nor is our Patriarch whiter than his Snow.
Their company's the worst that ever·played,
And their religion all but masquerade.
The conscious Primate therefore did not err,
180   When for a church he built a Theatre.
    A congruous dress they to themselves adapt,
Like smutty stories in clean linen wrapped.
Do but their pie-bald lordships once uncase
Of rochets, tippets, copes, and where's their Grace?
An hungry chaplain and a starvèd rat,
Eating their brethren, bishop grow and cat.
But an apocryphal Archbishop Bel
Like snakes, by swall'wing toads, does dragon swell.
    Strange was the sight, that Scotch two-headed man
190   With single body, like the two-necked swan;
And wild disputes betwixt those heads must grow
Where but two hands to act, two feet to go.
Nature in living emblem then expressed
What Britain was between two kings distressed.
    But now when one head does both realms control,
The bishop's noddle perks up cheek by jowl.
They, though no poets, on Parnassus dream,
And in their causes think themselves supreme.
King's-head saith this, but bishop's-head that do;
200   Does Charles the Second reign, or Charles the Two?
Well that Scotch monster and our bishops sort,
(It was musician too, and lived at court).
    Hark, though at such a distance what a noise
Shattering the silent air disturbs our joys:
The mitred hubbub against Pluto moot,
That cloven head must govern cloven foot.
Strange boldness! Bishops even there rebel,
And plead their *jus divinumn* though in Hell.

    Those whom you hear more clam'rous yet and loud,
210 Of ceremonies wrangle in the crowd,
    And would, like chemists fixing mercury,
    Transmute Indifference to Necessity.
    To sit is necessary in Parliament,
    To preach in diocese, indifferent;
    'Tis necessary bishops have their rent,
    To cheat the plague-money, indifferent.
    New oaths 'tis necessary to invent,
    To give new taxes is indifferent.
    'Tis necessary to rebabel Paul's,
220 Indifferent to rob churches of their coals.
    'Tis necessary Lambeth never wed,
    Indifferent to have a wench in bed;
    Such bishops are with all their complement,
    Nor necessary, nor indifferent.
    Incorrigible among all their pains,
    Some sue for tithes of these Elysian plains.
    Others attempt (to cool their fervent chine)
    A second time to ravish Proserpine.
    Even Father Dis, though so with age defaced,
230 With much ado preserves his postern chaste.
    The innocentest mind there thirst alone,
    And, uninforced, quaff healths in Phlegeton.
    Luxury, malice, superstition, pride,
    Oppression, avarice, ambition, Id-
    Leness, all the vice that did abound
    When first they lived, still haunts them underground.
    Had it not been for such a bias strong,
    Two nations ne'er had missed the mark so long.
    The world in all does but two nations bear,
240 The Good, the Bad, and those mixed everywhere:
    Under each Pole place either of the two,
    The Bad will basely, Good will bravely do.
    And few indeed can parallel our climes
    For worth heroic, or heroic crimes.
    The trial would, however, be too nice,
    Which stronger were, a Scotch or English vice,

Or whether the same virtue would reflect
From Scotch or English heart the same effect.
   Nation is all but name – a shibboleth –
250 Where a mistaken accent causes death.
In paradise names only Nature showed,
At Babel names from pride and discord flowed;
And ever since men with a female spite,
First call each other names, and then they fight.
Scotland and England! Cause of just uproar,
Do man and wife signify rogue and whore?
Say but a Scot, and straight we fall to sides,
That syllable like a Pict's wall divides.
Rational man! Words, pledges all of peace,
260 Perverted, serve dissension to increase.
For shame, extírpate from each loyal breast,
That senseless rancour against interest.
One king, one faith, one language, and one isle,
English or Scotch, 'tis all but cross and pile.

   Charles, our great soul, this only understands,
He our affections both and will commands.
And where twin sympathies cannot atone,
Knows the last secret how to make us one.
Just so the prudent husbandman who sees
270 The idle tumult of his factious bees,
The morning dews, and flowers neglected grown,
The hive a comb-case, every bee a drone,
Powders them o'er, till none discern his foes,
And all themselves in meal and friendship lose;
The insect kingdom straight begins to thrive,
And each work honey for the common hive.

   Pardon, young hero, this so long transport,
(Thy death more nobly did the same exhort).
My former satire for this verse forget,
280 The hare's head against the goose giblets set.
I single did against a nation write,
Against a nation thou didst single fight.
My differing crime does more thy vertue raise,
And such my rashness best thy valour praise.

Here Douglas, smiling, said he did intend
After such frankness shown to be his friend,
Forewarned him therefore lest in time he were
Metempsychosed in some Scotch presbyter.

Inscribenda Luparae

Consurgit Luparae dum non imitabile culmen,
  Escuriale ingens uritur invidia.

Aliter
Regibus haec posuit Ludovicus templa futuris;
  Gratior ast ipsi castra fuere domus.

Aliter
Hanc sibi sydeream Ludovicus condidit aulam;
  Nec se propterea credidit esse deum.

Aliter
Atria miraris, summotumque aethera tecto;
  Nec tamen in toto est arctior orbe casa.

Aliter
Instituente domum Ludovico, prodiit orbis;
  Sic tamen angustos incolit ille lares.

Aliter
Sunt geminae Jani portae, sunt tecta tonantis;
  Nec deerit numen dum Ludovicus adest.

TO BE WRITTEN ON THE LOUVRE

While the inimitable roof of the Louvre rises,
  The huge Escorial burns with envy.

An Alternate
Louis built this temple for future kings,
  But the camp was a more pleasing home to him.

Another

Louis built this starry palace for himself,
 Nor did he believe on that account that he was a god.

Another

10 You marvel at the halls, and the sky pushed up by the
   roof;
 Yet there is not in the whole world a less roomy house.

Another

Louis founding this house, the world came forth;
 Yet thus he inhabits a cramped household.

Another

These are the double gates of Janus, these are the roofs of
   the Thunderer;
 Nor is divinity lacking while Louis is present.

On Mr Milton's 'Paradise Lost'

When I beheld the poet blind, yet bold,
In slender book his vast design unfold,
Messiah crowned, God's reconciled decree,
Rebelling Angels, the Forbidden Tree,
Heaven, Hell, Earth, Chaos, all; the argument
Held me a while, misdoubting his intent
That he would ruin (for I saw him strong)
The sacred truths to fable and old song,
(So Sampson groped the temple's posts in spite)
10 The world o'erwhelming to revenge his sight.
  Yet as I read, soon growing less severe,
I liked his project, the success did fear;
Through that wide field how he his way should find
O'er which lame faith leads understanding blind;
Lest he perplexed the things he would explain,
And what was easy he should render vain.
  Or if a work so infinite he spanned,
Jealous I was that some less skilful hand

    (Such as disquiet always what is well,
20   And by ill imitating would excel)
    Might hence presume the whole Creation's day
    To change in scenes, and show it in a play.
      Pardon me, Mighty Poet, nor despise
    My causeless, yet not impious, surmise.
    But I am now convinced that none will dare
    Within thy labours to pretend a share.
    Thou hast not missed one thought that could be fit,
    And all that was improper dost omit:
    So that no room is here for writers left,
30   But to detect their ignorance or theft.
    That majesty which through thy work doth reign
    Draws the devout, deterring the profane.
    And things divine thou treat'st of in such state
    As them preserves, and thee, inviolate.
    At once delight and horror on us seize,
    Thou sing'st with so much gravity and ease;
    And above human flight dost soar aloft,
    With plume so strong, so equal, and so soft.
    The bird named from that paradise you sing
40   So never flags, but always keeps on wing.
      Where couldst thou words of such a compass find?
    Whence furnish such a vast expense of mind?
    Just heaven thee, like Tiresias, to requite,
    Rewards with prophecy thy loss of sight.
      Well mightst thou scorn thy readers to allure
    With tinkling rhyme, of thine own sense secure;
    While the *Town-Bayes* writes all the while and spells,
    And like a pack-horse tires without his bells.
    Their fancies like our bushy points appear,
50   The poets tag them; we for fashion wear.
    I too, transported by the mode, offend,
    And while I meant to *praise* thee must *commend*.
    Thy verse created like thy theme sublime,
    In number, weight, and measure, needs not rhyme.

*Illustrissimo Viro Domino Lanceloto Josepho
de Maniban Grammatomanti*

TO A GENTLEMAN THAT ONLY UPON THE SIGHT OF
THE AUTHOR'S WRITING HAD GIVEN A CHARACTER
OF HIS PERSON AND JUDGEMENT OF HIS FORTUNE.

Quis posthac chartae committat sensa loquaci,
   Si sua crediderit fata subesse stylo?
Conscia si prodat scribentis litera sortem,
   Quicquid et in vita plus latuisse velit?
Flexibus in calami tamen omnia sponte leguntur
   Quod non significant verba, figura notat.
Bellerophonteas signat sibi quisque tabellas;
   Ignaramque manum spiritus intus agit.
Nil praeter solitum sapiebat epistola nostra,
10   Exemplumque meae simplicitatis erat.
Fabula jucundos qualis delectat amicos;
   Urbe, lepore, novis, carmine tota scatens.
Hic tamen interpres quo non securior alter,
   (Non res, non voces, non ego notus ei)
Rimatur fibras notularum cautus aruspex,
   Scripturaeque inhians consulit exta meae.
Inde statim vitae casus, animique recessus
   Explicat; (haud genio plura liquere putem.)
Distribuit totum nostris eventibus orbem,
20   Et quo me rapiat cardine sphaera docet.
Quae Sol oppositus, quae Mars adversa minetur,
   Jupiter aut ubi me, Luna, Venusque juvent.
Ut trucis intentet mihi vulnera cauda draconis;
   Vipereo levet ut vulnera more caput.
Hinc mihi praeteriti rationes atque futuri
   Elicit; astrologus certior astronomo.
Ut conjecturas nequeam discernere vero,
   Historiae superet sed genitura fidem.
Usque adeo caeli respondet pagina nostrae,
30   Astrorum et nexus syllaba scripta refert.
Scilicet et toti subsunt oracula mundo,
   Dummodo tot foliis una Sibylla foret.

Partum, Fortunae mater Natura, propinquum
  Mille modis monstrat mille per indicia:
Ingentemque uterum qua mole puerpera solvat;
  Vivit at in praesens maxima pars hominum.
Ast tu sorte tua gaude celeberrime vatum;
  Scribe, sed haud superest qui tua fata legat.
Nostra tamen si fas praesagia jungere vestris,
40 Quo magis inspexti sydera spernis humum.
Et, nisi stellarum fueris divina propago,
  Naupliada credam te Palamede satum.
Qui dedit ex avium scriptoria signa volatu,
  Sydereaque idem nobilis arte fuit.
Hinc utriusque tibi cognata scientia crevit,
  Nec minus augurium litera quam dat avis.

TO THAT RENOWNED MAN LORD LANCELOT JOSEPH DE MANIBAN GRAPHOLOGIST

Who after this would commit his thoughts to babbling
    paper,
If he thought that his fate would be exposed by his pen?
And if the guilty handwriting might proclaim the fortune
    of the writer,
What thing in life would he more wish to have hidden?
Nevertheless, in the turnings of the reed-pen all things are
    read spontaneously.
What the words do not signify, the shape makes known,
And each signs for himself Bellerophontean letters;
A spirit within drives the unknowing hand.
My letter savoured of nothing beyond the ordinary,
10 And was a sample of my simplicity,
A narrative such as delights pleasant friends,
All full of the city, wit, news, poetry;
Yet this interpreter, than whom no other is surer,
(Neither the subject matter, the words, nor I known to
    him)
A cunning haruspex, examines the entrails of my writing
And, poring, consults the inwards of my script.

Then immediately the events of my life, the recesses of
    my mind
He unfolds. (I doubt that more things are apparent to my
    guardian spirit.)
He divides the whole zodiac into my fortunes

20 And teaches with what constellation I am carried around,
What misfortunes the Sun in my opposition, or Mars may
    threaten,
Or when Jupiter, the Moon, and Venus may aid me,
How the tail of the malignant dragon threatens wounds to
    me,
And how his head, like a viper's, may assuage the wounds.
Hence, interpretations of the past and future
He elicits; an astrologer more certain than an astronomer.
Although I may not be able to distinguish conjectures from
    truth,
Yet the natal star is more reliable than history,
So much does the page of the heavens correspond to ours,

30 And the written syllable refer to the patterns of the stars.
And no doubt all things in the world are subject to
    prophecies,
Provided that one Sibyl be in so many leaves.
An approaching birth, Nature, the mother of Fortune,
Shows in a thousand ways, through a thousand signs,
By which child-bearing labour she may ease her vast
    womb;
Yet the greatest part of mankind lives in the present.
But you, the most distinguished of seers, rejoice in your
    lot;
Write, but there is no one living who may read your fate.
Yet, if I may join my prognostications to yours,

40 The more you have gazed at the stars, the more you scorn
    the earth.
And, unless you are the divine offspring of the stars,
I shall believe you descended from Nauplian Palamedes,
Who gave written symbols from the flight of birds,
And was likewise renowned in the starry art.
Hence the related knowledge of both has increased in you,
The letter gives no less augury than the bird.

Additional Latin and Greek Poems

This Appendix includes Marvell's Latin and Greek
juvenilia and the commendatory verses in Latin which
accompanied the set of English verses appearing on
page 62 and the Latin poems for which there are
English counterparts (appearing on pages 100–102).

Ad Regem Carolum Parodia

Jam satis pestis, satis atque diri
Fulminis misit pater, et rubenti
Dextera nostras jaculatus arces
        Terruit urbem.
Terruit cives, grave ne rediret
Pristinum seclum nova monstra questum,
Omne cum pestis pecus egit altos
        Visere montes;
Cum scholae latis genus haesit agris,
10 Nota quae sedes fuerat bubulcis;
Cum toga abjecta pavidus reliquit
        Oppida doctus.
Vidimus Chamum fluvium retortis
Littore a dextro violenter undis
Ire plorantem monumenta pestis,
        Templaque clausa.
Granta dum semet nimium querenti
Miscet uxorem vagus et sinistra
Labitur ripa, Jove comprobante,
20   Tristior amnis.
Audiit coelos acuisse ferrum,
Quo graves Turcae melius perirent;
Audiit mortes vitio parentum
        Rara juventus.
Quem vocet divum populus ruentis
Imperi rebus? Prece qua fatigent
Doctior coetus minus audientes
        Carmina coelos?

Cui dabit partes luis expiandae
30 Jupiter, tandem venias, precamur,
Nube candentes humeros amictus
            Auxiliator.
Sive tu mavis, Erycina nostra,
Quam jocus circumvolat et Cupido,
Tuque neglectum genus et nepotes
            Auxeris ipsa.
Sola tam longam removere pestem,
Quam juvat luctus faciesque tristis,
Prolis optata reparare mole
40   Sola potesque.
Sive felici Carolum figura
Parvulus princeps imitetur, almae
Sive Mariae decoret puellam
            Dulcis imago.
Serus in coelum redeas, diuque
Laetus intersis populo Britanno,
Neve te nostris vitiis iniquum
            Ocior aura
Tollat. Hic magnos potius triumphos,
50 Hic ames dici pater atque princeps,
Et nova mortes reparare prole
            Te patre, Caesar.

A PARODY: TO KING CHARLES

Already the father has sent enough of plague
and enough of his dire thunderbolt;
striking our citadels with glowing hand,
        he has terrified the city.
He terrified the citizens, lest the harsh first age,
groaning with new horrors, should return,
when the plague drove the whole throng
        to the high mountains.
When the schoolish sort stuck in the broad fields,
10 formerly known only to the ploughman;

when the pale scholar, casting off his gown,
    fled from the city.
We beheld the Cam, its waters
violently recoiling from its right bank,
flow bewailing the monuments of the plague
    and the closed churches.
While Granta joins his spouse in too much lamenting,
and flooding over his left bank
with Jove's permission, glides,
20   a sadder river.
Our scanty offspring has heard heaven sharpen against us
    the sword
by which the menacing Turks should have more fitly
    perished.
They have heard of the deaths caused
    by their fathers' vices.
What god shall the people invoke
when the state collapses? With what prayer
may a more learned group weary the heavens,
    unheedful of their pleas?
You to whom Jove will give the role
30 of expiating the pestilence, come at last, we pray,
your gleaming shoulders mantled with cloud,
    our helper.
Or if you are willing, our Erycina,
whom Mirth and Love attend,
do you also aid
    your forgotten people.
You alone are able to end the long plague,
which is pleased by our mourning and sad faces;
you alone are able to renew
40   our generations.
Whether a little prince shows
the happy features of Charles,
or the sweet image of Mary
    graces a daughter.
Late may you return to heaven,
long may you live happy among the British people.

Nor may any ruder blast steal you,
  indignant at our vices, from us.
Here rather celebrate great triumphs;
50 here may you delight to be called prince and father,
and with new birth make good our losses,
    Caesar.

Πρὸς Κάρολον τὸν βασιλέα

Ω Δνσαριστοτόκος, Πέντ᾽ ὦ δύσποτμος ἀριθμός!*
  ῎Ω Πέντε στυγερὸν, Πέντ᾽, ἀΐδαο πύλαι!†
᾽Αγγλῶν ὦ μέγ᾽ ὄνειδος, ὦ οὐρανίοισιν ἀπεχθές!
  ᾽Αλλ᾽ ἀπελύμαινες Κάρρολε τοῦτον ἄνα.
Πέμπτον τέκνον ἔδωκε μογοστόκος Εἰλείθυια
  Πέντε δὲ Πένταθλον τέκνα καλοῦσι τεόν.
Εἰ δὲ θέλεις βίβλοις ταῖς ὀφιγόνοισι τίεσθαι,
  Πεντήτευχον ἔχεις παιδία διογενῆ.
῎Η ὅτι θεσπεσίης φιλέεις μήστωρας ἀοιδῆς,
  ῾Αρμονίην ποιεῖς τὴν Διὰ πέντε Πάτερ.

᾽Ανδρέας ὁ Μαρβέλλου, ἐκ τοῦ τῆς Τριαδος.

TO KING CHARLES

O ill-fated mother of the best of offspring, Five, O
ill-omened number, O hateful five, five, gates of Hades.
  O great reproach of the English, O hateful to the gods!
But thou, O Charles, didst wipe out this disgrace. Helping
Ilithyia has granted a fifth birth, and five children name
thy pentathlon.
  If you wish to be honoured in the books of later
generations, you have in these five divinely born children
your Pentateuch. Or because you love the masters of
divinely inspired song, you make here the fifth harmony,
Father.

Andrew Marvell, Trinity College

* 5 November
† 5 August

Dignissimo Suo Amico Doctori Witty
de Translatione 'Vulgi Errorum' D. Primrosii

Nempe sic innumero succrescunt agmine libri,
   Saepia vix toto ut jam natet una mari.
Fortius assidui surgunt a vulnere preli:
   Quoque magis pressa est, auctior hydra redit.
Heu quibus Anticyris, quibus est sanabilis herbis
   Improba scribendi pestis, avarus amor.
India sola tenet tanti medicamina morbi,
   Dicitur et nostris ingemuisse malis.
Utile tabacci dedit illa miserta venenum,
10   Acri veratro quod meliora potest.
Jamque vides olidas libris fumare popinas:
   Naribus O doctis quam pretiosus odor!
Hac ego praecipua credo herbam dote placere,
   Hinc tuus has nebulas Doctor in astra vehit.
Ah, mea quid tandem facies timidissima charta?
   Exequias siticen jam parat usque tuas.
Hunc subeas librum sancti seu limen asyli,
   Quem neque delebit flamma, nec ira Jovis.

TO HIS DISTINGUISHED FRIEND DOCTOR WITTY

On the Translation of the Vulgar Errors *of Primrose*

Truly, books are increasing in such an endless stream
That now scarcely one cuttle fish swims in the whole sea.
Unceasing presses spring more strongly from the wound:
And the more it has been pressed, the larger the hydra
    returns.
Alas, by what Anticyras, by what herbs is curable
This violent plague, this fierce love of writing!
India alone holds medicines for so great a disease,
And she is said to have groaned for our afflictions.
Compassionate, she gave the useful poison of tobacco,
10 Which is more efficacious than sharp hellebore.

And now you see smelly clouds smoke from books:
Oh, to learned nostrils what a precious odour!
I believe the herb pleases because of this special property;
From here your doctor carries these clouds to the stars.
Ah, my fearful pages, what, pray, will you do?
The musician even now prepares your obsequies.
May you enter this book as the threshold of a sacred
    refuge,
Which neither the flame nor the wrath of Jove will destroy.

Hortus

Quisnam adeo, mortale genus, praecordia versat?
Heu palmae, laurique furor, vel simplicis herbae!
Arbor ut indomitos ornet vix una labores;
Tempora nec foliis praecingat tota malignis.
Dum simul implexi, tranquillae ad serta Quietis,
Omnigeni coeunt flores, integraque sylva.
   Alma Quies, teneo te! et te germana Quietis
Simplicitas! Vos ergo diu per templa, per urbes,
Quaesivi, regum perque alta palatia frustra.
10 Sed vos hortorum per opaca silentia longe
Celarant plantae virides, et concolor umbra.
    O! mihi si vestros liceat violasse recessus
Erranti, lasso, et vitae melioris anhelo,
Municipem servate novum, voto que potitum,
Frondosae cives optate in florea regna.
    Me quoque, vos Musae, et, te conscie testor Apollo,
Non armenta juvant hominum, circique boatus,
Mugitusve fori; sed me penetralia veris,
Horroresque trahunt muti, et consortia sola.
20   Virgineae quem nonsuspendit gratia formae?
Quam candore nives vincentem, ostrumque rubore,
Vestra tamen viridis superet (me judice) virtus.
Nec foliis certare comae, nec brachia ramis,
Nec possint tremulos voces aequare susurros.
    Ah quoties saevos vidi (quis credat?) amantes

Sculpentes dominae potiori in cortice nomen?
Nec puduit truncis inscribere vulnera sacris.
Ast ego, si vestras unquam temeravero stirpes,
Nulla Neaera, Chloe, Faustina, Corinna, legetur;
30 In proprio sed quaeque libro signabitur arbos.
O charae platanus, cyparissus, populus, ulmus!
  Hic Amor, exutis crepidatus inambulat alis,
Enerves arcus et stridula tela reponens,
Invertitque faces, nec se cupit usque timeri;
Aut exporrectus jacet, indormitque pharetrae;
Non auditurus quanquam Cytherea vocarit;
Nequitias referunt nec somnia vana priores.
  Laetantur superi, defervescente tyranno,
Et licet experti toties nymphasque deasque,
40 Arbore nunc melius potiuntur quisque cupita.
Jupiter annosam, neglecta conjuge, quercum
Deperit; haud alia doluit sic pellice Juno.
Lemniacum temerant vestigia nulla cubile,
Dum Veneri myrtis Marti dum fraxinus adsit.
Formosae pressit Daphnes vestigia Phoebus
Ut fieret Laurus; sed nil quaesiverat ultra.
Capripes et peteret quod Pan Syringa fugacem,
Hoc erat ut calamum posset reperire sonorum.

Desunt multa

Nec tu, opifex horti, grato sine carmine abibis:
50 Qui brevibus plantis, et laeto flore, notasti
Crescentes horas, atque intervalla diei.
Sol ibi candidior fragrantia signa pererrat;
Proque truci Tauro, stricto pro forcipe Cancri,
Securis violaeque rosaeque allabitur umbris.
Sedula quin et apis, mellito intenta labori,
Horologo sua pensa thymo signare videtur.
Temporis O suaves lapsus! O otia sana!
  O herbis dignae numerari et floribus horae!

THE GARDEN

What madness so stirs the heart of man?
Alas, madness for the palm and the laurel, or for the
    simple grass!
So that one tree will scarcely crown his curbless efforts,
Nor wholly circle his temples with its scanty leaves.
While at the same time, entwined in garlands of tranquil
    Quiet,
All flowers meet, and the virgin woods.
    Fair Quiet, I hold you! And you, sister of Quiet,
Innocence! You a long time in temples, in cities
I sought in vain, and in the palaces of kings.
10 But you in the shaded silences of gardens, far off,
The green plants and like-coloured shadow hide.
    Oh, if I am ever allowed to profane your retreats,
Wandering about, faint, and panting for a better life,
Preserve your new citizen, and me, having attained my
    wish,
Leafy citizens, accept in the flowery kingdom.
    Me also, you Muses – and I call you, omniscient Apollo
    as witness –
Herds of men do not please, nor the roaring of the circus,
Nor the bellowing of the forum; but me the sanctuaries
    of spring,
And silent veneration draw, and solitary communion.
20   Whom does the grace of maidenly beauty not arrest?
Which, although it excels snows in whiteness and purple
    in redness,
Yet your green force (in my opinion) surpasses.
Hair cannot compete with leaves, nor arms with branches,
Nor are tremulous voices able to equal your whisperings.
    Ah, how often have I seen (Who would believe it?)
    cruel lovers
Carving the name of their mistress on bark, which is more
    worthy of love.
Nor was there a sense of shame for inscribing wounds on
    sacred trunks.

But I, if ever I shall have profaned your stocks,
No Neaera, Chloe, Faustina, Corinna shall be read:
30 But the name of each tree shall be written on its own bark.
O dear plane tree, cypress, poplar, elm!
    Here Love, his wings cast aside, walks about in sandals,
Laying aside his nerveless bows and hissing arrows,
And inverts his torches, nor does he wish to be feared;
Or he lies stretched out and sleeps on his quiver;
Nor will he hear, although Cytherea call;
Nor do idle dreams report previous iniquities.
    The gods rejoice, the tyrant ceasing to rage,
And although they have known nymphs and goddesses
        many times,
40 Each one achieves his desires better now in a tree.
Jupiter, forgetful of his wife, languishes for the aged oak;
Juno has not suffered thus for another rival.
No traces dishonor the bed of Vulcan,
[So long as the myrtle is at hand for Venus and the ash
    for Mars.]
Apollo pursued beautiful Daphne
That she might become a laurel; but he had sought
    nothing more.
And though goat-footed Pan fell upon fleeing Syrinx,
This was that he might procure a sounding reed.

Desunt multa

And you, maker of the garden, shall not depart without a
    grateful song:
50 You who in the brief plants and joyous flowers have
    indicated
The growing hours and intervals of the day.
There the sun more bright passes through the fragrant
    signs;
And fleeing the fierce Bull, the Crab's threatening claw,
Glides toward the safe shadows of roses and violets.
And the sedulous bee, intent on its sweet labour,
Seems to mark its duties with the thyme as horologe.
O sweet lapse of time! O healthful ease!
    O hours worthy to be numbered in herbs and flowers!

Ros

Cernis ut eoi descendat gemmula roris,
   Inque rosas roseo transfluat orta sin.
Sollicita flores stant ambitione supini,
   Et certant foliis pellicuisse suis.
Illa tamen patriae lustrans fastigia spherae,
   Negligit hospitii limina picta novi.
Inque sui nitido conclusa voluminis orbe,
   Exprimit aetherei qua licet orbis aquas.
En ut odoratum spernat generosior ostrum,
10   Vixque premat casto mollia strata pede.
Suspicit at longis distantem obtutibus axem,
   Inde et languenti lumine pendet amans,
Tristis, et in liquidum mutata dolore dolorem,
   Marcet, uti roseis lachryma fusa genis.
Ut pavet, et motum tremit irrequieta cubile,
   Et quoties zephyro fluctuat aura, fugit.
Qualis inexpertam subeat formido puellam,
   Sicubi nocte redit incomitata domum.
Sic et in horridulas agitatur gutta procellas,
20   Dum prae virgineo cuncta pudore timet.
Donec oberrantem radio clemente vaporet,
   Inque jubar reducem sol genitale trahat.
Talis, in humano si possit flore videri,
   Exul ubi longas mens agit usque moras;
Haec quoque natalis meditans convivia coeli,
   Evertit calices, purpureosque toros.
Fontis stilla sacri, lucis scintilla perennis,
   Non capitur Tyria veste, vapore Sabae.
Tota sed in proprii secedens luminis arcem,
30   Colligit in gyros se sinuosa breves.
Magnorumque sequens animo convexa deorum,
   Sydereum parvo fingit in orbe globum.
Quam bene in aversae modulum contracta figurae
   Oppositum mundo claudit ubique latus.
Sed bibit in speculum radios ornata rotundum;
   Et circumfuso splendet aperta die.

Qua superos spectat rutilans, obscurior infra;
   Caetera dedignans, ardet amore poli.
Subsilit, hinc agili poscens discedere motu,
40   Undique coelesti cincta soluta viae.
Totaque in aereos extenditur orbita cursus;
   Hic punctim carpens, mobile stringit iter.
Haud aliter mensis exundans manna beatis
   Deserto jacuit stilla gelata solo:
Stilla gelata solo, sed solibus hausta benignis,
   Ad sua qua cecidit purior astra redit.

DEW

See how a little jewel of orient dew descends
And, sprung from the rosy breast of Dawn, flows onto the
   roses.
The flowers stand, opened in solicitous desire,
And strive to entice with their leaves.
Yet that drop, surveying the heights of its native sphere,
Disdains the painted threshold of its new dwelling.
And enclosed within its shining globe,
It shapes the waters of the ethereal sphere as it can.
See how it, more noble, scorns the odorous purple,
10   And scarcely presses the soft resting place with its pure
   foot.
It looks up at the distant heavens with a long gaze.
And, desiring that place, hangs with a faint glow,
Sad, changed by sorrow into liquid sorrow,
It is spent, like a tear upon a rosy cheek.
Restless, how it trembles and quivers on its troubled
   couch,
And, as often as the air stirs with a breeze, rolls about.
Just as fear seizes a naive girl
If she returns home at night alone.
Thus the drop, shaken in tiny storms,
20   Now in its virginal shyness fears everything,
Until the engendering sun warms its hovering form

With gentle rays and draws it back to splendour.
Such, if it could be seen in the human flower,
Is the exiled soul, constantly aware of long delays;
It too, thinking of the feasts of its native heaven,
Overturns the drinking cups and purple banquet couches.
A drop of the sacred fountain, a glimmer of eternal light,
It is not caught in Tyrian robe or scent of Saba,
But withdrawing completely into the fortress of its own
    light,
30 It draws inward, closing upon itself.
Conforming in its nature with the arching heaven of the
    great gods,
It builds a starry heaven in its small sphere.
How well contracted into a little image of the heavens,
It shuts up everywhere its side opposed to the world.
But, ornate, it drinks the rays of the sun into its rounded
    mirror,
And shines, open to the surrounding light.
Glowing where it faces the gods, but darker below;
Scorning all else, it burns with love of the heavens.
It leaps up, desiring to depart quickly,
40 Fully ready, freed for its heavenly journey.
And, its whole surface stretched in aerial course,
[Here it touches by a point, seeking its easy way.]
Not otherwise did manna, overflowing with blessed
    nourishment,
Lie, a frozen drop, on the desert soil:
A frozen drop on the ground, but drawn by propitious
    suns,
It returns, purer, to the stars whence it fell.

APPENDIX 2
Uncertain Attribution

[*Blood and the Crown*]

When daring Blood his rents to have regained,
Upon the English diadem distrained,
He chose the cassock, surcingle, and gown,
(No mask so fit for one that robs a crown).
But his lay-pity underneath prevailed
And while he spared the Keeper's life, he failed.
With the priest's vestments had he but put on
A bishop's cruelty, the crown was gone.

Bludius et Corona

Bludius ut ruris damnum repararet aviti,
   Addicit fisco dum diadema suo:
Egregium sacro facinus velavit amictu:
   (Larva solet reges fallere nulla magis).
Excidit ast ausis tactus pietate prophana,
   Custodem ut servet, maluit ipse capi.
Si modo saevitiam texisset pontificalem,
   Veste sacerdotis, rapta corona foret.

Other Attributions

Found apparently among Marvell's papers and copied in
Eng. poet. d. 49 are the following additional satires:

The Second Advice to a Painter
The Third Advice to a Painter
Clarendon's Housewarming
The [King's] Vows ('When the plate was at pawn')
Upon the Cutting of Sir John Coventry's Nose
Upon Sir Robert Viner's Setting up the King's Statue ('As
   cities that to the fierce conquerors yield')
Upon the City's Going in a Body to Whitehall ('The
   Londoner's gent')
The Statue at Charing Cross ('What can be the mystery')
The Checker Inn
Scaevola Scoto-Britannus
The Doctor Turned Justice
On the Monument

Advice to a Painter to Draw *the Duke by* *Britannia and Ralegh*	both have been crossed through and ascribed to John Ayloffe.

Of these twelve pieces George deF. Lord (*Poems on
Affairs of State*) attributes six to Marvell on the strength
of their inclusion in *Eng. poet. d. 49*. They are:

The Second Advice to a Painter *The Third Advice to a Painter*	both assigned to Sir John Denham in the early printings and in the *State Poems*, 1689, 1697, though the latter adds about the *Second Advice* 'but believed to be writ by Mr Milton'.
Clarendon's Housewarming	not attributed to Marvell until 1726

Upon Sir Robert Viner's Setting up the
  King's Statue (or *On the Statue*
  Erected by Sir Robert Viner)
	not attributed in
	any manuscript or
	in the *State*
	Poems; first
	assigned in 1776.

Upon the City's Going in a Body to Whitehall (or
  Upon His Majesty's Being Made Free of the City) not
  attributed to Marvell in any manuscript or in the earliest
  printing; first assigned in 1697.

The Statue at Charing Cross not attributed until *The
  Poetical Remains of the Duke of Buckingham*, etc., 1698;
  the attribution was removed in the 1704 and 1716
  editions of the *State Poems*.

The other six poems in *Eng. poet. d. 49* Lord rejects:

The [King's] Vows not ascribed in the manuscripts; an
  undated printing assigns it to the Duke of Buckingham
  (Margoliouth).

Upon the Cutting of Sir John Coventry's Nose attributed in
  1776.

The Checker Inn attributed in 1776.

Scaevola Scoto-Britannus attributed in 1776.

The Doctor Turned Justice attributed in 1776.

On the Monument not attributed in the *State Poems* nor
  by Thompson in 1776.

He also accepts the *Further Advice to a Painter* which is
not included in *Eng. poet. d. 49* and was first attributed to
Marvell in the *State Poems*, 1697. (However, in his
Andrew Marvell (Modern Library College Editions, 1968)
he accepts *The [King's] Vows* as Marvell's but rejects the
Further Advice to a Painter.)

Other satires which on occasion have been attributed to
Marvell include:

Nostradamus' Prophecy attributed in *State Poems*, 1689,
  1697, but not in the manuscripts.

A Dialogue between the Two Horses attributed in *State
  Poems*, 1689, 1697, but not in the manuscripts.

Upon His [Clarendon's] House attributed in 1726.

Upon His [Clarendon's] Grandchildren attributed in 1872.

Oceania and Britannia attributed in *State Poems*, 1697;
  alludes to events after Marvell's death.

Margoliouth's observation made in 1927 remains a sound
guideline: 'it seems to me a great mistake to continue to
print among Marvell's poems inferior stuff which has
long been considered spurious.'

Notes

ABBREVIATIONS AND SIGLA

BNYPL	*Bulletin of the New York Public Library*
EA	*Études Anglaises*
FP	*Flagellum Parliamentarium*
FQ	*Faerie Queene*
MLN	*Modern Language Notes*
MLR	*Modern Language Review*
MP	*Modern Philology*
N & Q	*Notes and Queries*
PL	*Paradise Lost*
PQ	*Philological Quarterly*
RES	*Review of English Studies*
RQ	*Renaissance Quarterly*
SR	*Studies in the Renaissance*
Tilley	M. P. Tilley, *A Dictionary of the Proverbs in England*
TLS	*Times Literary Supplement*

The sigla used in the notes refer to the texts discussed in the introductory note to each poem. They include the Folio (abbreviated *F*), the manuscripts cited by name, and the early printings cited by dates or, in the case of certain of the anthologies, by the last name of the compiler; Thompson is abbreviated *Th*.

A DIALOGUE BETWEEN THYRSIS AND DORINDA

The popularity of this pastoral dialogue is attested by three manuscripts and four printed versions which antedate the Folio. Among these early versions are settings by three different composers, a fact which reflects the current interest in adapting a dramatic form consisting of alternate questions and answers to a musical setting designed for two voices, usually treble and bass, with a concluding brief duet. Though musical licence and manuscript circulation account for a host of minor variants, the several versions fall into two main groups, a shorter form which exists only in manuscript and a longer form which is represented mainly in the printed texts.

The earliest version of the poem (*BM Add. MS. 31432, f. 6*^v) is in the autograph of the musician William Lawes (d. 1645). Except for the final thematic couplet, it is substantially the same as that appearing in a seventeenth-century manuscript in the Bodleian (*Rawl. poet. 199, f. 27*^v), where it is ascribed to 'H. Ramsay'. The earliest printed version, representing the longer form, appeared with a setting by John Gamble (*Airs and Dialogues. The Second Book*) in 1659. It appeared again in the 1663 reprint of Samuel Rowland's *A Crew of Kind London Gossips* where it was included among appended 'Ingenious Poems' with six additional verses inserted after line 22; and again in 1672 in a collection of poems (*New Court Songs and Poems*) by Robert Veel, which, according to the dedicatory epistle, derived for the most part from one 'TD'. In 1675, and subsequently, the music publisher John Playford included it with a setting by Matthew Locke (d. 1677) in *Choice Airs, Songs, and Dialogues*. The manuscript version of Locke's setting (*Bod. MS. Sch.c. 96, f. 6*^v), while it shows a few variants from Playford's text, mediates between the earliest printed version (Gamble, 1659) and the Folio. Curiously, the poem is not in *Eng. poet. d. 49*.

The text of the Folio is inferior both to *Bod. MS. Sch. c. 96* and to the earlier printed versions in that some of the lines are incomplete or misassigned. Its placement between two late political poems rather than among the other pastorals is also odd. If the earliest extant version (36 lines) – that set by William Lawes, together with the related one (34 lines) ascribed to H. Ramsay – is Marvell's, it would represent his earliest datable poem in English.

Variants from the three manuscript and the four printed versions are listed only when my reading represents a departure from the text of the Folio.

title] *1659, 1675, F*; others vary slightly.

1   *part*] *1659, Mus. Sch. c. 96, 1633, 1675*; snatch *F*+, i.e., all others not specified.

7   *to our home*] *Rawl. poet. 199, Mus. Sch. c. 96, 1633*; to my home *Add. 31432*; one, our home *1659, 1672, 1675, F*.

8   *cell*] not in *F*.

9   *Turn*] *1659, Mus. Sch. c. 96, 1663, 1672, 1675*; Cast *Add. 31432, Rawl. poet. 199, F*.

22 *There's no wolf, no fox, no bear*] Free from the wolf and horrid bear *Add. 31432*, *Rawl. poet. 199*; these two manuscripts then conclude with fourteen and twelve lines respectively which have no equivalents in the other texts. *1633* has a six-line insertion after l. 22:

No wars unless our rams well fed
Butt at each other's curlèd head;
No work unless perhaps you find
Bees dig in king-cups [buttercups] golden mine;
No fold to keep one lamb from harms,
Only, Dorinda, thee mine arms.

25 *oat-pipe's ... thy ears*] *1659, 1672*; oat-pipe *Mus. Sch. c. 96, 1675*; thine ears *1663*; thy cares *Mus. Sch. c. 96*; And there most sweetly thine ear *F*.

26 *May sleep ... spheres*] *1659, Mus. Sch. c. 96, 1672, 1675*; Shall sleep ... spheres *1663*; May feast ... sphere *F*.

27 *Oh sweet! Oh sweet!*] *1659, Mus. Sch. c. 96, 1675*; Sweet! Sweet! *1663*; O sweet! *1672*; *not in F*.

28 *antedate* accelerate, as in *Young Love*, l. 23.

29 *to*] *not in F*.

32 *sweetest*] *1659+*; softest *F*.

33 *consorts* (a) in accord and (b) in display of harmony; 'consort' and 'concert' were confounded in this period.

34 *Cool*] *1659+*; Cold *F*.

43-4 *Thyrsis*] *misassigned to Dorinda in F*.

44 *I'll*] *1659, Mus. Sch. c. 96, 1663, 1675*; Would *1672*; Will *F*.

45-8 *Chorus*] *misassigned to Dorinda in F*.

45 *Corillo*] *Mus. Sch. c. 96, 1663*; Corilla *1659, 1672*; Clorillo *1675*; Corellia *F*. *Corillo*, as Margoliouth noted (*TLS* 19 May 1950, p. 309), is probably a corruption of *Carillo* found in the *Diana*, a popular Spanish romance written by the Portuguese Jorge de Montemayor (d. 1561).

CLORINDA AND DAMON

This pastoral dialogue with its religious theme (cf. the Christianized Pan in l. 24 with E.K.'s gloss in *The Shepheardes Calender* for May, 'Great Pan is Christ, the very God of all shepherds') was first published in the Folio and links up with other examples in form and with *Thyrsis and Dorinda* and *A Dialogue between the Resolved Soul and Created Pleasure* in theme. Leishman (pp. 118–19) argues that in writing this lyric Marvell was recalling Spenser's *Faerie Queene* II.12.50.

3-4 *a grassy scutcheon ...| Where Flora blazons all her pride* The goddess of flowers depicts in a meadow her armorial insignia.

5   *aim*   intend.

8   *Seize . . . ere they vade*   *vade*, used often as a variant of fade (l.7), is also used in the sense of the Latin *vadere*, to go, as in Richard Braithwaite's *Barnaby's Journal* (1638), K4:

Beauty feedeth, beauty fadeth.
Beauty lost, her wooer vadeth.

AMETAS AND THESTYLIS MAKING HAY-ROPES

This pastoral dialogue ties in with Marvell's other two examples designed to be set to music (*A Dialogue between Thyrsis and Dorinda* and *Clorinda and Damon*) but differs in theme and tone; it was first published in the Folio.

13-14   *What you cannot constant hope | Must be taken as you may*   a punning adaptation of the proverb, 'Everything is as it is taken' (Tilley T31).

A DIALOGUE, BETWEEN THE RESOLVED SOUL AND CREATED PLEASURE

This dialogue, first published in the Folio, may connect in date of composition with the *Dialogue between the Soul and Body* since it is often taken as the obverse expression of ideas found in that poem. It is given the title *A Combat between the Soul and Sense*, with the disputants labelled accordingly in a seventeenth-century manuscript (*Bod. MS. Rawl. A176*, which shows minor variants and omits ll. 15-16). Citing the differentiation in metrical patterns between the two participants (iambic octosyllables and trochaic heptasyllables) and the division of the poem into two parts by means of the Chorus, Leishman argues (pp. 203-9) that, in contrast to the *Dialogue between the Soul and Body*, it was intended to be set to music. On this basis it should be coupled with the *Dialogue between Thyrsis and Dorinda* for which settings by three composers exist, the earliest of which is to be dated pre-1645; but Marvell's changes in mood or style or thematic emphases, as Margoliouth observed many years ago, may as well have been recurrent as progressive.

Pleasure offers first the traditional attractions of the five senses, culminating in the appeal to the sense of hearing which provides the one pleasure that could tempt the Resolved Soul (ll. 41-4), and then the attractions of beauty, wealth, glory, and knowledge.

2-4   *immortal shield . . . helmet bright . . . sword*   The 'shield of faith', the 'helmet of salvation' and the 'sword of the spirit' are specified by St Paul (Ephesians vi 16-17) in his enumeration of a Christian's armour.

8   *let it shine*   the referent is to 'that thing divine' (l. 7).

9   *wants*   (a) needs and (b) lacks.

18   *bait*   refresh (myself).

21–22 *roses strewed so plain| Lest one leaf thy side should strain* Seneca (*De Ira*, II, 25.3) tells the story of the Sybarite who complained that he felt worse because the rose petals on which he had lain were crumpled.

plain evenly.

39 *Which the posting winds recall* an inversion, 'which recall the posting winds'.

44 *chordage* of 'charming airs' (l.38), with a pun on cordage.

51 *soft*] *Eng. poet. d. 49, Rawl. A176*; cost *F*.

61 *a price* assigned worth.

68 *captive* (a) take captive and (b) captivate.

69 *Thou shalt know each hidden cause* '*Felix qui potuit rerum cognoscere causas*' (Virgil, *Georgics II*, 490).

FLECKNOE, AN ENGLISH PRIEST AT ROME

Priest, incorrigible poetaster, and traveller, Richard Flecknoe (d. ?1678) was in Rome during Lent (l. 46) of 1645 and 1646, and thus the occasion for Marvell's visit to him would have fallen within this period though composition of the poem need not necessarily have coincided; it was first published in the Folio. Marvell (ll. 1–3) assigns to Flecknoe the triple role of priest, poet, and musician and takes him to be descended from 'some branch of Melchizédek' (in Gen. xiv 18 King of Salem and Priest of the most high God). In his *Mac Flecknoe*, probably written in 1678, Dryden was again to satirize Flecknoe as well as his putative son Thomas Shadwell and assign them the triple roles of prophets (i.e., poets), priests, and kings of Dullness.

4 *my Lord Brooke* Fulke Greville, first Lord Brooke, 'servant to Queen Elizabeth, councillor to James, and friend to Sir Philip Sidney', died in 1628. Following the posthumous publication of Greville's *Remains* in 1670, Flecknoe was to include commendatory verses (*On the Works of Fulke Greville, Lord Brooke*) in the 1671 edition of his *Epigrams* (pp. 10–11), and in 1675 he was to couple him with Sidney among 'the prime wits and gallants' of the times (*A Treatise of the Sports of Wit*, p. 8ᵛ).

6 *The Sad Pelican* Characterized as feeding its young with the flesh and blood of its 'tender bosom' (cf. ll. 127–8), it became a symbol of Christ and hence a 'subject divine'. In *The Rehearsal Transpros'd* (Smith, p. 260), Marvell makes the same play on the name: 'But where was his Shop? *Ad insigne Pelicani*. A very Emblematical sign. . . .'

12 *nor ceiling, nor a sheet* neither hangings (or wainscoting), nor a winding (or a bed) sheet.

18 *stanzas . . . apartément* It. *stanza* means both room and stanza (cf. Donne's *Canonization*, l. 23, 'We'll build in sonnets pretty rooms' where room has been suggested as a pun on *stanza*). Fr. *appartèment*: suite of rooms.

20 *in*] *Eng. poet. d. 49*; and *F*.

28 *The last distemper of the sober brain* Cf. Milton's *Lycidas* (1638), l. 71, 'Fame . . . (That last infirmity of noble mind)'.

48 *of generous* used as an absolute means a noble.

55 *him scant*] *G. A. Aitken*; him: Scant *F*.
    scant intelligent.

57 *our*] *Eng. poet. d. 49*; *not in F*.

63 *basso relievo* It., bas relief – with length and breadth but scant depth.

64–5 *Who as a camel . . . | The needle's eye thread without any stitch* 'It is easier for a camel to go through the eye of a needle, than for a rich man to enter the kingdom of God' (Matt. xix 24).
    stitch (a) of pain; (b) of clothing; and (c) in sewing.

74 *sottana* It., cassock.

75 *an antique cloak* The spellings 'antique' and 'antic' were indistinguishable in the seventeenth century; cf. 'antic cope' in *Upon Appleton House*, 591.

76 *Torn*] *Eng. poet. d. 49*; Worn *F*.

92–3 *I . . . Will make the way here* The visitor's 'I will' signifies determination; the persona of the poem wilfully interprets it as meaning 'I will clear the way for you'. See l. 105.

98 *Delightful* delighted.

98–101 *There can no body pass | . . . nor can three persons here | Consist but in one substance* These lines satirize a current philosophic dispute as to whether two bodies could occupy the same space at the same time (cf. *Horatian Ode*, ll. 41–4, where Marvell employs the same notion in order to compliment Cromwell), and allude as well to the Trinitarian doctrine of the union of three persons in one substance.

104 *By*] *Eng. poet. d. 49*; But *F*.

108 *Obliged* (a) made us morally responsible and (b) ironically, conferred a benefit.

126 *Nero's poem* 'While he was singing, it was not permitted to any man to depart the theatre, upon any occasion though never so necessary, insomuch that it is reported women were delivered there, and several persons so tired . . . that they either leaped privately over the wall or else fell down and dissembled themselves dead that they might be carried out as to their burials' (Suetonius, *The History of the Twelve Caesars*, 1672, a translation ascribed to Marvell in a contemporary hand in a copy at the Bodleian).

130 *foul copies* rough drafts.

137 *chancres and poulains* ulcers and sores resulting from venereal diseases Fr., ulcers etc.

152 *Perillus in's own bull* Having devised a brazen bull in which a victim would be roasted alive while his screams simulated the roaring of the animal, Perillus presented it to the tyrant Phaleris and then fell victim himself to its first use.

156 *is no lie* and, as a result, no occasion for a challenge to combat.

158 *'twas*] *Eng. poet. d. 49*; was *F*.

169–70 *Have made the chance be painted; and go now | To hang it* To signify his escape, the speaker, like a person who has made a miraculous recovery, wishes to deposit the record of his experience as a votive offering.

TO HIS NOBLE FRIEND MR RICHARD LOVELACE, UPON HIS POEMS

These commendatory verses appeared in the first edition of Richard Love-lace's *Lucasta*, 1649, together with the contributions of thirteen others, some of whom like Marvell were also Cambridge men. The lines (21ff) on the 'barbèd censurers' indicate that he wrote before the book had been licensed (4 February 1648; entered Stationers' Register 14 May 1649; probably published in June), and thus he must have returned from his European travels before the earlier date.

By a juggling of the order of the signatures (letters, in alphabetical order, printed at the bottom of a leaf to indicate to the binders the correct sequence of the text), Marvell's contribution was shifted in some copies from a position near the middle of the commendatory group to pride of place at the beginning, a shift which could have been made as late as 1657, since copies of *Lucasta* were still being advertised for sale in that year. However, it should be noted that Marvell's elegy on Lord Hastings, included in a collection entitled *Lachrymae Musarum* (see p. 230), was also shifted in the second issue (1650) from the end of the volume to a position nearer to the front. The two instances therefore suggest that the publishers felt Marvell's name was one to be reckoned with as early as 1649 and 1650.

Lovelace's acquaintance with Marvell and the other Cambridge men represented in the volume may have dated from 1637 when he was incorporated at that university.

2 *with*] R. G. Howarth, *N & Q* CXCVIII, 1953, 330; which *1649*.

8 *the bays* a reward for poetry.

12 *civic crown* a reward of oak leaves given to one who had saved the life of a fellow citizen in time of battle. Cf. *The Garden*, l. 2: 'To win the palm, the oak, or bays'.

15 *caterpillar* metaphorically, one who preys on society.

21 *The barbèd censurers* who enforced the Printing Ordinance that books must be licensed.

22 *grim consistory* court of presbyters; the 'young presbýtery' (l. 24) had been established in 1643.

28 *House's Privilege* Parliamentary privilege of free speech.

29-30 *you under sequestration are, | Because you writ when going to the war* Committed to Peterhouse Prison some six months earlier, apparently for precautionary reasons, Lovelace was discharged 10 April 1649. While sequestered, according to Anthony Wood, 'he framed his poems for the press'. The second song in the volume was *To Lucasta, Going to the Wars*.

31-2 *because Kent | Their first petition by the author sent* Lovelace had been committed to the Gatehouse in 1642 for presenting to the House a petition framed by Sir Edward Dering and others of Kent to restore the King's rights.

36 *He who loved best* Wood also reported that Lovelace was much beloved by the female sex.

40 *Sallied* sortied.

AN ELEGY UPON THE DEATH OF MY LORD FRANCIS VILLIERS

The *Elegy* for Lord Francis Villiers exists in an apparently unique copy in the library of Worcester College, Oxford. Its ascription to Marvell was made by George Clark (1660-1736), a scholarly collector and political figure who amassed a large collection of books and manuscripts, including many pamphlets and papers relating to the Civil Wars.

  Posthumous son of George, first Duke of Buckingham (see ll. 29-38), Francis Villiers was killed 7 July 1648 in a Royalist uprising near Kingston-on-Thames (see l. 7: 'the safe battlements of Richmond's bowers').

16 *Fairfax* Ferdinando, second Baron Fairfax, a military and political leader of the Parliamentary forces, had died 14 March 1648 after a short illness. He was father of Thomas (the General) and grandfather of Mary whom Marvell was to begin tutoring in languages in 1650 or 1651.

25 *Buckingham, whose death* ... Royal favourite of James I and Charles I, he had been assassinated in 1628 by a disgruntled naval lieutenant.

31-2 *As the wise Chinese ... a more precious clay entomb* Cf. *First Anniversary*, ll. 19-20:

Their earthy projects under ground they lay,
More slow and brittle than the China clay.

59-61 *Bright Lady ... | Fair Richmond* Francis's sister Mary had become Duchess of Richmond by her (second) marriage to James Stuart.

69 *Clora* probably Mary Kirke, daughter of the poet Aurelian Townsend (E. E. Duncan-Jones, *N & Q* CXCVIII, 1953, 102). On his death Lord Francis was found wearing a lock of her hair in a ribbon. Cf. also the Clora of *Mourning* (p. 37) and of *The Gallery* (p. 40).

81 *modest plant* *Mimosa pudica* or sensitive plant.

96 *eleven thousand virgins* A literary glance at the maidens associated with St Ursula, a British princess (according to one version of the legend) who was massacred with her companions when returning from a pilgrimage to Rome.

111 *him* Villiers.

MOURNING

If the subject of this poem is to be connected with the Clora of Marvell's *Elegy* on the death of Lord Francis Villiers, as seems likely, composition would have followed sometime after July 1648; it was first published in the Folio.

3 *these infants* To reflect oneself in the pupils of another person's eyes was traditionally known as 'to look babies', from the pun on *pupilla*.

9 *moulding of the watery spheres* Cf. ' Like its own tear, / Because so long divided from the sphere' (*On a Drop of Dew*, ll. 13–14).
   moulding shaping.

20 *Herself both Danaë and the shower* Pouring through the roof into her bosom, Jupiter wooed Danaë in the guise of a golden shower.

30 *dive*] *Eng. poet. d. 49*; sink *F*. The tonal effect of the single line as given in the Folio is appealing. Yet *dive* fits into the alliterative pattern of the whole stanza at least as well and is more appropriate to the action described, stressing (in contrast to the languidness of *sink*) the propulsion required of the Indian slaves to reach the bottom of deep seas before they can come up with pearl. Cf. the use of the verb in *Upon Appleton House*, l. 377, 'men through this meadow dive' and *The Last Instructions*, l. 702, 'the ships . . . were taught to dive'.

32 *And not of one the bottom sound* affords a syntactical pun – *sound* as verb and adjective.

THE FAIR SINGER

First published in the Folio, *The Fair Singer* is in the genre of the courtly compliment paid to a lady to commend her skill in singing, playing an instrument, or dancing, a form practised by Cavalier poets like Carew, Waller, and Lovelace. As such, its composition perhaps dates from the period of Marvell's courtly lyrics.

9 *the curlèd trammels of her hair* Cf. Michael Drayton, 'In the curlèd trammels of thy hair' (*The Muse's Elizium*, 'Second Nymphal', l. 236).

18 *She having gainèd both the wind and sun* military allusions to getting to windward of another ship or to the sunward side of an enemy.

THE GALLERY

First published in the Folio, *The Gallery* may well have been written before July 1650, when Charles I's collection of paintings was sold by Act of Parliament: the near-rhyme resulting from the use of the past tense in l. 48 suggests that the line may have been revised after dispersal of the collection. The apostrophe to Clora links up with the grieving figure in *Mourning*, which, in turn, may link with the 'matchless Clora' of the *Elegy upon the Death of My Lord Francis Villiers*.

As the title indicates, the poem follows in the iconographical tradition (*ut pictura poesis*) represented by Giambattista Marino's *La Galeria* (1619). But Marvell internalizes the scene by making his soul the gallery hung with images he has 'contrived' of Clora in her several aspects and thus objectifies his varied responses to her. The apostrophe gives an added psychological dimension in that the subject is invited to view herself depicted as a series of art objects. This sophisticated attitude is then countered in the final stanza with the lover reverting to the usual acknowledgement of love at first sight.

11   *Examining*   testing.

14   *a*] *Thompson; not in F.*

42   *do store*] *Eng. poet. d. 49*; doth store *F.*
      store   stock as in *Upon the Death of Lord Hastings*, l. 3; and *The Coronet*, l. 9.

48   *Whitehall's or Mantua's*   Charles I had purchased the paintings belonging to Vincenzo Gonzaga, Duke of Mantua, to supplement his own impressive collection.

THE UNFORTUNATE LOVER

This emblematic and conceited lyric depicts the unfortunate lover (yet fortunate in that only unhappy lovers become famous) in a progressive series of disasters from before his birth to his projected death. First appearing in the Folio, it was written some time after 1648 or 1649 since, as Margoliouth noted, ll. 57–8 echo two lines in Lovelace's *Dialogue – Lucasta, Alexis*:

Love near his standard when his host he sets,
Creates alone fresh-bleeding bannerets.

Marvell had contributed commendatory verses to Lovelace's volume before its publication (see p. 226).

17   *those*] *Eng. poet. d. 49*; these *F.*

18   *wears*] *Eng. poet d. 49*; bears *F.*

36   *bill*   peck.

40   *amphibium*   a creature of ambiguous position.

43–4   *to play | At sharp*   to fight with unbated swords.

48 *Ajax, the mad tempest braves* Having offered violence to Cassandra, Ajax (the son of Oileus) was punished on the voyage from Troy by Minerva who destroyed his ship with the thunder of Jupiter and the tempests of Neptune; he escaped to a rock only to have it split by Neptune's trident.

55 *'says* aphetic form of *assays*, attempts.

57 *banneret* a title and rank conferred for deeds done in the king's presence (here the 'tyrant Love').

64 *a field sable a lover gules* a heraldic device of a scarlet lover in a black field.

DAPHNIS AND CHLOE

First published in the Folio, *Daphnis and Chloe* is a pastoral insofar as the names are pastoral and a dialogue insofar as Daphnis utters a complain tto his companion; thus it is related to the other examples of pastoral dialogue despite its difference in tone. Parodying the extremes of lovers' psychology, the poet introduces a reversal in the final two stanzas to place both figures in a cynical light.

10 *niceness* scrupulousness.

12 *comprised* included.

13 *use* manipulate.

27 *than legacies no more* (they were) no more than legacies.

61 *alone* by itself.

78–80 *the gourmand Hebrew ... does through the desert err* a reference to the desert wanderings of the now long-dead Israelites before they reached the Promised Land (*Num.* xi).

79 *with*] *Cooke* +; *he F.*

80 *He*] *Cooke* +; *And F.*

83–4 *casts the seed* | *And invisible him makes* If found on St John's Day, the fern seed was reputed to make its finder invisible.

103 *This night for Dorinda kept* both (a) watched for and (b) reserved.

107 *the laws* of Nature, see ll. 13–15.

UPON THE DEATH OF THE LORD HASTINGS

Marvell's elegy was first published in the collection *Lachrymae Musarum*, assembled by Richard Brome in 1649 following the death on 24 June of the young Lord Hastings, heir to Ferdinando, Earl of Huntingdon. A small octavo, it included among its contributors Robert Herrick, Charles Cotton and John Denham. On signature E8^v of the first issue the printer inserted a note stating that the poems which followed were written and sent in after the earlier ones had been printed, and (on F1) he apologized to the writers for naming them without their titles or contrary to their degree or quality. In this 'Postscript', Marvell's name heads the list of eight additional contributors; that of Dryden, who was then a student at Westminster School, appears in fourth place.

A second issue of *Lachrymae Musarum* appeared in 1650. A 'Catalogue' on the verso of its black-bordered title page brings together the names of all the contributors; here Marvell's name appears a little before the middle of the list though without the page reference characteristic of the other entries, and his contribution was accordingly transferred to this new position. As with the *Elegy* on the Lord Francis Villiers, this meant an interruption of the orderly sequence of the signatures (see p. 226). Not only did the printer reset the poem on two unsigned and unnumbered leaves (though retaining the now inappropriate catchword), but he also printed a few spaces below the last line of verse a notation to the binder reading, 'Place this after fol. 42.' Signatures F1 and F2, where Marvell's contribution originally appeared, were cancelled.

A copy of this second issue in the Henry E. Huntington Library has a bookplate of the Hastings family and includes a twenty-one line elegy on the flyleaf written by Lucy, Countess of Huntingdon, Hastings' mother. That she recorded her verses in a copy of the second issue suggests no great time elapsed between publication of the two issues despite the change in year on the title page, a point further supported by the make-up of a second copy in the Huntington Library: despite its 1649 title page with the usual partial listing of contributors on the verso, the volume has Marvell's elegy in its reset version following folio 42, and signatures F1 and F2 have been cancelled. Such a 'mixed' copy suggests indiscriminate binding of the two issues as a result of their contemporaneity.

12 *remora* The *Echeneis remora* (sucking fish) was believed to stay the course of a ship to which it had attached itself. A comparable rhyme (way / remora) appears in the *Second Advice to a Painter*, ll. 199–200 (attributed to Sir John Denham).

18 *But weigh to man the geometric year* apportion a man's fate in accord with his rate of progress through the earthly cycle.

34 *carousels* knightly tournaments which often included plays and entertainments.

38 *happy names* of the elect. In the verses written by Hastings' mother (see above), she too refers to this theological doctrine.

40 *his Mother's name* Lucy, Countess of Huntingdon, was the daughter of Sir John Davies:

Thus I die living, thus alas mine eyes,
My funeral see, since he before me dies
Whom I brought forth . . . (ll. 3–5 of her elegy).

43-4 *Hymeneus . . . for sad purple, tears his saffron coat* The god of marriage was traditionally garbed in a saffron robe and carried a nuptial torch; the purple pall was used both to denote persons of rank and to cover a coffin or a tomb. Hastings died on the eve of his marriage to a daughter of the King's physician Sir Theodore Turquet de Mayerne. See ll. 48 and 52.

47 *Aesculapius* the patron deity of medicine.

49 *chemist* an alchemist (cf. his 'golden harvest') as well as a follower of Paracelsus; a French Protestant, De Mayerne was early involved in a medical controversy in which, like Paracelsus, he championed the use of chemical remedies.

50 *leap* break.

60 *art . . . is long, but life is short* a dictum attributed to the celebrated Greek physician Hippocrates.

THE DEFINITION OF LOVE

First published in the Folio, this lyric falls into the category of 'definition' poems (see Rosemond Tuve, *Elizabethan and Metaphysical Imagery*, pp. 301-2) with the emphasis not on defining love in general but on distinguishing the speaker's love in particular. Marvell's own explanation of 'definition' as a term in logic affords a witty application to stanza 8: 'it always consists, as being a dialectic animal, of a body which is the genus, and a difference, which is the soul of the thing defined' (*Defence of John Howe*, Grosart IV, 183). It is also to be linked with 'absence' poems such as Donne's *A Valediction: forbidding Mourning*, Carew's *To My Mistress*:

Yet let our boundless spirits meet,
And in love's sphere each other greet (ll. 9-10),

and Lovelace's *To Lucasta, Going beyond the Seas*:

Our faith and troth
Like separated souls
All time and space controlls, (ll. 14-16),

but it exhibits Marvell's distinctive hyperbolical and paradoxical cast.

2 *object* both (a) that which excites the emotion and (b) objective.

5 *Magnanimous Despair* An oxymoron; *magnanimous* meaning resolute and qualifying *Despair* (without hope) is contrasted with *feeble Hope* of l. 7.

10 *my extended soul is fixed* *extended* means (a) directed to; (b) held out; and (c) possessing extension, a qualification of matter, not mind or soul, so that the phrase is also an oxymoron.

fixed (a) directed towards and (b) firmly established.

11 *But Fate does iron wedges drive* The *wedges* have been identified with the 'heavy nails and wedges' attributed by Horace to Necessity or Fate (*Carmina* I, 35. 17-18).

14 *close* unite.

15 *Their union would her ruin be* the union of the lovers in spite of the intervention of Fate would be to counter her powers and decrees (l. 17).

18–19 *Us as the distant Poles have placed,* | *(Though Love's whole world on us doth wheel)* Though by decree of Fate the lovers are as far apart as the two Poles, yet the world of Love whirls around the imaginary line ('the Axle-tree of Nature', *The Rehearsal Transpros'd*, Smith, p. 230) extending between the Poles. Cf. the diction in *Tom May's Death*:

the wheel of empire whirleth back,
And though the world's disjointed axle crack (ll. 67–8).

24 *Be cramped into a planisphere* Planisphere is a chart formed by the projection of a sphere onto a plane. The two Poles could come together only if the charted world were collapsed.

25 *lines . . . oblique* inclined at any angle (other than a right angle).

27 *parallel* (a) equidistant and (b) corresponding, which points to the 'conjunction of the mind' in l. 31.

31 *conjunction* (a) the coming together in the same sign of the zodiac of two heavenly bodies and (b) union.

32 *opposition of the stars* Opposition is the position of two heavenly bodies at diametrical opposites. Literally and metaphorically, the phrase means 'star-crossed'. Cf. 'Souls in conjunction should, like stars, send kind influence' (Edward Benlowes, *Theophila*, 1652, XII, 13).

TO HIS COY MISTRESS

This invitational lyric, cast in syllogistic form (If . . . But . . . Therefore), was first published in the Folio and should perhaps be grouped in time of composition with other examples of courtly lyrics. Using the ancient theme of *carpe diem*, the poet blends together a blazon, reduced to a bare arithmetical recital of the lady's beauties (ll. 13–18), with echoes of a Greek epigram (ll. 25–32) in proffering his invitation, which is stated in terms of a direct inversion of the equally ancient theme of *tempus edax* (ll. 38–44).

4 *long love's day* Love's day picks up two meanings of loveday, that is, a day devoted to love-making and a day designated for settling personal disputes; in either case, the specificity is in contrast to the conditional – geographical and temporal – expressed in l. 1. But the first two elements may also be read as a unit ('long-love's') indicating duration, in which case, in qualifying a short span of time, the phrase is an oxymoron.

6–7 *tide* | *Of Humber* Tide originally meant time (as in the reduplicative phrase 'time and tide'); then tide of the sea. Allusion to the Humber estuary in Yorkshire recalls the poet's residence at Hull.

8–10 *the flood . . ./the conversion of the Jews* Though Biblical historians and millenarians could supply dates in the remote past and in the distant future for these two events, they fall within the literary convention of the catalogue of impossibilities (*adunata*). Roger Sharrock (*TLS* 31 October 1958; 16 January 1959) and E. E. Duncan-Jones (*TLS* 5 December 1958) suggest possible dates for the poem on the basis of these allusions.

11 *vegetable love* characterized only by growth (in accord with the doctrine of the three souls, vegetative, sensitive, and rational).

13–18 *And hundred years should go . . ./herat* Cf. *The Diet*, stanza 3, from Cowley's *Mistress* (1647):

On a sigh of pity I a year can live.
One tear will keep me twenty at least.
Fifty a gentle look will give,
An hundred years on one kind word I'll feast;
A thousand more will added be
If you an inclination have for me;
And all beyond is vast eternity.

24 *vast eternity* a popular phrase used, for example, by Herrick (*Eternity* in the *Hesperides*, 1648) and Benlowes (*Theophila*, 1652, V, 12) as well as by Cowley (see above).

25–30 *Thy beauty shall . . .* Leishman compares the epigram of Aesclepiades in the *Greek Anthology*, V, 85; 'Thou grudgest thy maidenhead? What avails it? When thou goest to Hades thou shalt find none to love thee there. The joys of love are in the land of the living, but in Acheron, dear virgin, we shall lie dust and ashes' (trans. W. R. Paton, Loeb Classical Library, 1916, I, 169).

29 *quaint honour* proud chastity (or reputation for it). Some editors find a pun by connecting the adjective *quaint* with the Middle English noun *queynte*: pudenda.

33 *glue*] *Eng. poet. d. 49*; hue *F*. It is to be noted that the reading *glue* (in this much debated couplet) appears in rhyme position in both *Eng. poet. d. 49* and in *F*. In the Folio, however, its transposition to l. 34 has resulted in a reading editors almost invariably have emended. Nonetheless, its appearance there attests to its presence in the manuscript used by the printer.

The reading given in *Eng. poet. d. 49* is also found in a short version of the lyric copied in 1672 (*Bod. MS. Don.b.8*, pp. 283–4, a miscellany compiled by Sir William Haward of Tanridge); this copy is discussed by W. Hilton Kelliher (*N & Q* CCXV, 1970, 254–6), who argues that despite obvious corruptions in the transcription, the poem was remembered with some accuracy.

Moreover, the sense of *youthful glue* is entirely consonant with the theme of the poem as the following quotation makes clear: 'Life is nothing else but as it were a glue, which in man fasteneth the soul and body together' (William Baldwin, *Moral Philosophy*, 1547, cited in the *OED*).

34 *dew*] *Eng. poet. d. 49*, Cooke + ; glue *F*. This reading, it should be noted, is also found in *Bod. MS. Don.b.8* (1672) referred to above.

40 *slow-chapped* slowly devouring; the noun *chap* is used in reference to a jaw or to a bill, particularly of a bird of prey, the latter probably suggested by 'amorous birds of prey', l. 38.

41–2 *roll all our strength, and all | Our sweetness, up into one ball* This image of a concentration of properties is frequent in Benlowe's *Theophila* (see n. to l. 24), where he has 'universal ball'; 'time's ball'; and 'earth's ball' (VIII. 18; XII. 86, 93).

44 *grates*] *Eng. poet. d. 49*; gates *F*. The phrase 'iron gates' has come to have the ring of idiom from the popularity of the poem in its Folio version. Yet the varieties of interpretation, ranging from the notion that the image suggests the reach of the Danube (Margoliouth) to metaphoric *labia* (Dennis Davison), points to its problematical basis and indicates a somewhat desperate search for signification.

In terms of literary tradition, the adjectives most commonly associated with gates are *horn* and *ivory*, whereas *iron* is commonly used with *grates* (see *OED*). Moreover, the traditional figurative phrase was 'gates of death' (*mortis januae*) not 'gates of life'. Used both in Roman times and in England from the time of Wycliffe, the phrase became proverbial in the sixteenth and seventeenth centuries. See Tilley D140 and D162.

The one literary example I know that specifies a 'gate' into life (as well as death) is found in Spenser's account of the Garden of Adonis (*F Q* III, vi, 31–2). Here the poet describes a cyclical process where a 'thousand thousand naked babes' issue from the Garden into a state of mortality and then return to the Garden by a 'hinder gate' to 'grow afresh'. The Garden is described as girt in with 'two walles on either side', the 'one of yron, the other of bright gold'.

And double gates it had, which opened wide,
By which both in and out men moten pas;
Th' one faire and fresh, the other old and dride.

The adjectives describing the double gates in this circular wall, one notes, accord with the condition of the men who pass through them. The gate in the 'bright gold' wall is 'faire and fresh' to accord with the condition of the 'naked babes' who exit from it, while that in the iron wall is 'old and dride' to accord with their condition on re-entry into the Garden. Thus in Spenser's scheme the gate into life is gold (whatever the 'fleshly corruptions' that ensue); the gate into death is iron.

One may also recall Tennyson's comment that he could fancy *grates* would have intensified Marvell's image (Hallam Tennyson, *Tennyson, A Memoir*, 1897, II, 501).

45-6 *we cannot make our sun | Stand still* as Joshua did in the war against Gibeon (*Joshua*, x 12). See the explicit use of this allusion in *A Poem upon the Death of . . . the Lord Protector*, ll. 191-2.

46 *yet we will make him run* Perhaps suggested by i 5 in Ecclesiastes, a book in which the *carpe diem* motif figures largely (see especially ix 7-12): 'The sun also ariseth, and the sun goeth down, and hasteth [literally 'pants'] to the place where he arose.'

EYES AND TEARS

In the convention of 'tear poetry', this lyric, first published in the Folio, links up with other examples of the conceited, argumentative strain of poetry that developed with the Counter-Reformation. Crashaw's *Saint Mary Magdalen or The Weeper* (first published in 1646, altered and extended in 1648 and 1652) is often suggested as the impetus for *Eyes and Tears*, but Marvell focuses on the more general proposition that since weeping is the inevitable result of seeing, it is therefore a superior activity (a kind of *post hoc ergo propter hoc* argument); the allusion to the Magdalen (stanza 8) is thus only one among a number of ingenious examples introduced to demonstrate this point. A manuscript copy in *Bod. Tanner 306*, which is ascribed to Marvell, shows minor variants and omits stanza 9.

3 *having viewed the object vain* a syntactical pun with *vain* used as an adjective meaning empty or futile or as an adverb (vainly, as in 'these roses strewed so plain', l. 21, *A Dialogue, between the Resolved Soul and Created Pleasure*); cf. also the 'self-deluding sight' of l. 5.

4 *We*] *Eng. poet. d. 49*, Tanner 306; They *F*.

5 *Thus*] *Eng. poet. d. 49*; And *F*, Tanner 306.

5-6 *the self-deluding sight, | In a false angle takes each height* Cf.:

The tree erewhile foreshortened to our view,
When fall'n shows taller yet than as it grew (*A Poem upon the Death of . . . the Lord Protector*, ll. 269-70).

11 *poise* balance.

20 *No honey but these tears, could draw* could elicit no honey (a) except these tears (b) only these tears.

22 *chemic* alchemic.

23 *But finds the essence only show'rs* The verb 'is' understood. The alchemists used the term *essence* for the fifth essence (quintessence), which they believed was capable of being distilled.

29–32 *So Magdalen ... her Redeemer's feet*   The Latin version of this stanza was appended in 1681; see ll. 57–60, and translation below.

35 *Cynthia teeming*   the moon at full. *Eng. poet. d. 49* reads *seeming*.

41–2 *the incense ... | Not as a perfume*   Cf.

> The tears do come
> Sad, slowly dropping like a gum. |
> So weeps the wounded balsam: so
> The holy frankincense doth flow (*The Nymph Complaining*, ll. 95–8).

48 *But only human eyes can weep*   The Nymph's fawn (as Margoliouth notes) is capable of doing so, see *The Nymph Complaining*, l. 95.

57–60 *Magdala ... pedes*

> Thus, when Magdalene dismissed her wanton lovers
> And dissolved her sultry eyes into chaste waters,
> Christ stood fixed in a flowing bond of tears,
> His sacred feet held in a liquid chain.'

THE CORONET

As a lyric in the religious pastoral mode, *The Coronet*, first published in the Folio, shows a thematic and generic link with the early dialogue *Thyrsis and Dorinda* and with *Clorinda and Damon*; this offers the only clue to its date of composition. Although Herbert's *The Wreath* provides an analogue, the diction of the poem, particularly in ll. 14 and 22, suggests that Marvell had also been reading in the sixteenth-century poets. Its convoluted style and tortuous syntax serve to suit the manner to the matter.

7 *towers*   high headdresses.

14 *twining in*   entwining.
    speckled breast   from Spenser's *Faerie Queene*, I. xi. 15.

15 *fold*   wind.

16 *wreaths*   coils.

22 *curious frame*   ingenious structure (the chaplet), a phrase taken from Sidney's Sonnet 28 in *Astrophel and Stella* where it is applied derisively to allegory; this borrowing lends support to the interpretation of the coronet as a metaphorical garland of poetry.

23 *these*   flowers, understood here and in the next line.
    so that   provided that.

25 *spoils*   (a) sloughing of a snake's skin and (b) plundering.

AN HORATIAN ODE UPON CROMWELL'S RETURN FROM IRELAND

The topical reference in the title to Cromwell's return (May 1650) and ll. 105–8, looking forward to an invasion of Scotland (which Cromwell entered on 22 July), limit the date of composition to the months of June and July. Refusing to invade Scotland, General Fairfax (whose daughter Marvell was to tutor) resigned his post in mid-June as commander-in-chief of the Parliamentary forces, and Cromwell as lieutenant-general was then advanced to the command.

Initially included in the Folio, the *Ode* was cancelled in most copies (*British Museum C.59.1.8* and *Huntington 79660* are exceptions) and not printed again until Thompson's edition of 1776. On the basis of the similarity of a line in Robert Wild's *Death of Mr Christopher Love* (beheaded by Cromwell 22 August 1651) to two lines of the *Ode*, Cleanth Brooks (*English Institute Essays*, New York, 1947, repr. in *Andrew Marvell*, ed. John Carey, Penguin Critical Anthologies) suggests that Marvell's poem was being handed about among Royalists at that date. The several minor differences from the Folio in *Eng. poet. d. 49* accord with Thompson's text.

The *Ode* has stirred up much critical debate, in part occasioned by Marvell's use of what L. D. Lerner (in *Interpretations*, ed. John Wain, Routledge & Kegan Paul, pp. 59–74) has termed 'double-edged' and 'poised' readings, the first permitting alternative readings, the second reflecting dual attitudes. The literary influence of Horace's *Odes* (particularly I. 35, 37; IV. 4, 5, 14, 15) and Lucan's *Pharsalia* (particularly book I) has been traced by R. H. Syfret (in *RES*, n.s. XII, 1961, 160–72) and John S. Coolidge (in *MP*. LXIII, 1965, 111–20), who detect a blending of the two earlier poets' attitudes toward the ambiguities of power and of right in Marvell's *Ode*. Verbal echoes seem to indicate he knew the popular contemporary translation of the *Pharsalia* by Thomas May, who was to die in November 1650, and become the object of Marvell's early satirical mode. (See notes to *Tom May's Death*, pp. 241–3.) Cf. ll. 5–8, 9–24, and 113–14 of the *Ode* with the following three passages characterizing Caesar from May's translation:

But restless valour, and in war a shame
Not to be conquerour; fierce, not curbed at all,
Ready to fight, where hope, or anger call
His forward sword; confident of success,
And bold the favour of the gods to press:
O'erthrowing all that his ambition stay,
And loves that ruin should enforce his way;
As lightning by the wind forced from a cloud
Breaks through the wounded air with thunder loud,
Disturbs the day, the people terrifies,
And by a light oblique dazzles our eyes,
Not Jove's own temple spares it; when no force,
No bar can hinder his prevailing course,
Create waste, as forth it sallies and retires,
It makes and gathers his dispersèd fires.

[Caesar]   'Fortune, I'll follow thee.
No more we'll trust: War shall determine all':
This said, by night the active general
Swifter than Parthian back-shot shaft, or stone
From Balearic slinger, marches on
To invade Ariminum; . . .

The young men rose, and from the temples took
Their arms, now such as a long peace had marred.
And their old bucklers now of leather bared:
Their blunted piles not of a long time used,
And swords with the eatings of black rust abused.
(A3ᵛ–A5, 1631; other complete editions in 1635, 1650)

1 *forward* (a) eager; (b) presumptuous.
appear emerge on the public scene.

3–4 *sing | His numbers languishing* suggests love poetry, hence private and unacclaimed.

9 *cease* remain at rest (intrans.).

13–16 *lightning . . . | Did thorough his own side | His fiery way divide* Conceived as an elemental force like lightning opening its way through the clouds which produced it, Cromwell after 1644 also opened a way for himself among rival Parliamentary leaders.

15 *thorough*] *Eng. poet. d. 49*, *Th*; *through F.*

19–20 *And with such to inclose | Is more than to oppose* This difficult and elliptical reading may mean 'And with such [a one as Cromwell], to contain [him] is more [galling to him] than to contend with [him].' If the reading looks back to the two immediately preceding lines, it could mean that although to a Cromwell the act is 'all one', 'to contain rivals or enemies is more [a greater achievement] than to contend with either of them', a comment reflecting Cromwell's emerging power within his own party set forth in ll. 13–16.

23–4 *Caesar's . . . laurels blast* Although lightning, according to tradition (Pliny, *Natural History* II. 56), does not strike the laurel tree, Cromwell, after rending the palaces and temples, has struck down Charles I.

29–33 *from his private gardens . . . | Could . . . climb* Cromwell's pattern of action from retirement to military activity parallels that suggested for the 'forward youth' (ll. 1–8).

32 *bergamot* a fine species of pear known as 'prince's pear' or the 'pear of kings' (John Bodaeus's commentary on Theophrastus' *Historia Plantarum*, 1644, cited by W. R. Orwen, *N & Q* CC, 1955, 340–41). These epithets should be considered in light of the 'highest plot' of the preceding line. Cromwell, before the 1640s, had been a wheat farmer in Huntingdon and then a grazier in nearby St Ives.

35 *kingdoms*] *Eng. poet. d. 49*, *Th.*; *kingdom F.*

38-40 *And . . . ancient rights . . . do hold or break | As men are strong or weak.*
Men is used inclusively (a) for the king who has not been able to maintain the
'ancient rights' (cf. his 'helpless right', l. 62); (b) for those like Cromwell
who have been able to abrogate them; and (c) for the people who have com-
plied with this state of affairs. The phrase 'ancient rights' also appears in *Tom
May's Death*, l. 69.

41-42 *Nature, that hateth emptiness, | Allows of penetration less* Though
averse to a vacuum, Nature is even more averse to the occupation of the same
space by two bodies at the same time (*penetration*). Cf. *Flecknoe*, ll. 98-101, for
a similar usage of this debated topic.

51-2 *That Charles himself might chase | To Carisbrooke's narrow case* In
1647 the King fled to Carisbrooke Castle on the Isle of Wight where he was
then betrayed to the Governor (see *The Last Instructions to a Painter*, l. 156
and n.).
    chase hurry (intrans.), *or* (trans.).

59-60 *But with his keener eye | The axe's edge did try* Brooks compares with
these two verses the line from Robert Wild's *Death of Mr Christopher Love*,
'His keener words did their sharp axe exceed.'
    try put to the test.

66 *assured* ensured.

69-72 *A bleeding head . . . | Did fright the architects . . . | And yet . . . the
State | Foresaw its happy fate* In digging the foundations of the temple of
Jupiter Capitolium, the excavators turned up 'a man's head, face and all,
whole and sound: which sight . . . plainly foretold that [Rome] should be the
chief castle of the empire and the capital place of the whole world' (Livy,
Annals I. 55. 6, tr. Philemon Holland, 1600, El^v). The story is related also
by Pliny (*N.H.* XXVIII. 4) and Varro (*De lingua latina* V. 41). The adjective
bleeding is Marvell's addition as is the *fright* of the architects.

73-4 *the Irish are . . . tamed* Landing at Dublin in August, 1649, Cromwell
systematically and savagely set about 'taming' the country.

82 *still* always.

83-4 *How fit he is to sway | That can so well obey* a commonplace attributed
to the Greek lawgiver Solon.

85 *Commons'*] *Eng. poet. d.* 49, Th.; *Common F.*

100 *crowns*] *Eng. poet. d.* 49, Th.; *crown F.*

101-2 *A Caesar he, ere long . . . an Hannibal* invaders of Gaul and Italy. The
use of *Caesar* here is to be contrasted with its application to Charles in l. 23.

104 *climactéric* fatal; epochal; critical.

105-8 *The Pict . . . his parti-coloured mind | . . . Shrink underneath the plaid*
Using Pict for Scot as if derived from Latin *picti*, painted or tattooed, Marvell
puns on *parti-party-coloured* and *plaid*. *F* has the spelling 'party'.

107 *sad* steadfast.

110 *mistake* because of the camouflage.

111 *lay his hounds in near* put the dogs on the scent.

118 *spirits of the shady night* including those ruined by Cromwell's 'industrious valour,' those who fell in the Civil Wars, and, inevitably, the dead king (E. E. Duncan-Jones, *EA* XV, 1962, 172–4, who cites the magical powers ascribed to the drawn sword in Homer, *Ody*. XI. 48 and Virgil, *Aen*. VI. 260).

TOM MAY'S DEATH

The death on 13 November 1650 of Thomas May, poet, dramatist, and translator, occasioned this satire, first published in the Folio (though omitted from *Eng. poet. d. 49*). His most important and popular work, a translation of the *Pharsalia*, had appeared in 1627 in ten books (a work Marvell recalled in writing the *Horatian Ode*, see p. 238), followed three years later by his continuation of Lucan's history relating events down to the death of Caesar. Initially a Royalist – May dedicated three works to King Charles – he became in the 1640s official apologist for the Parliamentary cause, publishing a *History of the Parliament* (see l. 23) and a *Breviary of the History of the Parliament* which stopped short of recounting the death of the King (see ll. 75–6). His enemies attributed this shift in allegiance to vexation at not gaining the laureateship (cf. ll. 57–8).

Since May was a disciple of Ben Jonson, who contributed laudatory verses to the *Pharsalia* (cf. ll. 19–24), which were reprinted in *Underwoods*, his expulsion from the Elysian Fields by the literary arbiter of the age carries double force. Marvell may have taken a few hints, if he needed any, from an incident in *The Great Assises Holden in Parnassus by Apollo and His Assessors* (1645), sometimes ascribed to George Wither. Here Jonson is a 'fat keeper' (cf. ll. 10–12) and here May is charged by a fellow 'gazette-writer' (cf. ll. 59–60) with having abused the King and having been guilty of ingratitude; calling down on himself the punishments of the giants or of Ixion's wheel (cf. ll. 91–4) should he be guilty, May is then absolved of the charges by Apollo who acknowledges (in contrast to ll. 55–6) that they have been prompted by 'mere malice'.

1 *As one put drunk into the packet-boat* May was reported to have suffocated in his sleep after a drinking bout.

    packet-boat mail boat.

6 *Stephen's Alley* the street, notorious for its taverns (cf. The Pope's Head and The Mitre, l. 7), where May lived.

8 *still* always.

10 *Ayres* apparently a contemporary tavern-keeper.

14 *layed* sang a lay.

17 *And*] *Cooke*; *But F*.

18 *Brutus and Cassius, the people's cheats* as conspirators against Caesar.

21–4 *Cups . . . | I sing . . . | In his own bowels sheathed the conquering health* adapts the opening lines of May's translation of the *Pharsalia*:

Wars more than civil on Emathian plains
We sing: rage licensed; where great Rome distains
In her own bowels her victorious swords.

25–6 *May to himself and them was come, | He found he was translated, and by whom* Having recovered consciousness as well as having reached his destination, the translator recognizes he has been translated by death as well as by Jonson.

27 *with foot as stumbling as his tongue* May, according to a contemporary, suffered from a speech defect which inhibited his discourse except among close friends.

37–8 *he whipped him . . . | Like Pembroke* A contemporary reports that when members of the Inns of Court were performing before the King in February 1634, the Lord Chamberlain, Philip Herbert, Earl of Pembroke, broke his staff of office over the shoulders of May whom he did not know; after apologizing to him the next morning, he presented the poet-translator with £50.

41 *Polydore, Lucan, Alan* 'Mercenary' seems to be the linking element in these names. The Italian churchman Polydore Vergil compiled his *Historia Anglica* at Henry VII's request in 1505 and then purportedly burned his sources (see *The Rehearsal Transpros' d*, Smith, p.316); Lucan despite his hatred of Nero inserted an adulatory passage in book I of the *Pharsalia*; the Alani, a Scythian people, joined with their conquerors the Huns to invade the Eastern and Western empires. Cf. the summary of the charges directed at May, ll. 71–4.

50 *As Bethlem's House did to Loreto walk* A house dedicated to the Virgin was believed to have been miraculously transported from Palestine (Nazareth, not Bethlehem) to Illyria and hence to Loreto, Italy.

53 *lay* sang, as in l. 14 above.

54 *Those but to Lucan do continue May* those measures, both as dimensions (l. 52) and as heroic verse, though purporting to continue Lucan's work, do no more than continue May's; he wrote his *Continuation of Lucan's Historical Poem* in both Latin and English.

57–8 *some one . . . more worthy wears | The sacred laurel* After Jonson's death in 1637, Sir William D'Avenant (see ll. 77–8) was appointed poet laureate.

60 *gázette-writer* Among contributors to the periodical *Mercurius Britannicus*, John Taylor the Water Poet termed May in 1643 'the contriver and chief engineer' (*Mercurius Aquaticus, or, The Water Poet's Answer to All That Hath or Shall Be Writ by Mercurius Britannicus*, sig. 2).

61–2 *must we | As for the basket, Guelphs and Ghib'llines be?* Must we poets become partisans for a fee?
  basket Latin *sportula*, a basket used for distributing alms or a dole, then

signifying a gratuity or gift. Cf. (a) basket-scramblers; (b) basket-clerks (used by Milton in *Considerations . . . to Remove Hirelings Out of the Church*); and (c) basket-justices, proverbial (Tilley, B103) for those who dispensed justice for a fee. In the lines that follow Marvell contrasts the incorruptible poet with the craven judge and churchman in a 'disjointed' world.

Guelphs and Ghib'llines   political parties in medieval Italy, the former opposing, the latter favouring, imperial rule.

69   *ancient rights*   as in the *Horatian Ode*, l. 38.

74   *chronicler to Spartacus*   A 'Thracian fencer', as May calls him in his notes to the *Pharsalia*, Spartacus led an uprising of slaves against the Romans. Topical identification since G. A. Aitken's edition (1901) has been with the Earl of Essex *or* Thomas Fairfax *or* 'the Parliamentary armies in general'. On the basis of May's enthusiastic remarks in the *Breviary of the History of the Parliament*, Cromwell would seem the most likely referent.

81   *Poor poet . . . and grateful senate*   The Council of State ordered May's interment in Westminster Abbey at a charge not to exceed £100; in 1661 Charles II was to order the body exhumed.

85–6   *where Spenser lies, / And reverend Chaucer*   These lines contrast pointedly with the tribute Jonson renders to Shakespeare in his own voice: 'I will not lodge thee by / Chaucer, or Spenser. . . .' (*To the Memory of My Beloved . . . Master William Shakespeare*, ll. 19–20.)

88   *As th' eagle's plumes from other birds divide*   *Divide* is used both in its English and its Latin sense – that is, to mark out and to destroy. Tradition has it that the feathers of eagles 'being mixed with the feathers of other birds . . . do waste and consume them' (Francis Willoughby, *Ornithology*, tr. John Ray, 1678, p. 56).

90   *Phlegethon*   the fiery river of Hades.

91   *Cerberus*   the triple-headed dog stationed at the entrance to Hades.

92   *Megaera*   one of the Furies, often represented as brandishing a torch in one hand and a scourge of snakes in the other.

93   *Ixion's wheel*   the ever-revolving fiery wheel to which Ixion was bound by brazen bands for having attempted to seduce Juno.

94   *perpetual vulture*   fed on the constantly renewing liver of Prometheus for his having stolen fire from heaven.

IN LEGATIONEM DOMINI OLIVERI ST JOHN AD
PROVINCIAS FOEDERATAS

Though first published in the Folio, composition of this epigram can be assigned to February 1651 (note the subjunctive in l. 6) when Oliver St John, together with Walter Strickland, was instructed on 14 February to arrange an alliance with the United Provinces of the Netherlands which he visited in early

March. After three months of negotiation, the embassy ended in failure, much to the exasperation of St John who, according to tradition, set about on his return to initiate action against Dutch trade.

9 *hoc Martis* St John, as author of the apocalyptic Book of Revelation, prophesying the Second Coming.

pacis nuntius illo Oliver, identified with the olive, symbolic of peace; cf. *First Anniversary*, l. 258.

10 *Jani ferrea claustra* The gates of the temple of Janus Quirinus in Rome were left open in war but closed in times of peace to keep wars within; cf. *Inscribenda Luparae*, l. 11. As presiding deity of gates (*januae*), Janus was usually represented holding a key in one hand and a staff in the other.

16 *Antiochus gyro non breviore stetit* Directed by the Roman consul Popilius to desist from war with the Egyptians, Antiochus responded evasively, whereupon Popilius, drawing a circle around him in the sand, ordered him not to step out of it until he had committed himself. Marvell alludes to this incident again in *Mr Smirk: or the Divine in Mode* (1676), Grosart IV, 38.

TO HIS WORTHY FRIEND DOCTOR WITTY UPON HIS TRANSLATION OF THE 'POPULAR ERRORS'

Marvell contributed these verses to the translation of James Primrose's Latin text which his friend Robert Witty, a physician at Hull, published in 1651 as *Popular Errors or The Errors of the People in Matter of Physic*. For his verses in Latin composed for the same occasion, see p. 203. Both sets are signed 'Andrew Marvell. A. F.' (Andreae Filius).

4 *cypress* a transparent fabric.

15–16 *Here he maketh blots | That mends* a typical inversion: here he that mends makes blots.

17 *Celia* perhaps Mary Fairfax, whom Marvell commends in *Upon Appleton House* (ll. 707–10) for her aptitude in languages.

27–9 *I slide | . . . into error . . . | Women must not teach here* a teasing allusion to the verses explicating the frontispiece of the volume which describe, as an example of popular error, 'a woman' prescribing such remedies as a pepper posset and a caudle.

30 *Stint them to caudles, almond-milk* limit them to warm drinks of gruel and emollients of sweet almonds and water.

33 *hasting*] hastning *F*. Marvell also uses it in *Flecknoe*, l. 167 and *A Poem upon the Death . . . of the Lord Protector*, l. 72.

THE PICTURE OF LITTLE T.C. IN A PROSPECT OF FLOWERS

First published in the Folio, this lyric with its pastoral ambience perhaps dates from the early 1650s. Margoliouth (*MLR* XVII, 1922, 351-61) has suggested that 'little T. C.' may be Theophila (cf. the 'Darling of the Gods', l. 10) Cornewall, who was baptized on 26 September 1644, the second daughter of that name in the family; the first Theophila had died two days after birth, a fact which may add a circumstantial touch to the last stanza.

title Prospect (a) landscape; (b) (mental) survey.

17 *compound* come to terms.

36 *Flora* Roman goddess of flowers.

YOUNG LOVE

Addressed to a not yet nubile young girl, this argumentative lyric perhaps connects with *The Picture of Little T.C. in a Prospect of Flowers* in time of composition. It was first published in the Folio.

6 *beguiled* (a) charmed and (b) deceived.

9 *stay* wait for.

17-18 *time may take | Thee before thy time away* Cf. *The Picture of Little T.C.*, ll. 36-40.

23 *antedate* accelerate; cf. *Thyrsis and Dorinda*, l. 8.

24 *prevent* act in anticipation of.

THE MATCH

The Celia of this poem, first published in the Folio, may be the same girl alluded to in *To His Worthy Friend Doctor Witty* (1651).

The word *match* in the title afforded multiple meanings in seventeenth-century idiom: antagonist, counterpart, equal, contest, pairing, alliance, and, aptly for the second half of the poem, the wick used to ignite gunpowder (cf. the 'nitre' or saltpetre of l. 22).

19 *magazine* arsenal.

29 *vicinity* (a) likeness; (b) propinquity.

THE NYMPH COMPLAINING FOR THE DEATH OF HER FAWN

The lament for the death of a favourite pet is an ancient literary tradition dating back to Catullus (on the death of Lesbia's sparrow, I. 3) and Ovid (on the death of Corinna's parrot, *Amores* II. 6). An example in the early sixteenth century in England is John Skelton's *Philip Sparrow* which exploits the mock-heroic and mock-religious possibilities of the form, which was practised on the continent later in the century by such poets as Ronsard and Du Bellay. Like Skelton, Marvell plays up the youthful aspects of his heroine, who is at the same time depicted at the acute psychological juncture when her grief for the loss of her lover merges with her grief for the loss of her pet and, like Skelton, he exploits religious diction. The poem was first published in the Folio, and its composition may date from the period Marvell spent at Nun Appleton.

1 *troopers* used in reference to the Scottish Covenanting Army which invaded England in 1640 in support of Presbyterianism.

13 *It cannot die so* that is, with its murder unavenged.

17 *Else men are made their deodands* Otherwise men would become forfeits. According to English law any personal chattel which caused the death of a human being was forfeited in expiation.

19 *doth part* is sundered.

32 *dear* Like heart: hart, l. 36, a common pun.

70 *four* dissyllabic (as in *Upon Appleton House*, l. 323).

99–100 *The brotherless Heliades | Melt in such amber tears* Disconsolate at the death of Phaëthon, his sisters were turned into poplar trees and their tears into amber.

104 *Then place it in Diana's shrine* as goddess of chastity as well as of the chase.

106 *turtles* turtledoves.

113 *Let it be weeping too* The weeping statue recalls the fate of Niobe slain by the arrows of Diana and Apollo for her excessive pride in her children.

UPON THE HILL AND GROVE AT BILBROUGH

This topographical and complimentary poem clearly dates from Marvell's residence at Nun Appleton (perhaps beginning in late 1650 and extending to the end of 1652), where, according to Milton, he had been employed to instruct General Fairfax's daughter in languages. It thus connects with the descriptive and complimentary Latin epigram on the two mountains Almscliff and Bilbrough (see p. 73). The extravagant personified account of this Fairfax property, located five miles from Nun Appleton, serves as a means to praise the owner and his lady and as an oblique comment on the politcail situation (see stanzas 9, 10). Fairfax had resigned as commander-in-chief of the Parliamentary forces and retired to his Yorkshire estates in June 1650.

5 *pencil* paintbrush; the language is that of the art of portraiture (cf. brow, model, ll. 5, 7).

9 *mountains more unjust* irregular, in accord with the typical Renaissance attitude of considering jutting mountains as disfiguring the earth (see, for example, Drayton's *Polyolbion*, Song IX, ll. 105–22).

13–14 *For ... | Nature must a new centre find* Owing to the mountains' irregularities, the earth is no longer a perfect circle.

28 *heaven-daring Tenerife* a peak of more than 12,000 feet in the Canaries which had long served as a landmark to sailors; Bilbrough Hill, in contrast, had a height of 145 feet.

34 *plump*] *Margoliouth*; plum *F*; plume *Cooke*.

38 *great Master's terror* the ability of its owner to inspire terror.

42–3 *the great Nymph ... | Vera* Lady Ann Fairfax was the daughter of Sir Horace Vere, a distinguished military leader.

45–6 *And on these oaks engraved her name; | Such wounds alone these woods became* For a different point of view about carving on trees, see *The Garden*, ll. 23–4.

52 *genius* tutelary spirit of the place (*genius loci*).

56 *As under this. . . .* 'Lord Fairfax' must be understood.

69 *civic garlands* of oak leaves, see *The Garden*, l. 2.

73 *ye*] *Eng. poet. d. 49*; the *F*.

74 *oracles in oak* The trees in the grove are implicitly compared with those at Dodona, site of the most ancient oracle in Greece.

EPIGRAMMA IN DUOS MONTES AMOSCLIVIUM ET
BILBOREUM: FARFACIO

This descriptive epigram in Marvell's favourite elegiacs (dactylic hexameters alternating with dactylic pentameters) serves as a compliment to General Fairfax and is thus parallel to *Upon the Hill and Grove at Bilbrough*. The contrast between the two Yorkshire landmarks reflects dual aspects of the general's character while the concluding lines gracefully acknowledge his daughter as the presiding deity of a new Parnassus.

7 *Atlanteo ... vertice* Atlas supported the heavens on his head.

8 *humeros ... Herculeos* Hercules supported them on his shoulders.

11 *Pelion Ossa* the two mountains which were heaped on top of each other to enable the giants to scale heaven.

12 *Pindi* a chain of mountains separating Thessaly from Epirus.

21 *Alcidae ... columnae* located at the Straits of Gibraltar. The reference to the 'Northern Hercules' is a compliment to General Fairfax.

24 *Maria* Fairfax's daughter was born in 1638 and so would have been twelve years of age in 1650, the year Marvell is presumed to have begun tutoring her. If the poet is alluding to her under the name Celia (in *To His Worthy Friend Doctor Witty*, 1651, ll. 17–26), she appears to have proved an apt pupil.

UPON APPLETON HOUSE

Connected with *Upon the Hill and Grove at Bilbrough* in its topographical motif (and presumably in time of composition), *Upon Appleton House* also falls within the category of the 'country house poem' designed to describe and praise a house, a family and a way of life. The genre shows classical influence, particularly that of Horace (Epode II 'Beatus ille'), Martial (III. 58), and Statius (*Silvae* I. 3; II. 2), but its English development with Jonson, Carew, and Herrick (as traced by G. R. Hibbard, 'The Country House Poem of the Seventeenth Century,' *Journal of the Warburg & Courtauld Institutes* XIX, 1956, 159–74) stresses the social context of the house with its environs and the personal context of the individual with his environment. Elements of other genres (well catalogued by R. Colie, '*My Ecchoing Song*', pp. 181–294) intrude, and numerous *topoi* are glanced at. The fantastic play of imagination and the hyperbole which set the tone are accounted for (by Leishman, pp. 267–73) as showing the influence of the very popular John Cleveland (particularly his *Upon Phyllis Walking in a Morning before Sunrise*).

The Yorkshire estate of Nun Appleton, a Cistercian Priory whose history is recorded in ll. 81–280, had come to the Fairfax family at the dissolution. In 1637 or 1638 the grandfather of the Lord General seems to have begun construction of a new house which was probably not completed until some years after the General had given up his military duties (alluded to in ll. 345–60) and retired to Yorkshire; for, as John Newman pertinently notes (*TLS* 28 January, 1972), the poet's description of the house (particularly stanzas 4, 5) would more aptly accord with the original residence cobbled up out of part of the nunnery (see ll. 87–8) than with the later brick mansion. In this country retreat the Lord General assumed his social responsibilities (ll. 65–70), nurtured his daughter Mary (ll. 649–768), and wrote verses (see note to ll. 71–2), among these a translation of Saint-Amant's *Solitude* (*circa* 1617), which some critics feel may have influenced Marvell's poem.

Although *Upon Appleton House* is written in couplets, the stanzaic divisions which characterized its first publication in the Folio serve a necessary function in marking off the poet's organization of what is his longest and most disparate (nonpolitical) poem.

6 *Did for a model vault his brain* 'A house being a mere artificial and no natural thing hath its first subsistence in the idea of man's brain, according to whose model, good or ill, the house so built proves good or ill' (Henry Hawkins, *Partheneia Sacra*, 1633, p. 166, cited in Scoular, *Natural Magic*).
    vault arch.

12 *equal nest* one proportionate to themselves; see ll. 7–8.

22 *mote*] *Eng. poet. d. 49*; mose *F*.

24 *the first builders failed in height* builders of the Tower of Babel frustrated in their attempt to make it reach to heaven (Gen. xi 1–9).

30 *loop* opening.

36 *Vere* Lady Fairfax, the Vera of *Upon the Hill and Grove*, l. 43.

40 *Romulus his bee-like cell* alluding to the thatched cottage on the Palatine where the founder of Rome reputedly had lived.

45 *t'immure* to inclose.

47 *holy mathematics* The circle symbolized perfection and the square variously vertue, righteousness, prudence, religion, justice.

52 *grows spherical* in reference to the cupola surmounting the hall.

56 *That* its humility.

64 *invent* find out.

65–6 *frontispiece of poor | Adorns . . . the open door* The poor awaiting alms embellish the opening to the house.

71–2 *And for an inn to entertain | Its Lord a while* apparently recalled in the Lord General's verses *Upon the New-built House at Appleton* which include the line 'This house's a stay but as an inn.'

73–4 *Bishop's Hill or Denton . . . | Or Bilbrough* other (more commodious) dwellings which Fairfax had inherited.

77 *neatly* elegantly.

90 *the blooming virgin Thwaites* In 1518 the heiress Isabel Thwaites was to marry William Fairfax of Steeton. When she was confined by her guardian the prioress, her future husband was forced to obtain an order for her release (l. 234) and then seize her by force (ll. 257–60).

100 *hedge . . . about* (a) restrict and (b) defend.

105 *shining armour white* the Cistercian habit.

106 *Like virgin Amazons do fight* This assertion is illustrated in stanza 32.

107–8 *our chaste lamps . . . | Lest the great Bridegroom find them dim* an allusion to the parable of the wise and foolish virgins (Matt. xxv 1–12).

109 *orient* fresh.

122 *legend* life of a saint.

152 *devoto* (It. or Sp.) devotee.

169 *nice* fastidious.

179–80 *for the clothes, | . . . amber we compose* arrange ambergris for perfuming the altar cloths.

181 *grieved* injured.

182 *baits* (a) refreshments and (b) enticements.

198–9 *Religion that dispensèd hath | Which she henceforward does begin* Religion having provided a dispensation from Isabel's plighted troth, she then enters the convent; see also ll. 279–80.

221 *'state* estate.

232 *from a judge, then soldier bred* William Fairfax's father was a judge of Common Pleas; his mother the daughter of the (twelfth) Lord Roos who fell at the battle of Tournay.

233 *in the storm* in storming the priory.

241–2 *whose offspring . . . | Shall fight* The son of Isabel and William fought in Germany and Italy, their grandson in France, and their great-grandsons in Germany and Turkey.

245 *Till one . . .* a future but unidentified descendant.

248 *the great race would intercept* would cut off their posterity. Cf. *The Garden*, 'The gods . . . | Still in a tree did end their race' (ll. 27–8).

253 *disjointed* distracted.

268 *had*] *Eng. poet. d. 49*; hath *F*.

274 *escheat* reversion, since there was no heir.

281 *the hero* perhaps Sir Thomas Fairfax, the son of this marriage or perhaps the Lord General who had also fought in France. See l. 297 where the latter is called 'Governor'.

284 *His warlike studies could not cease* Cf. 'So restless Cromwell could not cease / In the inglorious arts of peace' (*Horatian Ode*, ll. 9–10).

292 *dian* (Fr. *diane*) reveillé.

295 *pan* part of the musket lock (which contains the priming).

296 *flask* powder flask; the flowers are presented as military personnel. See also stanzas 39 and 42–3.

301 *virgin Nymph* Mary Fairfax whom the poet was tutoring; she was at this time between twelve and fourteen years old.

303 *compare* vie (with). The injunction is addressed to the flowers (of l. 297).

320 *nor*] *Cooke* +; or *F*.

322 *garden of the world* Cf:

The garden of the world, wherein the rose
In chief commanded
(Mildmay Fane, *Anglia Hortus* in *Otia Sacra*, 1648, ll. 1–2).

It is likely, as Leishman notes, that the author had presented a copy of his privately printed volume to the Lord General who was his brother-in-law. Similarities between Fane and Marvell are traced by M. C. Bradbrook in 'Marvell and the Poetry of Rural Solitude', *RES* XVII, 1941, 37–46.

323 *four* dissyllabic as in *The Nymph Complaining*, l. 70, and *The Loyal Scot*, l. 162.

336 *Switzers of our Guard* in reference to the black, yellow, and red stripes of the Swiss papal guard.

341 *stoves* hot houses.

349 *Cinque Ports* five ports on the southeast coast of England under the charge of a Lord Warden. In 1650 Parliament turned over this responsibility (together with the powers of the Lord High Admiral, a fact which explains l. 352) to the Council of State of which the Lord General was a member until his resignation in June. Poets frequently used the term metaphorically (see Scoular, *Natural Magic*, p. 134, n.1).

351 *spanned* restrained.

356 *earthy*] *Eng. poet. d.* 49; earthly *F*. Familiar from the Biblical phrase (I Cor. 15, 47–9) 'of the earth, earthy' also rendered 'of the earth, earthly', the two forms were interchangeable in this sense in the sixteenth and seventeenth centuries.

   want (a) lack and (b) need.

358 *that which shrinks at every touch* the sensitive plant; cf. *An Elegy upon the Death of My Lord Francis Villiers*, ll. 81–2.

363 *Cawood Castle* a seat of the Archbishop of York, located two miles from Nun Appleton.

365 *quarrelled* found fault with (trans.).

368 *graze*] *Eng. poet. d.* 49; gaze *F*.

372 *But grasshoppers are giants there* 'And there we saw the giants . . . and we were in our own sight as grasshoppers, and so we were in their sight'. (Num. xiii 33).

380 *or go* is going (forwards).

382 *show . . . the ground* show the nature of the ground.

385 *engines strange* devices for manipulating stage effects.

392 *crowd a lane to either side* crowd to either side to form a lane.

395 *rail* a small land bird.

402 *cates* provisions.

406 *He called us Israelites* See ll. 388–90.

408 *Rails . . . for quails, for manna, dew* After crossing the Red Sea, the Israelites came to a wilderness where they were miraculously fed: 'at even the quails came up . . . and in the morning the dew lay round about the host' (Ex. xvi 13). See Marvell's use of the allusion in *Daphnis and Chloe*, stanza 20.

413 *orphan parents'* a transferred epithet.

416 *sourdine* the low sound of the trumpet.

419 *traverse* track.

426 *hay* a country dance (with a pun).

428 *Alexander's sweat* 'The sweats of that great monarch were held to be perfumes; and why? Perhaps because they took some deity to be in him, for his so strange and prodigious conquests' (Hawkins, *Partheneia Sacra*, p. 61). A well-known source of the story is Plutarch's *Lives*.

439 *Roman camps* used for the tumuli (hillocks serving as burial mounds); they were actually of British origin.

444 *As cloths for Lely* the portrait painter Sir Peter Lely, who had come from Holland to England in 1641.
　cloths canvases

446 *table rase* blank tablet (*tabula rasa*).

447 *toril* for 'bullring'.

448 *Madril* Madrid.

450 *Levellers* a political party which, coming to the fore *circa* 1647, sought to establish social and economic equality.

451–2 *The villagers in common chase | Their cattle, which it closer rase* As the villagers use this level space for a common pasture, the cattle keep it closely cropped.

453 *increased* grew.

454 *beast*] *Eng. poet. d. 49*; breast *F*.

455–6 *painted world . . . | D'Avenant . . . the universal herd* alluding to William D'Avenant's description (*Gondibert* II, vi) of a painting of creation, where on the sixth day 'an universal herd' appears.

457–8 *They seem . . . | A landskip drawn in looking glass* (a) the cattle seem as if sketched in a landscape scene that is then reflected in a mirror (with consequent diminution of size, anticipating l. 459); or (b) they seem 'within the polished grass' as in a landscape scene that has been sketched in quicksilver.

461–2 *Such fleas, ere they approach the eye, | In multiplying-glasses lie* such as fleas appear in microscopes not yet brought into focus; this is the obverse of James Howell's statement (*Epistolae Ho-Elianae*, 1650), 'Such [multiplying] glasses can make a flea look like a cow' (Leishman, p. 222 n.).

466 *Denton . . . ope its cataracts* The estate of Denton (see l. 73) was located on the Wharfe River thirty miles from Nun Appleton.

472 *isles . . . round* to make an island around. Cf. a similar usage in *The Last Instructions to a Painter*, l. 968.
　astonished] *Eng. poet. d. 49*; astonish *F*.

474 *eels now bellow* having been swallowed by the ox when it was drinking.

475–6 *tails . . . | Turned . . . to leeches quick* alluding to the popular notion that a horsehair put in water would become live.

480 *pound* a fold for cattle.

485 *the first carpenter* Noah who built *his* ark of gopher wood (Gen. vi).

486 *pressed* commandeered; see ll. 493–4.

488 *in armies, not in pairs* in contrast to those in Noah's ark. The diction of the poem here as elsewhere evokes the Civil-War milieu.

491 *pedigrees* genealogical trees.

493 *Of whom though many fell in war* The referent seems to be (a) to the timber felled for war purposes and (b) to members of the Fairfax and Vere families.

498 *It seems . . . as wood not trees* an inversion of the proverb, Tilley W733.

499 *neighbourhood* proximity.

502 *a fifth element* supplementary to earth, air, fire, and water.

526 *Sad pair unto the elms they moan* a recollection of Virgil's line about the turtledove, *nec gemere aëria cessabit turtur ab ulmo* (*Ecl.* I, 58).

535 *stork-like* The stork popularly was believed to leave behind one of its young as a tribute to the owner of the house where it nested.

537 *hewel's* the hewhole's or green woodpecker's.

538 *holtfelster's care* woodcutter's concern.

563–4 *little now to make me wants | Or of the fowls, or of the plants* A typical inversion – there lacks little now to make me be either of the fowls or of the plants.

568 *I was but an inverted tree* A commonplace notion going back to Plato's *Timaeus* 90 A (see A. B. Chambers, 'I Was But an Inverted Tree' *SR* VIII, 1961, 291–9).

577 *sibyl's leaves* Ten in number, the sibyls were believed by the Greeks and Romans as well as certain of the Church Fathers (see l. 581) to have been divinely inspired; the most celebrated was the Cumaean who customarily recorded her predictions on leaves. Cf. *Illustrissimo Viro*, l. 32.

580 *plumes* feathers used to form 'Mexique paintings'.

582 *mosaic* the pattern formed by the trembling leaves. There is an implied contrast with the Mosaic books of the Bible which, in turn, is implicitly contrasted with 'Nature's mystic book' of l. 584.

586 *with a mask my studies hit* with a disguise or habit proper for my studies (see *The Rehearsal Transpros'd*, Smith, p. 71, for a comparable use); *mask* and *masque* were interchangeable in the period.

591 *antic cope* grotesque ecclesiastical vestment, but the spellings *antic* and *antique* were interchangeable. Milton uses the same derisive phrase ('it had no rubric to be sung in an antic cope upon the stage of a high altar') in *An Apology for Smectymnuus*, 1642.

592 *great prelate of the grove* a (self-)mocking echo of l. 366.

599 *shed* part.

601-2 *How safe ... behind | These trees have I encamped my mind* Cf. the words of the prioress, 'These walls ... hedge our liberty about' (ll. 99–100). The diction of the stanza evidences an intruding awareness of the Civil War.

610 *gadding vines* echoes Milton's use of the phrase in *Lycidas*, l. 40.

629-30 *No serpent ... nor crocodile | Remains behind our little Nile* a popular view, as in *Antony and Cleopatra* (II. vii. 29–31): 'Your serpent of Egypt is bred now of your mud by the operation of your sun: so is your crocodile.'

631-2 *Unless itself ... | Among these meads the only snake* *itself* refers to 'our little Nile'. The same image appears in the Lord General's translation of Saint-Amant's *Solitude*: 'Then gliding under the arbored banks, / As winding serpent in the grass' (M. A. Gibb, *The Lord General*, London, 1938, 283–7).

636 *slick* smooth.

639-40 *for his shade ... | Narcissus-like, the sun too pines* The youth Narcissus becoming enamoured of his own reflection in a fountain pined away until he was changed into a flower.
   shade shadow, as in *The Garden*, l. 5.

645 *sliding foot* as in *The Garden*, l. 49.

649 *quills* floats (made of the quill of a feather).

650 *angles* fishing rods and line.

657 *loose* lax.

659 *whisht* hushed.

660 *bonne mine* (Fr.) good appearance; *bonne* is disyllabic.

668 *eben shuts* black (ebony) shutters.

669-70 *halcyon ... | Flying betwixt the day and night* the kingfisher, as in *The Gallery*, ll. 35–6, where it is described as flying 'betwixt the air and water'.

675 *compacts* solidifies.

677 *stupid* stupefied.

679 *assist* attend.

681 *Maria such, and so ...* Maria, in like fashion. ... A lady's power over a landscape was a standard *topos*. Leishman (pp. 237–40) points to the possible influence on Marvell of *Sylvia's Park*, a translated version by Thomas Stanley (1651) of Théophile de Viau's 'country house' poem entitled *La Maison de Silvie*.

684 *star new-slain* a shooting star or meteor.

685-6 *giddy rockets ... | Which from the putrid earth exhale* either the fiery vapours exhaled from the earth or meteors, on occasion thought to be exhaled.

688 *vitrified* turned to glass like the crystalline sphere.

707-8 *to converse | In all the languages* Cf. *To His Worthy Friend Doctor Witty*, ll. 17–26, where the Celia who is complimented for her skill in languages probably represents Mary Fairfax.

713-14 *prevent | Those trains* anticipate the artillery.

729 *fond* foolish.

734 *black-bag* mask.

743-4 *her glad parents . . . make their destiny their choice* In 1657 Mary Fairfax married George Villiers, second Duke of Buckingham, the older brother of the Francis Villiers whose death in 1648 occasioned an elegy subsequently attributed to Marvell.

753 *Thessalian Tempe's seat* a vale in Thessaly celebrated by the poets as a place of delight (*locus amoenus*).

755-6 *Aranjuez . . . Bel-Retiro* Spanish royal residences noted for their gardens.

757 *Idalian grove* Cyprus, the favourite haunt of Venus.

765-6 *Your lesser world . . . in more decent order* The microcosm which is Nun Appleton is more orderly than the post-lapsarian world.

771 *like Antipodes in shoes* like the men who dwell opposite on the globe. Cf. 'The Antipodes wear their shoes on their heads' (Cleveland, *Square Cap*, 1647, 1651, l. 19, cited in Leishman, p. 221).

772 *shod their heads in their canoes* Fishermen transported the leathern boats ('coracles') on their heads.

774 *rational amphibii* The salmon-fishers are 'rational' creatures who are both of the land and of the water. Cf. the unfortunate lover in the poem of that name (l. 40) who is termed an 'amphibium of life and death'.

THE GARDEN

An example of the poetry of solitude, *The Garden* very probably dates from the period of Marvell's sojourn with General Fairfax: thematically, it is in harmony with his other poems extolling the Yorkshire locale and its owner's retirement from active life to Nun Appleton, while the ambiguous tone of stanza 1 is clearly harmonious with the *Horatian Ode* written in the summer of 1650. Mildmay Fane's *To Retiredness* (*Otia Sacra*, 1648) and Cowley's *Of Solitude* (*Works*, 1668) strike notes of similarity with *The Garden*, but its (slightly) serious undertone is established as well as offset by Marvell's manipulation of ideas (the inversion of myth in stanza 4) and of language (the many puns).

As in the case of *A Drop of Dew* and *Ros*, Marvell wrote a companion piece to *The Garden* in Latin which, while corresponding fairly closely to it, lacks the equivalent verses for stanzas 5 to 8 (see Appendix, p. 205), and the editor inserted in the text of *Hortus* the note *Desunt multa* indicating that he thought lines were missing from his copy. (Cf. the equivalent insert in *Eng. poet. d. 49* for *A Dialogue between the Soul and Body*.) In the light of this fact it is scarcely possible to determine the priority of one version or the other, but the English, surprisingly, is terser than the Latin, and it may thus reflect the poet's honing of his first ideas in a second effort.

1 *vainly* (a) futilely and (b) arrogantly; cf. the double meaning in 'vain head', *A Dialogue between the Soul and Body*, l. 10.

 amaze (a) perplex and (b) craze, a reading which accords with the Latin 'madness' (*furor*).

2 *the palm, the oak, or bays* awards for military, civic, or poetic achievement.

4 *single herb or tree* in contrast to 'all flowers and all trees' (l. 7) which supply multiple 'garlands.'

5 *vergèd shade* deflected shadow (the latter term as in *Upon Appleton House*, l. 639).

6 *prudently their toils upbraid* The diction is associative and ambiguous:

 prudently (a) with discernment, (b) discretion, and (c) politic awareness.

 toils (a) tasks and (b) snares (looking forward to the associative meaning of the verb).

 upbraid (a) censure and (b) braid up (the 'toils' which issue in the plaited wreath of leaves).

7 *close* unite (as in l. 14 of *The Definition of Love*).

13 *Your sacred plants, if here below* those symbolic of Quiet and Innocence, if they exist here on earth.

15 *all but rude* almost uncivil, an inversion of the normal view of 'society' and 'companies of men', but cf. Milton, 'For solitude sometimes is best society' (*PL* IX, 249) and the Ciceronian commonplace 'Never less alone than when alone' (Tilley, A 228).

17 *white nor red* here emblematic of the lady; in *Eyes and Tears* (stanza 5), the red, the white, the green are colours characterizing a garden.

19 *fond* (a) doting and (b) foolish.

25 *run our ... heat* (a) run our course and (b) quenched our ardour.

26 *retreat* withdrawal (a) as from a battle engagement and (b) from the world.

28 *Still* always.

 race (a) competition and (b) line. Cf. *Upon Appleton House*, l. 248.

29–30 *so, / Only that* for the one purpose alone.

29–32 *Apollo ... laurel ... Pan ... reed* The laurel which the god of poetry seeks is, of course, identical with the 'bays' of l. 2, while the reed which Pan seeks becomes his pipe (syrinx), symbolic of pastoral poetry.

33 *is*] *Thompson*; in *F*.

33–40 *What wondrous life . . .* In this catalogue of delights – a standard *topos* – it is the inanimate fruits and flowers that proffer their attractions.

37 *curious* choice.

41 *from pleasures less* from lesser pleasures.
pleasures] *Eng. poet. d. 49*; pleasure *F*.

43–4 *The mind, that ocean where each kind | Does straight its own resemblance find* alluding to the popular notion that the flora and fauna of the land have their parallels in the sea and perhaps also to the philosophic notion of pre-existent ideas.
straight without delay.

45 *these* looks back to 'each kind' and ahead to 'other worlds' and 'other seas'.

47 *Annihilating* reducing.

48 *a green thought in a green shade* The doubled use of *green* calls up con-notative meanings supplementary to its basic sense of colour – fresh, youthful vigorous, tender, innocent, immature. In his *Song* (l. 26) the Mower terms the meadows 'companions' of his 'thoughts more green', and the 'green shade' echoes Virgil's *Ecl.* IX. 20 (*viridi fontis induceret umbra*).

49 *sliding foot* as in *Upon Appleton House*, l. 645.

51 *vest* garment.

52 *My soul into the boughs does glide | . . . like a bird* As Renato Poggioli pointed out ('The Pastoral of the Self', *Daedalus*, 1959, LXXXVIII, 686–99), the metamorphosis here is more metaphoric than symbolic though the reference (l. 55) to the *longer flight* the 'bird-soul' will undertake (when its stay in this or another garden comes to an end) indicates the poet's awareness of the religious origin of the image.

54 *whets* preens, apparently a nonce use.

60 *What other help could yet be meet* what other aid could yet be suitable, deriving from Gen. ii 18, 20; ('helpmeet' as a *word*, it should be noted, dates chiefly from the nineteenth century).

61 *share* lot.

63–4 *Two paradises 'twere in one | To live in paradise alone* Cowley's line. (*Of Solitude*, *Works*, p. 94) serve to gloss this passage:

As soon as two (alas!) together joined,
The serpent made up three.

66 *dial* the garden set forth as a floral sun dial which thus serves as a daily and a seasonal clock.

67–8 *the milder sun | Does through a fragrant zodiac run* While it follows its course through the circle of aromatic flowers and herbs, the sun (although in the Latin poem it is 'more bright') here has its intense rays tempered by the flora through which they filter.

69–70 *the industrious bee | Computes its time as well as we*   The reminiscence of Horace (*Carmina* IV. 2, 27–9) – 'in the manner and mode of the Mantinian bee seizing the pleasant thyme' (*carpere thyma*) – which lies behind the Latin version (p. 205, ll. 55–6) offers a pun (*Horologo . . . thymo*) explicit only to an *English* reader and apparently suggested to the poet by the tag *carpe diem*.

72   *but with*   except by means of.

ON A DROP OF DEW

First published in the Folio, *On a Drop of Dew*, with *Ros* – its Latin counterpart – is assumed like *The Garden* with its Latin companion piece to date from Marvell's residence at Nun Appleton. It is an ingeniously extended descriptive poem in irregular form which makes an explicit comparison with the soul in ll. 19–26 and, as a result of its suggestive language, achieves an implicit comparison throughout. As with *Hortus* (*The Garden*), the Latin (see Appendix, p. 208) is more expansive, the diction more erotic; for example, the equivalent in Latin of 'the blowing roses' of l. 3 is 'The flowers stand opened in solicitous desire'. In some ways the Latin counterpart serves to sharpen our sense of the English.

1   *orient*   sparkling, as a pearl, hence pearl-like.

3   *blowing*   blossoming.

5   *For*   in favour of.

6   *Round . . . incloses*   roundly closes within itself.

8   *as it can*   so far as it can.

13   *Like its own tear*   Cf:

Each ruby there,
Or pearl that dare appear,
Be its own blush, be its own tear
(Crashaw, *Wishes. To His [Supposed] Mistress*, ll. 52–4).

24   *recollecting*   (a) re-collecting and (b) recalling (in allusion to the doctrine of reminiscence, the Platonic notion that the soul recovers knowledge which it had intuitively known in a former incorporeal existence).

26   *The greater heaven in an heaven less*   the greater . . . in a lesser heaven; cf. *Upon Appleton House*, l. 44.

27–36   *In how coy a figure . . . bend*   See ll. 35–42 of *Ros* and translation for a more explicit rendering of these lines.

27   *coy*   modest.

29   *the world excluding round*   (a) excluding the round world; (b) the world round (about it).

34   *girt*   prepared.

37   *manna's sacred dew*   alluding to the miraculous food provided for the Israelites in the wilderness which fell along with the dew (Ex. xvi; see also *Daphnis and Chloe*, ll. 78–80, and *Upon Appleton House*, ll. 406–8).

A DIALOGUE BETWEEN THE SOUL AND BODY

If it is linked with Marvell's other examples, this dialogue could date from any time between 1645 and 1652, though probably late rather than early in the period since it contrasts markedly with the countering *Dialogue between the Resolved Soul and Created Pleasure* in terms of intellectual and poetical compression; it was first published in the Folio. The irregularity of the form (three stanzas of ten lines followed by one of fourteen) has led some critics to doubt that the poem, as we have it, is complete; in *Eng. poet. d. 49* the unidentified corrector has crossed out the last four lines and added the notation *Desunt multa* to indicate, in his view, its incomplete state. (In the same manner the unidentified editor of the Folio indicated his view that lines – equivalent to stanzas 5–8 – were missing in *Hortus* by adding a similar notation.)

Deriving from the medieval débat, this lyric differs from characteristic examples in that Marvell focuses not on the question of the superiority of one participant to the other but on their mutually inhibiting capacities. He achieves this focus by a liberal use of paradoxes ('blinded with an eye') and verbal and syntactical puns ('vain head'; 'this ill spirit it possessed', where the words can serve different grammatical functions) as well as by a persistent transposing of normal word order to accord with the transposition of attributes proper to each participant (the Soul 'constrained . . . to endure / Diseases'; the Body perplexed by joy and vexed by sorrow).

For an account of the contemporary intellectual issues involved, see Kitty Scoular Datta, 'New Light on Marvell's *A Dialogue between the Soul and Body*', *RQ* XXII (1969), 242–55.

3–4   *that fettered stands | In feet, and manacled in hands*   who stands fettered in having feet and manacled in having hands. The root meaning of each of the verbals implies its attribute (fettered-foot, manacled-hand), so that the statement is a kind of tautology.

10   *vain*   (a) empty; (b) futile; and (c) conceited.

   double   characterized by duplicity, but it also suggests the physical aspect of double ventricles.

11–18   *O, who shall me deliver whole | From bonds of this tyrannic soul | Which . . . | Has made me live to let me die*   A transposing of Rom. vii 24: 'O wretched man that I am! who shall deliver me from the body of this death?'

14   *That mine own precipice I go*   in that I may make my own headlong fall (since the soul has caused the body to walk erect).

15   *needless*   not in want.

24   *I feel . . . the pain*   perceive.

34 *And then the palsy shakes of fear* a bold (if awkward) inversion with the modifier separated from its noun; cf. 'cramp of hope does tear' and 'pestilence of love does heat'.

43–4 *So architects do square and hew, | Green trees* Cf. Marvell's use of similar diction in a passage of prose – 'men, instead of squaring their governments by the rule of Christianity, have shaped Christianity by the measure of their government ... and bungling divine and human things together, have been always hacking and hewing one another, to frame an irregular figure of political incongruity' (*An Account of the Growth of Popery, and Arbitrary Government in England*, 1677, Grosart, IV, 281).

THE MOWER AGAINST GARDENS

The four Mower poems were first published in the Folio. While individually accenting different aspects of rural life, they are linked by milieu and the central figure and should perhaps be linked in time of composition, which is generally assumed to be during Marvell's tenure at Nun Appleton.

In treating the popular Renaissance topic of nature versus art (represented by horticulture as in Perdita's speech in *The Winter's Tale*, IV. 4. 79–100), Marvell may have used as his point of departure a seduction lyric by Thomas Randolph entitled *Upon Love Fondly Refused for Conscience' Sake*, editions in 1638, 1640, 1645, and 1652 (Frank Kermode, 'Two notes on Marvell' *N&Q* CXCVII [1952], 136–8, who reads Marvell's poem as a refutation of Randolph's). Here are found several notions that reappear in *The Mower against Gardens*: enclosures represent the invention of man (cf. ll. 1–8); the issue of man's sovereignty (cf. ll. 19–20); and the gardener's practice of grafting and inoculation relating to the art of husbandry (cf. ll. 9–30). Further, both poems have the same pattern of rhymed couplets of ten and eight syllables, which is a pattern Marvell used only on this occasion, and both poems use a diction marked by sexual overtones.

1 *Luxurious* voluptuous;
bring his vice in use (a) bring into practice; (b) establish as a custom.

5 *gardens square* a characteristic inversion of noun and adjective. The use of the plural pronoun in l. 7 and the plural nouns in the title and l. 38 supports the plural reading here (contrary to some editors who print 'garden's square').

6 *standing pool of air* A phrase used by Sir Henry Wotton in *The Elements of Architecture*, 1624, reprinted 1651 (M. Allentuck, 'Marvell's "Pool of Air"', *MLN* LXXIV, 1959, 587–9) and by James Howell in *Instructions for Foreign Travel*, 1642, reprinted 1650 (K. Datta, 'Marvell and Wotton: A Reconsideration', *RES* XIX, 1968, 403–5).

7 *luscious* (a) cloying; (b) voluptuous.

9 *The pink ... as double as his mind* a double bloom and a double-dealing mind. Cf. the 'double heart' in l. 10 of the *Dialogue between the Soul and Body*.

15 *onion root* bulb.

18 *Marvel of Peru* a flower of many colours from tropical America (*Mirabilis Jalapa*); the four o'clock.

21 *Had he not dealt between the bark and tree* proverbial for audacity and frequently applied in the seventeenth century to interference between man and wife (Tilley, H88).

22 *Forbidden mixtures* Legouis (*Andrew Marvell*, p. 43) refers this to the Mosaic law in Lev. xix 19 and Deut. xxii 9.

27 *seraglio* (a) enclosure and (b) Turkish palace.

30 *To procreate without a sex* vegetative propagation by grafting or budding (called *inoculation* as in *Hamlet*, Pelican, III, i, 117–18, '. . . virtue cannot so inoculate our old stock but we shall relish of it'; cf. Randolph's punning line, 'We may as well inoculate as plant').

31 *enforced* (a) constrained, in contrast with 'willing nature' in l. 33, and (b) ravished.

DAMON THE MOWER

Damon the Mower is in the ancient Theocritean tradition of the lovesick rustic represented by the complaint of the Cyclops Polyphemus for Galatea (*Idyl* XI) and its Virgilian derivative (*Ecl.* II). In the final stanzas Marvell adds sophisticated notions to the realistic scene.

9 *heats* in the plural, used for the hot season.

12 *hamstringed* disabled.

18 *Dog Star* Sirius in the constellation of the Greater Dog was supposed to cause excessive heat, giving rise to the 'dog-days'.
    inflame] inflame's *F*.

21 *mads*] *Eng. poet. d. 49*; made *F*. (as in *Richard II* V. v. 61, 'This music mads me'.)

22 *Phaëton* Offspring of the sun-god Helios and the nymph Clymene Phaëton set the world on fire when driving the chariot of the sun.

48 *cowslip-water* decoction made from cowslips and used medicinally.

54 *closes* enclosed fields.

57 *Nor am I so deformed* a reminiscence of Vergil's *nec sum adeo informis* (*Ecl.* II, 25).

79 *And there among the grass fell down* a play on the Biblical assertion 'All flesh is grass' (Isa. xl 6).

80 *By his own scythe, the Mower mown* The self-inflicted psychic wound of the lover becomes a literal wound.

83 *shepherd's-purse and clown's-all-heal* the *capsella bursa pastoris* or shep-
herd's bag and the *stachys palustris* or clown's-wound wort. The latter was so
named by the sixteenth-century herbalist John Gerard because of its efficacy
in healing a mower who had wounded himself with a scythe.

THE MOWER TO THE GLOWWORMS

Consisting of one sentence with three stanzas of apostrophes, *The Mower to the
Glowworms* may be indebted to Pliny's accounts of the glowworm, called
'the husbandman's star,' and the nightingale (see the translation of the *Natural*
History by Philemon Holland, 1635, bk. X, ch. 29; bk. XIX, ch. 27).

4 *Her matchless songs doth meditate* The verb *meditate* is perhaps intended
to recall Vergil's *Musam meditari* (*Ecl.* I, 2), though Pliny comments (in
Holland's translation) that 'the young nightingales study and meditate how
to sing.' Cf. Milton's similar usage in *Lycidas*, l. 66: 'And strictly meditate the
thankless Muse'.

9 *officious* (a) serving a useful office and (b) efficacious.

12 *foolish fires* (a) of love and (b) *ignes fatui* or will-o'-the-wisps.

THE MOWER'S SONG

The Mower's Song is the only instance of Marvell's use of a refrain, an alexan-
drine consisting entirely of monosyllables.

1 *survey* delineation.

3-4 *in the greenness...| Did see its hope's as in a glass* The colour green was
symbolic of hope.

19 *ought* owe.

26 *my thoughts more green* Cf. 'a green thought in a green shade', *The Garden*,
l. 48.

27-8 *the heraldry ... | With which I will adorn my tomb* Cf. the use of
heraldic depiction in *The Unfortunate Lover*, l. 64.
    will] Eng. poet. d. *49*; shall *F*.

MUSIC'S EMPIRE

As an example of the *laudes musicae* tradition, *Music's Empire* is an extended
metaphor, presenting the origin and progress of music in terms of a developing
sociol-political organization. First published in the Folio, its date of composi-
tion is uncertain. On the one hand, its subject matter links up with *The Fair
Singer* (perhaps dating from 1648 or 49), while l. 22, referring to a 'gentler
conqueror' echoes Marvell's tribute to the Lord General Fairfax in *Upon the*

Hill and Grove; this would suggest composition some time before 1652. On the other hand, in *The First Anniversary* (1654, printed 1655), Marvell presents the development of the Cromwellian state in terms of an extended musical conceit (ll. 45–74) which leads some critics to accept stanza 5 here as a tribute to the Protector rather than to Fairfax and a consequent later date of composition.

For accounts of the *laudes musicae* tradition, see James Hutton, 'Some English Poems in Praise of Music', *English Miscellany* II (1951), 1–63, and John Hollander, *The Untuning of the Sky: Ideas of Music in English Poetry, 1500–1700* (Princeton, 1961).

5 *Jubal* the inventor of musical instruments according to Gen. iv 21.

6 *tuned music's first jubilee* jubilee, a year of emancipation, proclaimed by the blast of trumpets; perhaps a mock pun in *Jubal – jubilee*.

first] *Eng. poet. d. 49*; *not in F* (eds. compensate by making *tuned* dissyllabic).

7 *sullen* gloomy.

9 *consort* (a) mate and (b) harmony.

15 *wire* stringed instruments.

18 *solemn* sacred.

20 *sphere* vault of heaven; Marvell thus excludes the music of the spheres so often invoked in the traditional *laus musicae* (see *The First Anniversary*, ll. 47–8).

23 *though he flies the music of his praise* Cf. 'That courage [Fairfax's] its own praises flies' (*Upon the Hill and Grove*, l. 76).

THE CHARACTER OF HOLLAND

Deane, Monck, and Blake (l. 150) served as Generals-at-Sea from November 1652 until the death of Deane in June 1653; Marvell's poem was written sometime during that period, probably, as Margoliouth suggested, a short time after 20 February 1653 when the English achieved a naval victory over the Dutch near Portland. Although it was anonymously published in part (ll. 1–100 plus an 8-line ending) in 1665, all copies of this edition seem to have disappeared; the satire becoming timely again, the same publisher brought out another edition in 1672. The full text appears in the Folio, though it is represented in variant states because of the cancellation of the following *Horatian Ode* from most copies.

2 *off-scouring* refuse.

5 *alluvion* inundation.

15 *those pills which sordid beetles roll* The tumble-dung beetle forms pills of dung about its eggs and rolls them into a hole.

19–20 *to the stake a struggling country bound, | Where barking waves still bait the forcèd ground* The imagery relates to bearbaiting.

21 *watery Babel* Probably stressing two aspects of the story (Gen. xi 1–9): (a) the presumption of the builders and (b) their lack of success because of the confusion of languages (see ll. 71–2). See *Upon Appleton House*, l. 24 and *The Loyal Scot*, l. 219 for other uses of the allusion.

26 *Mare Liberum* The title of a book by the Dutch jurist Hugo Grotius (1609) asserting the freedom of the seas; in claiming the right of dominion in British waters, the Commonwealth required foreign ships to salute (see 'vail', l. 107) the English flag.

28 *level-coil* a Christmas game in which each player is driven from his seat and supplanted by another (Fr. *lève-cul*).

32 *cabillau* codfish (Fr. *cabillaud*).

36 *duck and drake* a game of skipping stones.

43 *sees*] *Eng. poet. d. 49*; see *F*.

45 *leak* leaky.

48 *be magistrate*] *Eng. poet. d. 49*; be a magistrate *F*.

49 *dyke-grave* Dutch official in charge of sea-walls.

52 *Commission of the Sewers* officials in charge of maintaining ditches, dikes, banks, etc.

53 *Half-anders* not *Holl-anders* (whole-anders).

62 *Poor-John* dried salt fish.

65–6 *their Margaret, that laid down | For Hans-in-Kelder of a whole Hans-town* A Dutch countess reputedly had 365 children at one delivery, *Hans-in-Kelder* unborn child (Dutch)

Hans-town member of the Hanseatic League.

78 *chose a village* the Hague, which did not become a town until the time of Napoleon.

80 *Hogs, as all their subjects Bores* *Hoog-mogoden* 'high and mighty', the title used by the States-General (with a pun).

Bores punning on (a) Boers and (b) boars.

82 *Civilis* a Batavian leader who fought against the Romans, AD 69.

86 *chafing-dish* The Dutch carried stoves to church.

88 *a*] *1672*; not in *F*.

90 *western end* posterior, antedating the first instance cited in the *OED*.

95 *towns of Beer* punning on the common prefix *bier*.

96 *snick and sneer* for *snick and snee*, thrust and cut.

98 *Cut out each other's Athos to a man* carve each other's bulk into a human form, as an ancient sculptor proposed to carve Mount Athos into a representation of Alexander. Cf. ''Twas the Mount Athos carved in shape of man/ (As 'twas designed by the Macedonian)' (Cleveland, *To Prince Rupert*, 1647, ll. 109–10).

107 *vail* salute by lowering the flag; here countervail; in May 1652 Dutch ships had refused to salute the English in their own waters on two occasions, constituting a breach of sea-custom which initiated the long struggle between the two nations.

113 *Jus Belli & Pacis* alluding to a second work by Grotius entitled *Concerning the Law of War and Peace* (1625).

114 *burgomaster of the sea* Admiral Van Tromp.

115 *brand wine* brandy, a drink, according to a contemporary, 'very brisk' in the Dutch fleet even when wind or wine was lacking.

116 *linstock* staff designed to hold a lighted match.

120 *case-butter shot . . . bullet-cheese* canisters of small shot made of butter and bullets made of cheese.

123 *kindly* in accord with her nature.

124 *A wholesome danger drove us to our ports* (litotes). In November 1652 the Dutch inflicted a severe loss on the English in the Downs.

127 *That ours . . . at leisure might careen* The fleet was reinforced during the next few months before the expected return of the Dutch.

130 *Till the dear halcyon hatch out all its nest* It was believed that a short period of calm (halcyon days) occurred during the winter solstice to allow the halcyon (kingfisher) to nest.

133–4 *that very agitation laves | And purges* As a result of the November defeat, an inquiry into the action was instituted with subsequent discharge of certain of the officers.

135 *Bucentore* the state-galley (*Bucentaur*) used in the yearly celebration of the marriage of Venice and the sea.

136 *their*] *F* (*most copies*), *Eng. poet. d. 49*; the *F* (*Htn copy*); ll. 135–44 stress the contrast between *our* and *their*.

137 *now*] *Eng. poet. d. 49*; *how F*.
   their] *F* (*Htn. copy*), *Eng. poet. d. 49*; the *F* (*most copies*).
   hydra of seven provinces the multi-headed monster of the United Provinces of the Netherlands; the destruction of the hydra constituted Hercules' second labour.

138 *our infant Hercules* apparently alluding to the trial of naval strength in February 1653, when under the command of Deane, Monck, and Blake, the English gained a decisive victory over the Dutch.

139 *wants its vainly stretchèd neck* lacks its (a) futilely and (b) arrogantly extended neck (as a result of the English victory).

143–4 *Unless our Senate, lest their youth disuse | The war, (but who would?) peace, if begged, refuse* This difficult clause perhaps means 'Unless our Senate, for fear that their youth should discontinue the exercise of war, refuse peace if begged (but who would do so?)'. Marvell appears to be alluding (a) to the fact that *after* their defeat in the First Punic War, the Carthaginians then consented to negotiate a peace (ll. 141–2) and (b) to the current division within Parliament of a pro- and an anti-war party.

BERMUDAS

First published in the Folio, this psalmic and descriptive lyric was presumably composed sometime after July 1653 when Marvell went to Eton to assume a position as tutor to William Dutton, later a ward of Cromwell's. There he lodged in the house of the Puritan divine John Oxenbridge, a Fellow of Eton College, who in 1634 had been persecuted by Archbishop Laud (alluded to in l. 12) and had made two trips to the Bermudas. Thus Marvell could have had a firsthand account of the locale; he also seems to have known Waller's mock-epic *The Battle of the Summer Islands*, 1645 (as the Bermudas were sometimes called after the shipwreck there of Sir George Somers in 1609), and perhaps, as Margoliouth suggests, Captain John Smith's *The General History of Virginia, New England and the Summer Isles*, 1624.

7 *an isle so long unknown* the Bermudas were discovered in 1515 by Juan Bermudez.

9 *the huge sea-monsters wracks* apparently alluding to 'the dreadful fight' in Waller's poem between the Bermudans and two stranded whales.

15 *fowl*] *Eng. poet. d. 49*; fowl's *F*. Cf. the use of the singular 'orange' in l. 17.

17–28 *He hangs in shades* .... Cf. Waller I. 6–11:

That happy island where huge lemons grow,
And orange trees, which golden fruit do bear,
The Hesperian garden boasts of none so fair;
Where shining pearl, coral and many a pound,
On the rich shore, of ambergris is found.
The lofty cedar, which to heaven aspires,
The prince of trees! is fuel for their fires.

20 *Ormus* Hormuz, on the Persian Gulf.

23 *apples* pineapples.

28 *Proclaim* make known.
    ambergris the musky secretion of the sperm whale, called 'sea-born amber' in *Upon Appleton House*, (l. 180), and described in *The Gallery* (ll. 37–8) as a mass borne in on the rolling wave.

A LETTER TO DOCTOR INGELO

A Fellow of Eton, Nathaniel Ingelo accompanied Bulstrode Whitlocke, Ambassador Extraordinary, to the court of Queen Christina in the fall of

1653. Marvell had apparently met Ingelo shortly before his departure (see l. 2) and written him the epistle so that he might show it to the Queen, taking the occasion not only to commend Christina but also Cromwell and the political alliance (see ll. 97–104). The successful mission returned to London in July 1654; in 1658 Ingelo received the degree of D.D. from Oxford.

See W. Hilton Kelliher ('Marvell's A Letter to Doctor Ingelo', *RES* XX, 1969, 50–57) for an account of an eighteenth-century partial printing which may derive from the copy the ambassador showed to Queen Christina.

21 *mundi melioris ab ortu*   that is, from the beginning of the Christian era.

32 *nympha* Parrhasis (also called Callisto), an attendant of Diana, was seduced by Zeus who changed her into a bear and ultimately into the constellation Ursa Major.

36 *Delia*   a surname of Diana from her birthplace in Delos.

37 *Triviae*   a surname of Diana from her function of presiding over places where three roads met.

43–4 *nympharum . . . perque nives*   recalling *Aeneid* I, 498–501 and Ovid, *Metamorphoses* III, 182.
>   *Cynthi*   a mountain of Delos.
>   *perque*] *Cooke* +; *per F.*

48 *fovet*] *Grosart* +; *foret F.*

49–50 *Alcides . . . pelle Nemaea | . . . orbis onus*   After slaying the Nemean lion – his first labour – Hercules clothed himself in its skin; in quest of the apples of the Hesperides – his eleventh labour – he undertook for a time to hold up the heavens.

55 *chlamys*   short mantle.

57 *tribus spernat . . . certare deabus*   alluding to the judgement of Paris as to whether Juno, Minerva, or Venus was the fairest; to ensure her selection, Juno offered Paris the promise of a kingdom, Minerva intellectual and military renown – prizes which Queen Christina, according to the poet, already bears away though she scorns the bribe of love which Venus proffered.

74 *geminis . . . sonis*   Latin and Swedish.

81 *lacte . . . melle*   as in the Promised Land (Ex. iii 8).

82 *Salam*   located about forty miles from Upsala.

83 *Upsalides Musae . . .*   recalling Vergil's *Ecl.* IV, 1: *Sicelides Musae, paulo maiora canemus.*

92 *virgo Volsiniensis*   alluding to the drowning of St Christina in Lake Bolsena in AD 278.

97 *ille*] *Cooke* +; *illa F.*

99 *aquilam*   symbolizing the Holy Roman Empire.

100 *lupam*   symbolizing Rome and the Catholic Church.

105 *senior . . . Godfredus*   Godfrey of Bulloigne whose exploits in beseiging Jerusalem are recorded in Tasso's epic which Edward Fairfax, a relative of the Lord General's, had translated in 1600.

106 *Spina . . . comis*   Godfrey refused a crown of gold, as Cromwell was to do, and accepted a crown of thorns (Margoliouth); *canis . . . comis*, as Grosart points out, plays on the name of the ambassador Whitlocke.

132 *Rogerio*   Benjamin Rogers, a musician patronized by Ingelo who presented Queen Christina with some of his compositions.

IN EFFIGIEM OLIVERI CROMWELL

This epigram on Cromwell's portrait (*umbra*) is to be linked with the verses immediately following. See below.

IN EANDEM [EFFIGIEM OLIVERI CROMWELL]
REGINAE SUECIAE TRANSMISSAM

As the title indicates, these lines were intended as a companion piece to the preceding epigram and were occasioned by the portrait of Cromwell sent to the Queen of Sweden as a consequence of the treaty of alliance between England and Sweden signed at Upsala, 28 April 1654. Although they have sometimes been assigned to Milton, they were included in the Folio and again in *Chorus Poetarum* edited by Charles Gildon, 1694 (misdated 1674), where they are attributed to Marvell and 'Englished' by Sir F. S. whose translation follows the Latin text. Two manuscript copies (*B M Add. 32096* and *34362*) also ascribe the poem to Marvell. The picture itself (*umbra*, l. 7) is the persona of the poem.

THE FIRST ANNIVERSARY OF THE GOVERNMENT UNDER
HIS HIGHNESS THE LORD PROTECTOR, 1655

The First Anniversary was published anonymously in a quarto pamphlet in January 1655 in celebration of Cromwell's first anniversary as Protector which fell on 16 December 1654; although it was then reprinted in the Folio directly from the quarto, it was cancelled from most copies (but not from the British Museum's or Huntington's). In 1707 it appeared in *Poems on Affairs of State*, IV, where, however, it carries the ascription 'supposed to be written by Edmund Waller of Beaconsfield Esquire and printed in 1655'. Thompson then included it in his Addenda to volume 3, along with Marvell's other two poems on Cromwell which were also cancelled from most copies of the Folio.

A seventeenth-century manuscript (*Bod. MS. Eng. poet e. 4*), as well as *B M Burn. 390* ascribes its composition to Waller, but its appearance in the Folio and its insertion in manuscript within the printed portion of *Eng. poet. d. 49* is a sufficient guarantee of Marvell's authorship. Since there are some dubious readings in the quarto, followed by the Folio, it is questionable whether he saw the 1655 edition through the press.

The occasional nature of the poem is indicated in its title. John M. Wallace (*Destiny His Choice*, pp. 106–44) argues that instead of panegyric it comes within the category of a deliberative oration intended as an argument for Cromwell's accepting the crown and establishing a new dynasty of kings, while Joseph A. Mazzeo (*Renaissance and Seventeenth-Century Studies*, Columbia University Press, 1964, pp. 183–208) stresses its theme as that of Davidic King. Treating in the main both foreign and domestic affairs, the poem falls into seven divisions: ll. 1–48 celebrating Cromwell's vigour; ll. 49–116 his building of a harmonious state; ll. 117–58 the millennium delayed because of man's sin; ll. 159–220 the coaching incident; ll. 221–92 the answers to charges of Cromwell's abuse of power; ll. 293–324 the attack on the Fifth Monarchists; and ll. 325–402 the reaction of foreign princes.

title] *varies slightly*; F reads under O.C.

1 *curlings* undulations.

12 *the jewel of the yearly ring* the sun and the zodiacal circle; the analogy with the sun utilizes the conventional imagery of kingship.

14 *one year the work of ages acts* Cf. the different view ('ruin the great work of time') set forth in the *Horatian Ode*, ll. 34–6.

17 *Platonic years* Estimated at 26,000 to 36,000 solar years, the Platonic Year was to see the completion of the cycle of heavenly bodies at which time a new cycle would begin (*tempus recurret*). See *Timaeus* 39D.

20 *China clay* It was popularly believed that the preparation of Chinese porcelain entailed its being buried for a long period. Cf. the *Elegy . . . of My Lord Francis Villiers*, ll. 31–2.

21 *to*] *1655* +; on Eng. poet. d. 49, Th.

23–4 *some more active for a frontier town, Taken by proxy, beg a false renown* If active, a king may secure renown, though falsely, since the capture of a fortified area (frontier town) is due to the efforts of others (see l. 27).
    Taken by proxy, beg] Eng. poet. e. 4; Took in by proxy, begs *1655* +.

33–4 *They neither build the temple . . . | Nor matter for succeeding founders raise* recalling the fact that though God had elected Solomon to build the temple, King David by example and entreaty caused the people to offer contributions to it (I Chron. xxviii–xxix).

38 *of*] Th.; and *1655* +.

41 *image-like* as mechanical figures on a clock.
    an] *1655* +; and F.

47–8 *Learning a music . . . | To tune this lower to that higher sphere* The Pythagorean notion of the music of the spheres (as set forth in Plato's *Timaeus* 47B and *Republic* X. 617B) results from their ordered revolutions; by imitating that proportion, man, it was asserted, could regain from the *harmonia mundi* a comparable harmony (*musica humana*) within his soul and within the state.

49–56 *Amphion did the lute command, | Which the god gave him*   Given a golden lyre by the god Hermes, Amphion erected the walls of Thebes by causing the stones to respond to the tone of his instrument.

55   *stone was*] *Eng. poet. e. 4*; story *1655* +.

60   *joining*] *1655* +; joying *F*.

68   *ruling Instrument*   with a pun on the Instrument of Government which established the Protectorate in 1653.

69   *tedious statesmen many years did hack*   The reference is to the attempt in the previous years to frame a suitable constitution.
   hack   (a) to break a note in music and (b) to chop.

89–90   *The crossest spirits . . . take their part, Fastening the contignation*   The opposing tensions make for the strength of the walls just 'as with arches' (l. 96). Marvell is alluding to the 'mixed state' which incorporates opposing interests.
   contignation   frame.

93   *most equal*   an oxymoron.

99–100   *for his foot . . . a place had found, | He hurls . . . the world about him*   Archimedes is reported to have said that given a place for his foot, he could move the earth.

102   *in war*] *Eng. poet. e. 4*; a war *1655* +.

106   *Kiss the approaching, not yet angry Son*   recalling 'Be wise now therefore, O ye kings. . . . Kiss the Son lest he be angry, and ye perish from the way, when his wrath is kindled but a little' (Ps. ii 10–12).
   not] *Eng. poet. e. 4*; nor *1655* +.

110   *The great designs . . . for the latter days*   apocalyptic allusions to a Fifth Monarchy and the reigning of the Saints (Dan. vii 28) in the latter days (Dan. x 14).

113   *the whore*   of Babylon (Rev. xvii 5), identified with the Church of Rome.

115–16   *Indians . . . the Jew*   The millennium was to usher in a unity of nations; with this in mind Cromwell proposed in 1656 to readmit Jews to England.

116   *Nor*] *1655* +; Not *Eng. poet. d. 49, Th.*

123   *prevents the east*   anticipates the dawn.

125   *hollo*   call the hounds.

128–30   *the monster . . . Gnashes her gory teeth*   the scarlet-coloured Beast of the Apocalypse (Rev. xvii 3).

133   *still*   always.

140   *latest day*   the Day of Judgement.

151–2   *the dragon's tail | Swinges the volumes of its horrid flail*   recalling Milton's 'The old dragon . . . | Swinges [whips] the scaly horror of his folded tail' (*Ode on the Morning of Christ's Nativity*, ll. 168–72) and Rev. xii 3–4.

153–4 *did first suspend | The world* during the flood, see l. 157.

156 *the elected* Cf. the allusion to this doctrine in *Upon the Death of the Lord Hastings*, ll. 37–8.

161–2 *Whose saint-like mother . . . did. . . . Live out an age* Cromwell's mother Elizabeth died 16 November 1654 at the age of ninety-four.

166 *Yet*] *Eng. poet. e. 4*; But *1655* +.

171 *poniarding conspiracies* Various plots led by extremists such as the Levellers were directed at Cromwell.

175 *How near* by how little.

177–8 *Our brutish fury . . . | Hurried thy horses* on 29 September 1654, Cromwell, driving his own coach and six great horses in Hyde Park, overturned and narrowly escaped death; Marvell accounts for the incident on the basis of the sins of the people.

184 *purling ore* thread made of twisted gold or silver used for embroidery.

201–4 *Thou, Cromwell, falling . . .* This passage picks up the *topos*, standard in pastoral poetry, of nature grieving at an individual's plight. (See, for example, Virgil's *Ecl.* V, 20–28.)

203 *panic* as if derived from Greek πᾶν 'all'.

215–18 *But thee . . . the fiery car, And fiery steeds had borne . . . | Unto the kingdom blest* recalling the translation to heaven of the prophet Elijah, honoured for his moral righteousness and social justice, and the subsequent succession of the kingdom to his son Elisha (II Kings ii 11–15).

233–4 *at the seventh time thou . . . | As a small cloud, like a man's hand, didst rise* recalling Elijah's action in obtaining rains for Israel under King Ahab – 'And it came to pass at the seventh time, that [Elijah's servant] said, "Behold, there ariseth a little cloud out of the sea, like a man's hand" ' (I Kings xviii 44).

240 *yet*] *Eng. poet. e. 4*; it *1655* +. The reading 'yet' stresses the paradoxical elements.

249–54 *When Gideon . . . durst suppress, | With thorns and briars of the wilderness* alluding to Gideon's delivery of Israel with only 300 men from the Midianite invasion led by the two kings Zeba and Zalmunna; because of their refusal to supply food to his hungry men, Gideon on his return razed the tower of Penuel and tore the flesh of the Elders of Succoth with 'thorns of the wilderness and with briars' (Judges viii, ix).

256 *Yet would not he be Lord, nor yet his son* 'I [Gideon] will not rule over you, neither shall my son rule over you: the Lord shall rule over you' (Judges viii 23).

257–62 *Thou . . .| Didst (like thine olive) still refuse to reign . . .* recalling the parable of Jotham (Gideon's son) – when the olive, the fig, and the vine refused the crown, the fruitless bramble accepted, saying, 'If in truth ye anoint me king over you, then come and put your trust in my shadow: and if not, let fire come out of the bramble, and devour the cedars of Lebanon, (Judges ix 7–15).

262 *levelled* alluding to exponents of an egalitarian system (the Levellers; cf. *Upon Appleton House*, l. 450).

269 *Tritons* sea deities or monsters.

270 *corposants* balls of light seen on the mast or yard-arm of ships, also called St Elmo's Fire.
  tackling] *Eng. poet. e. 4*; tacklings *1655* +.

275 *artless* unskilful.

281 *bounders* limits.

283 *like Noah's eight* Cromwell's family at this date included his wife, two sons, and four daughters; Noah's 'eight' included his wife, his three sons and their wives.

286 *wouldst*] *1655* +; would *F*.

286–8 *thou . . . not drunken with its wine* in contrast to Noah (Gen. ix 21–2) who in drunkenness revealed himself in his nakedness (see ll. 291–2).

293 *Chammish* like Ham, the second son of Noah and progenitor of Nimrod.

297 *the fifth sceptre* that of the Fifth Monarchists who opposed Cromwell; two of their leaders – Feake and Simpson in l. 305 – had been imprisoned in 1654 on charges of sedition.

300 *so one were ten* provided each heresy could be equalled with ten soldiers.

302 *their religion . . . is to fall* with epilepsy (*morbus caducus* or *divus*), which Mahomet supposedly experienced during his revelations (see ll. 303–4).

307 *their rant* apparently alluding to the sect called Ranters (as *quake*, l. 298, probably alludes to the Quakers).

308 *tulipant* turban. Mohammedans, as well as Quakers, refused to remove their hats.

310 *Alcoraned* made into an inspired book (the Koran), a nonce use.

311–12 *Accursèd locusts . . . of the unbottomed pit* recalling the creatures from the bottomless pit, presided over by King Abaddon (called Apollyon in Greek), who were to torture men lacking the seal of God on their foreheads (Rev. ix).

313 *Munster's*] *Eng. poet. e. 4*; Munser's *1655* +. This city in Westphalia was taken over in the early sixteenth century by the Anabaptists; contemporary sectarians represent their 'dregs'.

316 *points and lace* for fastening hose (as in l. 49 in *On Mr Milton's 'Paradise Lost'*).

319 *act the Adam and the Eve* by going naked, like the Adamites.

325–42 *So when the first man did . . . | See the bright sun . . .* This allusion to how the first man reacted to the setting of the sun is traced back to Lucretius (V. 973–6) and Statius (IV. 282–4) by E. E. Duncan-Jones ('Marvell, Johnson, and the First Sunset', *TLS*, 3 April 1959, p. 193).

350   *both wars*   the Civil Wars and that with the Dutch in 1652–4.

352   *their*] Eng. poet. e. 4; our *1655* +.

355–6   *their fowl proceed | Of shedding leaves*   the notion of the equivocal generation of Solan geese was that they came from certain kinds of leaves which had fallen into water.

362   *brazen hurricanes*   bronze cannons.

366   *watery leaguers*   besiegers by sea.

374   *oak, and . . . treble brass*   recalling the *robor et aes triplex* of Horace's *Ode to Vergil* (I, 3, 9).

377   *in the day . . . in late night*] Eng. poet. e. 4; all the day . . . in late nights *1655* + (*all* clearly picked up from the preceding line).

381   *enchased*   inlaid.

391   *O*] *1655* +; or Eng. poet. d. 49. Th.

392   *that*] Eng. poet. e. 4; yet *1655* +.

398   *So that we both alike may miss our end*   provided that the foreign prince's hope (l. 392) fall as short of its goal as does the poet's praise.

402   *Troubling the waters, yearly mak'st them heal*   Echoing the phrase 'healing and settling' which Cromwell had used in the opening of his first Parliament.

UPON AN EUNUCH: A POET

This epigrammatic piece plays on the notion of the productive eunuch-poet; there is no evidence for its date of composition, but it was published in the Folio labelled 'Fragment'.

4   *monte*   either Pindus, Parnassus, or Helicon, all sacred to the Muses.

5   *modulos . . . nepotes*   verses.

THE SECOND CHORUS FROM SENECA'S TRAGEDY 'THYESTES'

Though first published in the Folio, copies of Marvell's translation appear in *BM Add. MS 29921* and *(Bodleian) Rawl. poet. 90 and 196*. The original consists of thirteen verses; in view of Marvell's revision of l. 2, it is interesting to compare the first few lines of Cowley's version (1668), which requires twenty-six lines to render, and Sir Matthew Hale's (1676), which requires twenty-two lines, with Marvell's.

Upon the slippery tops of human state,
  The gilded pinnacles of fate,
Let others proudly stand, and for a while
  The giddy danger to beguile,
With joy and with disdain look down on all. . . .
Cowley, *Works*, 1684, p. 97.

Let him that will, ascend the tottering seat
Of courtly grandeur, and become as great
As are his mounting wishes; as for me,
Let sweet repose and rest my portion be. . . .

Contemplations Moral and Divine, p. 285.

2 *Giddy favour's slippery hill*] *Eng. poet d. 49*; Tottering favour's pinnacle *F*.

IN THE FRENCH TRANSLATION OF LUCAN...

The passage from Georges de Brebeuf's translation of the *Pharsalia* (1655) which Marvell renders into Latin points up the popular *topos* of *ut pictura poesis*.

The first translation is by Sir Philip Meadows (who in 1653 received the appointment as Latin Secretary to Cromwell which Milton had requested for Marvell) and appears in manuscript in *Eng. poet. d. 49* following the French (which it corrects on several counts).

  title Lib 3] *Eng. poet. d. 49*; *not in F*.

1 *luy* the Phoenician who invented the alphabet.

7 *Conspicuamque ... charta*] *Eng. poet. d. 49*; *Et mentem chartis, oculis impertiit aurem F*; the translators render this: And he transferred thought to paper, hearing to the eyes.

AN EPITAPH UPON —

This epitaph on an unidentified person was first published in the Folio.

4 *When dead to offer were unkind* When she is dead, to offer courtly compliments would be unkind.

14 *No minute but it came and went* (presumably) on wings of prayer.

ON THE VICTORY OBTAINED BY BLAKE OVER THE SPANIARDS... 1657

Composition of this congratulatory poem to Cromwell, on the occasion of Admiral Robert Blake's remarkable victory at Santa Cruz (20 April), may be dated fairly precisely, that is between 28 May, when Blake's account reached England, and 10 August, when the news of his death three days earlier arrived.

Initial publication seems to have been in 1674 when John Bulteel included it without indication of authorship in *A New Collection of Poems and Songs* (reprinted 1678), but the indirect allusions to Cromwell were further disguised (for example, l. 14, 'you' becomes 'we') and ll. 39–52, extolling his imperialism, omitted. The Folio is thus the source for the original version; curiously, the poem (as with *Thyrsis and Dorinda* which follows it) is not represented in *Eng. poet. d. 49* either in printed or manuscript form.

title On the Victory over the Spaniards in the Bay of Santa Cruz, in the island of Tenerife *1674*.

4 *Freighted with . . . guilt, and guilt to come* with the (inevitable) pun on *gilt*; the Spanish fleet consisted of sixteen treasure ships returning from the West Indies.

25 *One* Tenerife, conspicuous by its peak (ll. 75–80) shaped like a 'sugar loaf' or 'Greek omega'.

40 *The best of lands. . . the best of kings* Cf. *The First Anniversary*, ll. 131–58.

47 *that league* The English and Spanish had been at peace from 1630 to 1655.

54 *of the gods the fancied drink* nectar.

64 *guilty* punning, as in l. 4.

66 *your present* 'conquests' understood.

117 *Bold Stayner* Captain Richard Stayner, Rear-admiral, led the attack on the Spanish ships (while Blake fought off the attack from the six or seven forts on shore); he was knighted by Cromwell on 11 June.

117–18 *this fleet's designed by fate | To give him laurel, as the last did plate* The victory at Santa Cruz added to the prestige of the English navy, but it provided no prize money in contrast with Stayner's earlier capture (in September 1656) of Spanish ships.

129 *aspire*] *1674*; a spire *F*.

TWO SONGS AT THE MARRIAGE OF THE LORD FAUCONBERG
AND THE LADY MARY CROMWELL

Marvell wrote these two occasional poems, cast in the form of pastoral dialogues, to celebrate the marriage, on 19 November 1657, of Cromwell's third daughter to Thomas Belasyse, second Viscount Fauconberg. In the first, Endymion represents the bridegroom, Cynthia the bride, and, inevitably, Jove (ll. 53–8) Cromwell himself. In the second, the bride and groom are alluded to under the pastoral guise of Damon and Marina. Both were first published in the Folio.

First Song

30–32 *Anchises was a shepherd too.* . . . Anchises (father of Aeneas) consorted with Venus on Mount Ida, but the topical allusion here is to the marriage of Frances Cromwell to Robert Rich, grandson and heir of the Earl of Warwick on 11 November 1657.

35 *Latmus' top* site of the wooing of Endymion and Cynthia.

Second Song

26 *silly* innocent.

35–6 *lesser beauties . . . meaner virtues* Cf. the 'meaner beauties' of Sir Edward Wotton's famous lyric on the Queen of Bohemia.

43 *hire* reward.

A POEM UPON THE DEATH OF HIS LATE HIGHNESS
THE LORD PROTECTOR

On 3 September 1658 Cromwell died; on 18 October his effigy was placed on view; and on 23 November the public funeral was held. Composition of Marvell's funeral elegy may reasonably be assigned within this period. On 20 January 1659 the publisher Henry Herringman entered in the Stationers' Register the title of a volume to include elegiac poems by Marvell, Dryden, and Sprat; when the volume appeared, by another somewhat obscure publisher, Waller's already published elegy was used in place of Marvell's poem. Its first publication was in the Folio where it was then cancelled from all copies except for one in the British Museum which includes only lines 1–184. Thompson then published the full text, with the other two poems on Cromwell, in the Addenda to volume 3, using a copy-text which (despite Margoliouth's assertion to the contrary) is closer, as the textual notes evidence, to *Eng. poet. d. 49* (in manuscript) than it is to the printed portion in the Folio.

title] *Eng. poet. d. 49*, Th.; *A Poem upon the Death of O.C.F.*

21 *'signed* aphetic for assigned.

22 *kind*] *Eng. poet. d. 49*, Th.; *mind F.*

30 *Eliza* Cromwell's second daughter, the wife of John Claypole, had died less than a month earlier (6 August 1658), and Marvell accounts for the Lord Protector's non-heroic end (see ll. 7–12) on the basis of his grief for her (l. 88).

41 *in*] *Eng. poet. d. 49. Th; and F.*

45 *not knowing* that is, not by knowing.

48 *his*] *Eng. poet. d. 49*, Th.; *her F.*

52 *This* this one.

54 *his tortured image* the suffering Eliza, a likeness of himself; cf. l. 78 below.

62 *feigns* dissimulates (in contrast with l. 259).

63 *skills* knowledge.

67–8 *Eliza's purple locks were shorn, | Where she so long her Father's fate had worn* adapting the story of the purple (or golden) lock belonging to Nisus, King of Megara, on which his life depended; it was cut off by his daughter Scylla (when she became enamoured of an enemy of her father).

72 *hasting* A common form of the verb in Marvell; cf. *Flecknoe*, l. 167, and *To . . . Doctor Witty*, l. 33.

79–80 *mournful swans, | Of halcyons kind, or bleeding pelicans* alluding to the popular notions that swans sing their own funeral songs, that halcyons nest in calm seas in winter (symbolizing the mutual affection of Ceyx and Alcyone before their metamorphosis), and that pelicans feed their young with their own blood.

106 *hollow seas* as in *Bermudas*, l. 27.

108 *celebrates*] *Eng. poet. d. 49*, *Th.*; celebrate *F*.

109–32 *But never yet was any human fate . . .* The convulsive response of nature to the death of a great person is conventional; cf. the description in Virgil (*Georgics* I, 464–97) of the conditions obtaining when Caesar was assassinated. A storm raged the day before Cromwell's death, leading Waller to entitle his elegy *Upon the Late Storm and Death of His Highness Ensuing the Same* and others to say that the Devil had come to spirit him away.

121 *lead*] Grosart +; dead *Eng. poet. d. 49*, *F.*, *Th.*

124 *a*] *Eng. poet. d. 49*, *Th.*; an *F*.

129–30 *the elements . . . where so exactly mixed* Cf. the tribute to Brutus:

. . . and the elements
So mixed in him that Nature might stand up
And say to all the world, 'This was a man!'
(*Julius Caesar* V, v, 73–5).

132 *universe*] world with throes *Th.*; this is Thompson's one conspicuous textual difference from *Eng. poet. d. 49*.

137 *stars that for him fought* Cf. 'Cromwell . . . | Urgèd his active star' (*Horatian Ode*, ll. 9–12).

139 *cast* calculate.

143–6 *But this . . . | Twice . . . him victor crowned | . . . Dunbar | . . . and through deep Severn* Twice on 3 September (his eternizing and immortalizing day, ll. 147–8), Cromwell scored two notable victories – at Dunbar (1650) and Worcester (1651) where he had used bridges of boats to convey his soldiers across the Severn.

153–4 *his victorious ghost | Gave chase to Ligny* At this time the French and English were allied against Spain, and on 21 July, a day of thanksgiving had been observed celebrating the abasing of Spanish troops under the Prince de Ligne and deliverance from the plague (see ll. 127–8 above).

156 *laurel shade* as in 'victory laurels'. One would expect *palm*; see *The Garden*, l. 2 and n.

162 *those of Moses hid from human eyes* Though Moses was buried in the land of Moab, 'no man knoweth of his sepulchre unto this day' (Deut. xxxiv 6).

173–4 *... the Flandric shore | And stretched our frontier to the Indian ore* alluding to the capture of Dunkirk from the Spanish by a joint French and English effort (1658) and to the acquisition of the Island of Jamaica (1655).

177–8 *Arthur's deeds | ... the Confessor exceeds* King Arthur, one of the Nine Worthies; King Edward, called The Confessor, because of his piety.

179 *He*] *misprinted* The *in Th.*

187 *Preston's field* site of Cromwell's victory over the Scots in August 1648.

188 *impregnable Clonmel* Cromwell's ineffectual siege of this Irish city, in May, 1650, was the most disastrous military experience of his career though the Irish were nonetheless forced to evacuate it. He left immediately after this for England where his arrival occasioned the *Horatian Ode*.

189–90 *where the sandy mountain Fenwick scaled, | The sea between, yet hence his prayer prevailed* On 4 June 1658, Cromwell and the Council maintained a day of fasting and prayer for the Dunkirk enterprise (see l. 173 and n. above); on that day the English regiments successfully attacked the Spanish who held a ridge of sand dunes between the sea and the high road to Dunkirk (the Battle of the Dunes). Colonel Roger Fenwick was mortally wounded in the battle (Margoliouth) and Colonel George Fenwick at Dunkirk.

191–2 *What man was ever so ... obeyed | Since the commanded sun o'er Gibeon stayed* alluding to Joshua (x 13–14), when he caused the sun and the moon to stand still – 'there was no day like that before it, or after it, that the Lord harkened unto the voice of a man'. Cf. Marvell's submerged use of this allusion in *To His Coy Mistress*, ll. 45–6.

194 *still* always.

201 *does claim*] *misprinted* desclaime *in Th.*

202 *The first foundation of his house and name* Sir Thomas Cromwell (later Earl of Essex), a statesman under Henry VIII, virtually adopted his nephew Richard Williams who duly became Sir Richard Cromwell and the paternal great grandfather of the Protector.

219 *as*] *Eng. poet. d. 49*; so (repeated from the previous line) *in Th.*

229 *refuse*] *Eng. poet. d. 49*; refuge *Th.*

234 *It seemed Mars broke through Janus' double gate* that is, presaging war but intending peace; when the gate of the temple of Janus was opened, it was the signal for battle; when closed, it was a pledge of peace. Cf. *In Legationem Domini Oliveri St John*, l. 10.

242   *As ungirt David to the ark did dance*   an action symbolic of his enthusiasm for the Lord (2 Sam. vi 13-15).

245   *Francisca*   Cromwell's youngest daughter (Frances), who had married Robert Rich in 1657; see the first of *Two Songs*, ll. 30-32 and n.

259   *feign*   imagine.

261-2   *the sacred oak which shoots | To heaven ... and through earth its roots* echoing Virgil:

aesculus ... quae quantum vertice ad auras
aetherias, tantum radice in Tartara tendit (Georgics II, 291-2).

264   *honoured wreaths*   The garland of oak was the award for civic achievement (as in *The Garden*, l. 2, and *To His Noble Friend Mr Richard Lovelace*, l. 12).

269-70   *The tree erewhile foreshortened ...*   Cf. *Eyes and Tears*, ll. 5-6, and 273-4.

273   *fall. The eye*] *misprinted* full the eye *in Th.*

275   *seat*] *misprinted* state *in Th.*

287   *pitch*   height (to which a falcon soars); the language throughout the passage relates to the art of falconry.

305   *Richard*   On the day of his father's death, he was proclaimed Protector; he resigned the title in April 1659.

324   *He threats no deluge, yet foretells a shower*   Cf. the same image used of the father in *The First Anniversary*:

And down at last thou poured'st the fertile storm,
Which to the thirsty land did plenty bring (ll.236-7).

THE LAST INSTRUCTIONS TO A PAINTER

This vigorous satire surveys political and Parliamentary affairs during the year 1666-7 as a backdrop to an account of the shocking incursion of the Dutch fleet into the Medway in June, 1667. Including, as it does, an attack on Henry Hyde, Earl of Clarendon, the poem seems to have been written just before the Lord Chancellor was forced to step down from his post (see l. 926). He resigned the seals 30 August 1667; on 29 November he fled to France, a fact which is not mentioned; nor is there any mention of the Parliament which opened on 10 October and was soon astir over the question of impeaching him. Thus the date assigned to the poem in *Eng. poet. d. 49* – 4 September 1667 – is probably correct.

The satire was attributed to Marvell at its first (?) appearance in print in *The Third Part of the Collection of Poems on Affairs of State* (1689), where it is called *Marvell's Further Instructions to a Painter* (apparently because *Advice to a Painter to Draw the Duke by* had been attributed to him in *The First Part* of the *State Poems*), and in all subsequent editions. Here most of the eighty-odd persons referred to are identified only by initial and final letters of their names. In one section of the poem (ll. 649–96) recounting the death of Captain Archibald Douglas during the Dutch attack, the poet asserts that if his verse serves, he will propagate the hero's name, a promise presumably fulfilled in *The Loyal Scot* which (in ll. 15–62) incorporates the earlier lines practically unchanged. *The Last Instructions*, with the names supplied, was published again, together with *The Loyal Scot*, in a pamphlet lacking title page and hence date in the extant copy in the Free Library of Philadelphia, though the two poems are signed with Marvell's initials. It next appeared, attributed to Marvell, in the 1697 edition of the *State Poems*, where the lines on Captain Douglas are omitted, presumably because they reappear in *The Loyal Scot* which immediately follows it in that edition; the text there follows the same misreadings found in the undated pamphlet, adding some of its own, which suggests that it derives from the pamphlet.

Though the satire is included in the manuscript portion of *Eng. poet. d. 49* (with the names supplied in large letters), this fact in itself is not conclusive proof of authorship in that non-Marvellian satires, apparently found among his papers, were also copied. There is also a seventeenth-century manuscript copy of it in the Osborn Collection (*P V* VIII) at Yale which lacks attribution. Ll. 29–48 (a portrait of St Albans) is in *B M Add. M S. 18220*, entitled *A Libel Taken out of the Painter, upon H. Jermyn Earl of St Albans*.

The genre which is adopted, as the title indicates, is that of the Advice-to-a-Painter in which the poet's instructions to the artist serve as a framework on which to drape much disparate topical matter. Introduced into England with Thomas Higgon's translation (1658) of Gian Francesco Busenello's poem celebrating the victory of the Venetians over the Turks after prolonged fighting (alluded to in ll. 401–2), the device was picked up by Edmund Waller who used it to write an encomium on the Duke of York and to comment on the Dutch Wars, concluding with an envoy directed to the King (*Instructions to a Painter*, 1666). Others were quick to adopt his pattern but for the purposes of satire, the notion of *satura* (a medley) serving to justify a wide range of subject and tone. Such topical commentary, often of a scurrilous nature, was necessarily circulated anonymously.

The year 1667 saw a spate of such poems – the *Second* and the *Third Advice* appearing individually and then together with the *Fourth* and *Fifth* (along with *Clarendon's Housewarming* 'By an Unknown Author') in a collection carrying Sir John Denham's name on the title page, an attribution which has persistently been doubted. Reprinted in 1689, the four *Advices* were again ascribed to Denham; in 1697 they appeared in the *State Poems* with an entry in the Table of Contents reading 'said to be written by Sir John Denham but believed to be writ by Mr Milton', and on occasion they have been attributed to Marvell. Most recently George deF. Lord has attributed the *Second* and *Third Advice* to Marvell. (His arguments for doing so appear in the *B N Y P L* LXII, LXIII, 1958, 1959; Ephim G. Fogel set forth an opposing view in the latter volume; both reprinted in *Evidence for Authorship*, (ed. D. Erdman and E. G. Fogel.)

A bibliography of the genre is M. T. Osborne's *Advice-to-a-Painter Poems, 1638–1856*.

The use of circumstantial detail in *The Last Instructions* is in accord with the technique of the genre, but the numerous succinct allusions to the men and matters involved in the House of Commons' sessions in 1666–7 clearly reveal the author to have been a Member of Parliament (a fact, as Margoliouth observed, not revealed in any one of the other *Advices*). As a result, the account of these sessions which John Milward recorded in his *Diary* (ed. Caroline Robbins) furnishes useful interpretative material.

The poem has five main divisions with two digressions to provide variety in tone: (1) portraits and character sketches of members of the court and House of Commons (ll. 1–104); (2) the Parliamentary sessions of 1666–7 (ll. 105–522); the Dutch attack 10–15 June, 1667, which includes the lyrical description of De Ruyter's progress up the Thames and the heroical account of the death of Captain Douglas (ll. 523–760); the effect of the ignominious defeat on the Commons and the court, leading up to the vision which appears to Charles II (ll. 761–948); and the envoy to the King (ll. 949–90). The copy-text is *Eng. poet. d. 49* with names of contemporary persons italicized at their first occurrence. *FL* is the siglum for the printed text in the Free Library and *Osb* for Osborn *PV VIII*.

title London . . . *1667*] not in *1689*; September: 1667 *Osb.*; 1667 *FL*.

1 *After two sittings* . . . Since three sittings, as Margoliouth points out, were the usual number for 'limning' a portrait, it is not necessary to connect this poem with the *Second* and *Third Advices*.

4 *If 't*] *Osb.*, *FL.*; It *Eng. poet. d. 49*, *1689*.

6 *without a fleet can fight* The fleet was inactivated in May; in June the Dutch made their raid on the Thames and the Medway (see ll. 523–760).

10 *aly-roof* ceiling of an ale-house.

14 *As th' Indians, draw our luxury in plumes* See *Upon Appleton House*, l. 580, for another allusion to feather painting.

15 *score out our compendious fame* mark out our short fame.

16–18 *Hooke . . . the new comptroller . . . a tall louse brandish the white staff* Robert Hooke included in his *Micrographia* (1665) illustrations of objects seen under a microscope, among them a louse climbing along a human hair. The new Comptroller of the Household, who carried a white staff in symbol of his office, was Lord Clifford of Chudleigh; he and Marvell had been at odds since 1662 (Margoliouth).

19 *pencil* brush (as in *Upon the Hill and Grove*, l. 5).

21–6 *The painter so, long having vexed his cloth* . . . Pliny tells this story, illustrative of the coincidence of art and fortune, about Protagenes when he attempted to depict a heavily breathing dog; unable to render the nature of froth – 'the only mark he shot at' – despite his industry and skill, he hurled his sponge in anger at the painting and by chance achieved the desired effect (*Natural History* XXXV. 10, tr. P. Holland, 1634, p. 542).

29 *St Albans* Henry Jermyn, created the Earl of St Albans in 1660, served as ambassador at the French court; in January 1667 he was again sent to Louis XIV to negotiate the Treaty of Breda.

32 *salt* salacious.

35-6 *title of St Albans ... Bacon never studied nature more* In 1621 Sir Francis Bacon received the title of Viscount St Albans; in contrast to his successor he directed his attention to physical rather than human nature.

38 *treat* (a) entertain and (b) negotiate.

40 *disavowing treaty, asks supply* See ll. 123-4; the intent was to negotiate a secret peace though Parliament was asked to supply funds to carry on the war.

41 *St James's lease* In 1664 St Albans had received an extensive grant of land in Pall Mall.

42 *Whose breeches wear the instrument of peace* a scandalous allusion to his reputed affair with Queen Henrietta Maria with a play on 'wear the breeches'.
wear] *Eng. poet. d. 49*; were *1689* +.

45 *the Most Christian should trepan* that Louis XIV would cheat.

46 *St Germain, St Alban* playing on the ambassador's name and title (see n. to l. 29).

49 *Her Highness* Anne Hyde, daughter of the Lord Chancellor, had married the Duke of York in 1660 and given birth to a son two months after the ceremony (see ll. 55-6); she was popularly accused of licentious conduct before and after her marriage.

50 *Philosopher beyond Newcastle's wife* Margaret Cavendish, wife of he Marquis of Newcastle, a Royalist officer, published several works on natural philosophy.

51 *Archimedes ... put down* outdo the celebrated mathematician and inventor. In ascertaining whether a gold crown contained an alloy of silver, he discovered the theory of specific gravity while bathing, and, according to popular account, ran naked into the street to announce his discovery. For another use of a popular story concerning Archimedes, see *The First Anniversary*, ll. 99-100.

52 *an experiment upon the crown* As Charles II lacked an heir, the children of his brother would be next in line.

53 *engine* device.

57-8 *Crowther . . . Of's Highness Royal Society* Dr Joseph Crowther, chaplain to the Duke of York, had performed the marriage; York was a charter member of the Royal Society.

60 *glassen Dukes* Perhaps, as Margoliouth suggested, a reference to her two children, the Duke of Cambridge and the Duke of Kendal, who died within a month of each other before either had reached the age of four. An epigram, on occasion attributed to Marvell, alludes to their early deaths while commenting on the fact that Lady Margaret Denham who had become York's mistress in 1665 was dead two years later:

Kendal is dead, and Cambridge riding post:
What fitter sacrifice for Denham's ghost.

65–8 *if China clay | Can . . . venomed juice convey, | Or . . . poison . . . of the pacao* Lady Denham died in January 1667, poisoned, it was asserted, with a cup of chocolate. The implication here is that it had been administered by the Duchess of York; see also l. 342.

72 *fawns* the young of an animal.

75 *Sidney's disgrace* Henry Sidney, at this time twenty-six years old and recently dismissed from the Duke of York's service, had been the Duchess's Master of the Horse.

79 *Castlemaine* Barbara Villiers, Countess of Castlemaine, a mistress of Charles II.

98 *in's fob* in his pocket.

102 *Jermyn* Henry Jermyn, the nephew of St Albans (l. 29).

103–4 *Alexander . . . this Campaspe thee, Apelles, give* The celebrated Apelles, requested by Alexander to paint Campaspe naked, became enamoured of her; out of admiration, Alexander gave her to the artist and 'the concubine of a king' became 'the bedfellow of a painter' (Pliny, *Natural History* XXXV. 10, trans. Holland, p. 539).

105–6 *a pair of tables . . . then | The House of Commons clattering like the men* The analogy is made between 'the men' used in the game and the members of the two factions – the Court and the Country – 'clattering' over the question of a general excise (see ll. 130 ff.).

    tables a board used for playing a variety of backgammon (named 'tric-trac' in l. 109).

    In the following identifications of the Members of Parliament, information derives, whenever possible, from the *Flagellum Parliamentarium*, a satirical roll call of 178 MPs compiled in 1671–2 and formerly attributed to Marvell.

114–16 *the cheat Turner . . . | Can strike the die* Sir Edward Turner served as Speaker of the House of Commons from 1661 to 1673.

    to strike the die to throw one of the dice in a cheating fashion.

119 *so too Rubens* The painter served as an envoy to England in 1629–30.

121 *The close Cabal* a small junta of the Privy Council known as 'The Committee for Foreign Affairs'.

126 *Goodrick silence and strike Paston dumb* The two were MPs (Sir John and Sir Robert); the first sometimes acted as teller for the Court party in the 1664–5 session; the second had earlier proposed an enormous appropriation for the war; the reward for this was, according to *FP*, 'worth to him £3000 per annum'.

129 *Hyde's avarice, Bennet's . . .* Henry Hyde, Earl of Clarendon (the Lord Chancellor).

   Bennet's Henry Bennet, Lord Arlington.

131–3 *Excise . . . | A thousand hands she has and thousand eyes* Having agreed to supply the King with the sum of £180,000 to carry on the war with the Dutch, Parliament then split into factions over the means to provide it: the Court party supported an excise on domestic goods (an 'imposition upon consumption', as one MP termed it); among the objections of the Country party was the number of officials required for collecting it, who, it was feared, would enrich themselves at the expense of the people.

136 *cassowar* the cassowary, a long-legged running bird related to the ostrich, noted for devouring whatever it was offered; the Dutch were credited with having introduced the species into Europe.

143 *Black Birch* Colonel John Birch 'marrying a rich widow, got into the House and is now a commissioner in all excises, and is one of the council of trade' (*FP*).

151–4 *Of early wittols . . . Denham . . . did head* See n. to l. 60.

156 *Ashburnham* John, 'he who belonged to the old king' (as Marvell described him, *Letters* II, 60) was an MP for Sussex from 1661 until his expulsion in November 1677. Together with Sir John Berkeley, he had made the arrangements for Charles to escape to the Isle of Wight and then, according to *FP*, 'betrayed' the King.

158 *But know the word* Cf. 'nor asks the word' (*Upon Appleton House*, l. 320).

160 *Stew'rd* Robert, an MP who chaired certain sessions in this Parliament. Though Marvell groups him with the turncoats, he was to make a long speech defining treason in November 1667.

162 *Wood . . . Knight of the Horn and Cane* Sir Henry, Clerk of the Spicery to Charles I (see l. 166), served now as Clerk Comptroller of the Board of Green Cloth and was thus responsible for maintaining order (? Knight of the Cane) in the palace and examining accounts (Margoliouth). The phrase 'horn and corn' was used metaphorically for provisions. Contemporaries remarked on his odd appearance.

167 *headless St Denys* patron saint of France beheaded in 272; according to tradition, he carried his head in his hands for six miles in order to place it at the site where his cathedral was to stand.

168 *both . . . French martyrs* Here, as elsewhere, *French* carries the suggestion of the French disease (syphilis).

169 *as used* as was customary.

170 *Fox* Sir Stephen, 'at the Restoration was made Paymaster to the Guards [see l. 172], where he has cheated £100,000 and is one of the Green Cloth' (*FP*).

173–5 *Progers . . . Brounker – Love's squire.* – Edward, 'a Bedchamber man, not born to a farthing' (*FP*).

Brouncker Henry, also a Gentleman of the Bedchamber, but to the Duke of York; they were both considered procurers for their royal masters. Brouncker was to be expelled from the House in April 1668.

178 *to teal preferring bull* teal . . . bull – a jest, playing on the name of John Bulteel, Clarendon's secretary.

180 *bloated Wren* Matthew, secretary first to Clarendon and then (in 1667) to the Duke of York.

181–2 *Charlton . . . whose coif does awe | The Mitre troop* 'Chief Justice of Chester, and the King's Sergeant' (*FP*).

Mitre a common name for an inn or tavern; cf. *Tom May's Death*, l. 7.

186 *Finch . . . and Thurland* Sir Heneage, Solicitor General (see l. 256), then Attorney General (1670), Lord Keeper (1673), and Lord Chancellor (1675). He was ultimately raised to the peerage as Earl of Nottingham.

Thurland Sir Edward was Solicitor to the Duke of York.

188 *Trelawney's care* Sir Jonathan Trelawney, 'a private forsworn cheat in the Prize Office, with the profit of which he bought the place of the Comptroller to the Duke of York; of the King's Privy Chamber' (*FP*).

193 *For chimney's sake . . . all Sir Pool obeyed* The Chimney or Hearth Money, a very unpopular tax of two shillings levied on the hearths in all houses except cottages, dated from 1662; in October 1666, Humphrey Orme had proposed the sale of this tax as one means of raising the supply. According to *FP* (though not Marvell), Sir Courtenay Pool was 'the first mover for Chimney Money, for which he had the Court thanks but no snip'.

197–8 *Higgons . . . | Mourning his Countess, anxious for his Act* Sir Thomas, a 'poor man's son' (*FP*), a courtier, and, later, an ambassador. The death of his wife, the widow of the Earl of Essex, in 1656 led to his attempt to recover some £4,500 (or £5,550, according to Marvell, *Letters* II, 50) which had been agreed on for her maintenance; the matter was debated in this session to the conclusion that it had been disposed of by Parliament 'in Oliver's time' and so fell under the Act of Oblivion.

199 *Sir Frederick and Sir Solomon* Hyde, sergeant-at-law; and Swale, high sheriff of Yorkshire, a Roman Catholic.

200 *politics* that is, politicians.

203 *Carteret* Sir George, Treasurer of the Navy, exchanged this office for that of Deputy-Treasurer for Ireland at the time the Dutch sailed into the Medway. His credit was sufficiently good so that he could borrow enough money in his own name to keep the fleet abroad during the plague (Margoliouth). See also ll. 343–4.

206 *Talbot* either Sir Gilbert (of Devon) 'The King's Jeweller. A great cheat at bowls and cards' or Sir John (of York), 'Captain in the Guards; an Excise Farmer, Commissioner of Prizes, and a great cheater therein' (*FP*).

207 *Duncombe . . . of the projectors chief* Commissioner of the Ordnance, Sir John, together with the other officers, was to be subjected to a Parliamentary investigation of the naval defeat inflicted by the Dutch; see ll. 609–10; 793–800.

projectors speculators.

208 *old Fitz-harding of the Eaters Beef* Sir Charles Berkeley, second Viscount Fitz-harding (Irish peerage), served as Treasurer of the Household; presumably he was in charge of the Yeoman of the Guard (Margoliouth).

212 *Apsley and Brod'rick . . . hand in hand* both 'Sir Allen'; the former was Treasurer to the Duke of York, the latter, according to *FP*, 'bribe-broker for his master the Chancellor'. Pepys records their arrival in the House 'drunk' on 19 December 1666, where they 'did speak for half an hour together, and could not be either laughed, or pulled, or bid to sit down and hold their peace'.

213–14 *Powell . . . weltering in his stride* 'Gentleman of the Horse to the Duchess of York' (*FP*).

weltering reeling.

218 *Cornb'ry* Henry Hyde, Lord Cornbury, the eldest son of the Lord Chancellor, 'Chamberlain to the Queen . . . had £3000 per annum Crown lands' (*FP*).

221–3 *Not the first cock-horse . . . | To rescue Albemarle from the sea-cod, | Nor the late feather-men, whom Tomkins fierce . . .* The passage is obscure; cock-horse perhaps picks up 'hobby horse' in l. 218.

Albemarle the Duke of, George Monck, General-at-sea, commended in *The Character of Holland*, l. 150.

sea-cod the Dutch.

Tomkins Sir Thomas, who opposed the notion of a standing army (see ll. 841–4), represented perhaps by 'feather-men' (see ll. 593–600, where there is allusion to 'our feathered gallants' in the account of the Dutch break through at Chatham).

225–8 *two Coventry's . . . Hector Harry steers by Will the Wit* the two sons of the Lord Keeper; Henry had just concluded an embassy to Sweden and was to be one of the negotiators of the Treaty of Breda; William, who had just given up his position as secretary to the Duke of York, was Commissioner of the Treasury and of the Navy and supported the concept of a standing army. See also ll. 934–6.

236 *The Speaker* Sir Edward Turner, see ll. 114–16.

245 *Strangeways* Colonel Giles, who represented Dorset; on his death in 1675, Marvell wrote sharply of him to his nephew (*Letters*, II, 319–21), perhaps because he disagreed with him on the matter of toleration (see Milward's *Diary*, p. 207).

249 *Roman Cocles* opposed, single-handedly, the army of Porsenna at the head of a bridge until his companions could cut it down behind him.

255-6 *Temple, conqueror | Of Irish cattle and Solicitor* Sir Richard supported the bill against importing Irish cattle, and in the debate on 5 October 1666 corrected the Solicitor-General (Sir Heneage Finch, l. 186), whose speech in opposition had 'reflected' on some members of the House. The Solicitor-General objected to the term 'nuisance' which became a leitmotif in all subsequent debates (see Milward's *Diary* and Marvell's *Letters*, II, 51).

257-8 *daring Seymour . . . | Had stretched the . . . Patent* Edward, who reported to the House (27 October 1666) the Committee's view that since the Corporation of the Canary Company was monopolistic and destructive of trade, its Patent should be recalled (Milward's *Diary*).

259-60 *Keen Whorwood . . . pierced the giant Mordaunt* Brome Whorwood helped in drawing up articles of misdemeanour against Viscount Mordaunt, Constable of Windsor Castle. On 2 November 1666, William Taylor 'an officer of Windsor' alleged he had been dispossessed because his daughter would not prostitute herself to Mordaunt (Margoliouth).

261 *Williams*] William *Osb.* Identity uncertain. Robbins (Milward's *Diary*) suggests Colonel Henry Williams (alias Cromwell), but his function as the bane of accountants is not established.

262 *Lovelace . . . of chimney-men the cane* John, opposed to the tax on hearths (see l. 193 and n.).

263 *Old Waller, trumpet-general* Edmund, who had initiated the Advice-to-a-Painter genre in English with his panegyric (1666) celebrating the Duke of York's victory in June 1665.

265 *How'rd . . . presumes*] Of birth, state, wit, strength, courage How'rd presumes *1689, Osb., FL.*

265-6 *How'rd . . . wears many Montezumes* Sir Robert; in 1664 he collaborated with Dryden in writing *The Indian-Queen*, the first heroic play (the hero is Montezuma) presented in London; in 1668 he was ridiculed in the character of Sir Positive At-All in Shadwell's *The Sullen Lovers.*

275-6 *Orlando . . . | Broached whole brigades* The hero of Ariosto's poem on one occasion pierces six of his opponents with his spear and then ('As that . . . his shaft may seem too short') strikes so great a blow with it a seventh falls dead (*Orlando Furioso*, tr. Sir John Harington, 1591, IX. 62-3).

287-99 *A gross of English gentry . . . Garway and great Littleton. | Lee* One of the means suggested in the House for raising the supply and one favoured by the Country party was a land tax (passed on 8 November) for a duration of eleven months; William Garway or Garraway (Chichester), Sir Thomas Littleton (Much Wenlock, Salop) and Sir Thomas Lee (Aylesbury) apparently were active in its support. As Margoliouth notes (in connection with John Ayloff's *Britannia and Raleigh*), Lee's name was frequently coupled with that of Garway.

301-2 *Sandys ... | St Dunstan ... tweaking Satan's nose*   Colonel Samuel (Worcester). St Dunstan served as Bishop of Worcester before becoming Archbishop of Canterbury in 959; tempted while at work at a forge by Satan in the guise of a beautiful girl, the monk attacked the Devil with a pair of pincers and forced him to flee.

306   *the Excise receives a total rout*   8 November 1666 (Milward's *Diary*).

313   *seamen's clamour*   In December 1666, the seamen had rioted over their payment, which was by the use of tickets, a system open to many abuses, and on 31 January 1667 a bill was introduced to prevent fighting and disorder at their pay-day (Milward's *Diary*).

327-8   *the loved King ... | Is brought to beg in public*   The House decided on 29 November to sit every day both forenoon and afternoon until 'the King's business was perfected'; on 18 January 1667, he appeared in the House of Lords to address the members (Milward's *Diary*).

336   *The House prorogued*   8 February 1667 until 10 October.

337   *decrepit Aeson*   the father of Jason rejuvenated by Medea's herbal brew to the vigour of forty years.

342   *mortal*   fatal, see ll. 67-8 and n.

345   *the Sad-tree*   a translation of *arbor-tristis*, the Night Jasmine of India, also called the Melancholy-tree.

352   *by hecatombs*   literally, a hundred oxen, used of a public sacrifice.

355   *his new palace*   Clarendon House near St James's (early nicknamed Dunkirk House because of the sale of the city in 1662 to France for some £400,000) was completed only a short time before the Chancellor went into exile.

357   *Buckingham*   George Villiers, the second Duke, together with certain members from the House, supported the Irish Cattle Bill in opposition to Clarendon; on 25 February 1667, he was arrested for treasonable practices.

359   *twelve Commons*   Commissioners appointed to take account of the monies raised for carrying on the war.

360   *roll in vain at Sisyphus's stone*   that is, perform a never-ending still-beginning task; Sisyphus was condemned by Pluto to roll a huge stone up a hill.

361   *braved*   vaunted.

367-8   *The Count ... | To play for Flanders*   St Albans; recalling and punning on the allusion in l. 38.

369-70   *two ambassadors | ... shall beg for peace*   In May 1667 Henry Coventry (see l. 225) and Denzil Holles were sent to Breda to negotiate terms with the Dutch.

377-86   *A punishment ...*   Called the 'Skimmington ride', it was meted out to meek husbands and 'masculine wives'.

397 *designment* enterprise.

398 *Isle of Candy* Canvey Island on the coast of Essex where the Dutch ships penetrated; in l. 402, however, it refers to Candia (Crete), which the Venetians had been defending against the Turks for 'twenty years'.

399 *Bab May ... Arlington* Baptist May, 'Keeper of the Privy Purse, and Pimp General' (*FP*).
    Arlington that is, Henry Bennet, see l. 129 and n.

403–4 *the first year our navy is but shown, | The next divided, and the third we've none* Margoliouth explains (a) in 1665 the navy failed to follow up the advantage of 3 June, occasioning an inquiry; (b) in 1666, the fleet was divided between Albemarle (Monck) and Prince Rupert, the latter arriving on the last day of the battle of the North Foreland (1–4 June); and (c) in 1667 the greater part of it was out of commission.

406 *Pilgrim Palmer* Roger, Earl of Castlemaine, travelled to the Levant after his wife became the King's mistress (see l. 407) and wrote an account of the war between the Venetians and the Turks; this situation, coupled with the fact that he was a Roman Catholic, accounts for the diction of the passage.

408 *Pasiphaë's tomb* in Crete (Candia); Pasiphaë was the wife of Minos and the mother of the Minotaur, also a horned creature.

409 *Morice ... demónstrates, by the post* Sir William served as joint Secretary of State with Arlington, who was also Postmaster-General.

420 *mure up* wall up.

422 *That Mordaunt, new obliged* See ll. 259–60 and n. With the proroguing of Parliament, his impeachment was not effected; on 22 January 1667, Marvell had written that he expected the case to be 'nipped in the bud' (*Letters* II, 52). The case was brought up again (with new charges) in October 1667 (Milward's *Diary*).
    That] *Eng. poet. d. 49*, used as a demonstrative; But *1689* +.

424 *so*] *Eng. poet. d. 49*; to *1689*, *FL*; *Osb. gives both variants*.

425 *The Bloodworth-Chancellor* alluding to the ineffectual conduct of Sir Thomas Bloodworth, the Lord Mayor of London, during the Great Fire ('not to be forgotten for his pissing out the Fire', *A Seasonable Argument* – a continuation, 1677, of *FP*.

431 *Dolman's disobedient* Colonel Thomas Dolman was in command of the Dutch land-troops; he had been ordered (October 1665) to give himself up by a certain day or be attainted of high treason.

435 *prove* try.

437 *De Witt and Ruyter* John de Witt (d. 1672), Grand Pensionary or first minister of the United Provinces.
    Ruyter Michael de Ruyter (d. 1676, see l. 532 where he is spoken of as old), Dutch admiral.

441 *near relation* as a result of his connection with Queen Henrietta Maria.

442 *character* credentials.

450 *Harry Excellent* Coventry, see ll. 369–70 and n.

454 *as the look adultery* 'implies' understood. 'Whosoever looketh on a woman to lust after her hath committed adultery with her already in his heart' (Matt. v 28).

457 *Presbyter Holles* Denzil, see n. to ll. 369–70.

460 *infecta re* with the matter unfinished.

461 *ordered*] *Osb., FL*; order *Eng. poet. d. 49, 1689*.

463–4 *The Dutch . . . commandment*] *not in Eng. poet. d. 49.*
     shent blamed.
     eleventh commandment see l. 454.

468 *None but himself must choose the King a Queen* The Privy Council had assessed a variety of choices for King Charles before the selection of Catherine of Braganza.

470 *That summons up the Parliament again* It met 25 and 29 July (1667) though it had been prorogued until 10 October (see l. 336 and n.).

471 *banned* cursed.

475 *then . . . him*] *Osb.*; in . . . he *Eng. poet. d. 49, 1689, FL*.

480 *To raise a two-edged army* Twelve infantry regiments and many troops of horse were mustered, but at the 25–29 July session, Sir Thomas Tomkins (see l. 223 and n.) expressed the fears of the House at the prospect of a standing army, and their disbanding was requested (see ll. 841–4).

488 *Myrmidons* originated as ants and then were changed to men; the term was often used in the period for 'hired ruffians'.

494 *banquiers banquerout* bankrupt bankers (with the suggestion of legal irregularities).

496 *sacramental* outwardly symbolic.
     wart here syphilitic wart (found near the 'yard' or phallus).

497 *Horse-leeches . . . at the hem'rrhoid vein* Cf.:

Sure England hath the hemerrhoids, and these
On the north postern of the patient seize,
Like leeches (Cleveland, *The Rebel Scot*, 1644, ll. 83–5).

499 *The kingdom's farm* farming of taxes.

502 *confiscate* 'Becomes' understood.

503 *scrip* (a) satchel and (b) scrap of paper.

513 *for nothing ill, like ashen wood* Cf. Spenser, 'the ash for nothing ill' (*FQ*, I, i, 9).

514 *Herb John* St John's wort.

518 *Monck* Albemarle, see l. 222 and n.

521-2 *the independent troops would close,* | *And ... his place dispose* See l. 480 and n.

527 *vain* futile.

547 *Aeolus* ruler of the winds.

550 *Sheppey Isle* at the mouth of the Thames.

560 *at Sheerness unloads its stormy sides* The Dutch having sailed up to Canvey Island (Candy) on 10 June, then returned to Sheppey where they bombarded Sheerness on the northwest of the island.

561 *Spragge* Sir Edward, a vice-admiral in command at Sheerness.

566 *bullet showers*] *Eng. poet. d. 49, 1689*; bullets showers *Osb.*, *FL*; a difficult reading – perhaps the intention is 'the cannon pours ... and [the] bullet showers'; perhaps 'bullet-showers' is used as the object of *pours*.

572 *Chatham* The chief navy arsenal, protected by a boom ('frail chain', l. 586).

581 *untack* detach.

600 *Cornb'ry* See l. 218 and n.

605 *Duncombe and ... Legge* See l. 207 and n.; William Legge was the Lieutenant-General of the Ordnance.

607 *Upnor Castle* Located two miles below Chatham, the castle was used as a military fortification, but at the time inadequately supplied with munitions.

611 *Royal Charles* As the largest vessel of the fleet (with 80 guns), it was the 'British Admiral' (l. 615); on this occasion it was captured by 'a sorry boat and six men'. In 1660 it had brought the King to Dover.

616 *their* referring to Monck and the ship.

631 *Daniel* Sir Thomas, apparently in charge of protecting one of the three ships fired by the Dutch.

636 *lac* crimson pigment (also called lake).

647-8 *unsinged ...* | *Like Shadrack, Mechack, and Abednego* Three companions of Daniel who refused to worship a golden image and were thrown into a fiery furnace by Nebuchadnezzar – 'upon whose bodies the fire had no power, nor was an hair of their head singed' (Dan. iii 27).

649 *brave Douglas* Archibald Douglas commanded a company of Scots, first in the French service (see l. 655) and then in England.

654 *Nor other courtship knew* Douglas was, in fact, married to the daughter of Andrew, seventh Baron Gray.

662 *at those that run away* In the later investigation, it was reported that of '800 men in pay for the King's service at Chatham, scarce twelve men were to be found there' (Milward's *Diary*).

663-4 *Nor other fear ... | Then, lest heaven fall ere thither he ascend* an assertion made by the Adriatic Celts to Alexander the Great (Strabo, *Geography* VII. 3. 8, cited by Margoliouth).

666 *birding* taking aim.

669 *The fatal bark* the *Royal Oak*.

691 *relics* bodily remains.

693-4 *Fortunate boy ... if my verse can propagate thy name* adapted from *Aen.* IX, 446-7; the promise was presumably fulfilled in *The Loyal Scot*.

695 *Oeta and Alcides* Alcides (Hercules), wearing the fatal shirt of Nessus, was brought to Mount Oeta where he intended to sacrifice himself on a blazing pyre but was then snatched to heaven in a thundercloud.

698 *The Loyal London now a third time burns* A man-of-war, the *London* was blown up in 1665; then the Great Fire destroyed the (loyal) city of London in 1666, and now in 1667 the *Loyal London* (a replacement for the earlier man-of-war) was one of the ships fired by the Dutch.

702 *the ships ... were taught to dive* Some were sunk so as not to be burned. Cf. *Mourning*, l. 30.

712 *Our merchantmen ... we drown* in order to stop the Dutch from penetrating to London.

715 *hole* hold.

722 *least navigable* 'where' understood.

735-6 *the feared Hebrew ... | Was ... the public scorn* 'And they called for Samson out of the prison house; and he made them sport' (Judges xvi 25).

747-50 *since first that happy pair was wed ...* Recounted by Spenser *FQ*, IV. xi.

761-2 *The court in farthing ... | And female Stuart there rules the four seas* Before her marriage in 1667 to the Duke of Richmond (l. 764), Frances Stuart was sought after by Charles II. She is reported to have served as the model for Britannia on certain coins, one of which, the farthing, carried the words *Quattuor maria vindico* (Margoliouth).

767 *All our miscarriages on Pett must fall* Peter Pett was the Commissioner of the Navy at Chatham. On 13 November the House drew up an impeachment ('for many high crimes and misdemeanours'); according to Milward (p. 108), Marvell had earlier spoken against returning him to the Tower where he had been ordered on 17 June following the Dutch attack.

771 *Who would not follow when the Dutch were beat* that is, follow up the advantage obtained in 1665. An inquiry in 1667-8 into the several 'miscarriages' of the war reflected on the Duke of York and Henry Brouncker, who was expelled from the House.

772 *Who treated out the time at Bergen* In 1665 also the English under Edward Montague, the Earl of Sandwich, had opportunity to attack a flotilla of Dutch ships from the East Indies in the neutral port of Bergen but let slip the advantage.

775 *prevented* anticipated.

776 *The fleet divided, writ for Rupert* The matter of the division of the fleet in 1666 between Monck and Prince Rupert, which left Monck alone to battle the Dutch in the Downs while Rupert was sailing to meet a rumored French attack, became one of the major aspects of the Parliamentary investigation of the miscarriages of the war. For other of the misdemeanours, see Milward's *Diary*, particularly pp. 89-93.

782 *Landguard . . . Gravesend* Landguard a fort at Harwich, also attacked by the Dutch in June 1667; Gravesend, a few miles from Chatham.

784 *Fanatic Pett* so-called because he had been a master shipwright at Chatham (see l. 785) during the Commonwealth and was credited with preserving the ships from revolting in 1648. The term was applied to sectarians.

793-4 *Southampton dead . . . much . . . fell to Duncombe's share* As a result of the death of Thomas Wriothesley, Earl of Southampton, in May 1667, the Treasury was put in a commission which included Sir John Duncombe (see l. 207 and n.), at a period, as Margoliouth notes, antecedent to the Dutch attack and the English 'miscarriages'.

797 *petre* saltpetre, used in gunpowder, alluding to his connection with the Ordnance.

799 *corn* grain of gunpowder.

801 *no chimneys, to give all is best* alluding to the Hearth tax and the matter of supply.

805 *in's brother May* the Keeper of the Privy Purse (see l. 399) was Duncombe's brother-in-law.

811 *Grave Primate Sheldon* the Archbishop of Canterbury who had a reputation for anything but 'grave' behaviour; see the allusion in l. 813 to the two court ladies Katherine Boynton and Jane Middleton.

816 *Convocation* assembly of the Clergy, organized like Parliament.

817 *De Ruyter*] *Osb., FL*; Ruyter *Eng. poet. d. 49, 1689.* three syllables required for the metre, though Marvell uses the form 'Ruyter' elsewhere.

820 *Harry* Coventry who had been negotiating a treaty at Breda (see ll. 369-70).

826 *Let them come up so to go down again* 'the MPs' understood. The proroguing of the House at its second meeting, 29 July, Milward reports, 'was not pleasing and satisfactory to all men'.

828 *vest* a long cassock designed by King Charles.

833 *adust* seared, a term from the doctrine of the humours.

837 *Turner* the Speaker, see l. 114 and n.

840 *And for three days thence moves them to adjourn* reporting the King's pleasure that the House should adjourn until Monday (29 July).

841 *Tomkins* See l. 223 and n.

846 *And long as cider lasts in Hereford* Tomkins was MP for Weobley, Hereford.

854 *Expects . . . till Turner's dressed* 'The Speaker came not until almost an hour after the King was come to the House of Lords' (Milward's *Diary*).
expects awaits.

855 *Ayton* Sir John, Gentleman Usher of the Black Rod to the House of Lords.

858 *Nor gave the Commons leave to say their prayers* 'We had not time to have prayers nor did I see the Chaplain' (Milward's *Diary*).

866 *mace's brain* alluding to the sceptre carried by the sergeant-at-arms and placed before the Speaker as a symbol of the authority of the House.

872 *a poll bill does like his apron look* Part of the supply was raised by a poll bill, the text presumably as spotted as a cook's apron.

882 *Norfolk* James, Sergeant-at-arms.

883–4 *Chanticleer . . . Pertelotte* the cock and 'Dame Partlet' the hen of Chaucer's tale.

889 *calm horror* Cf. the use of the phrase 'horror calm' to describe the period between day and night (*Upon Appleton House*, l. 671).

907 *startling* starting.

916 *with blue streaks infect the taper clear* indicative that a ghost is present; cf. *Richard III* V. iii. 179–80.

918 *grandsire Harry* father of Henrietta Maria, Henry IV had been assassinated in 1610.

927–8 *Castlemaine . . . / Bennet, and Coventry* opponents of the Lord Chancellor; see ll. 79, 129, and 225 and nn.

933 *False to his master Bristol, Arlington* formerly in the service of George Digby, second Earl of Bristol.

934–5 *Coventry . . . / who to the brother, brother would betray* in his former capacity as secretary to the Duke of York.

942 *Pett* a scapegoat, as in ll. 767–84.

944 *Poetic picture, painted poetry* Cf. *In the French Translation of Lucan*.

951 *please*] Eng. poet. d. 49, 1689, *FL*; press *Osb*.

968 *to isle our Monarch* Cf. 'isles the astonished cattle', *Upon Appleton House*, l. 472.

981–2 *The smallest vermin ... | And a poor warren once a city rased* Among beasts of warren are hares, conies, and roes. Pliny includes a short chapter (*Natural History* VIII. 29) describing 'the hurt and damage' coming from 'small contemptible creatures, which otherwise are of no reckoning and account' (trans. Holland, p. 212).

    vermin various wild beasts other than game.

THE LOYAL SCOT

Incorporating nearly fifty lines from the earlier *Last Instructions*, *The Loyal Scot* was probably written some two years after it. Of the new material, one topic deals with the desirability of a Parliamentary union between England and Scotland, a subject, as Margoliouth noted, under discussion in 1669–70; a second topic deals with the misdeeds of the Anglican clergy. Doubt that this latter portion is Marvell's has been expressed on several grounds: its mordant tone (equally illustrated in the early satires, in *The Last Instructions*, and in *The First Anniversary*, particularly ll. 311–20); its disruption of structural balance (though the conclusion has point only in terms of the preceding anti-clerical lines); and, generally, its 'unMarvellian' quality (a subjective matter).

The manuscript version in *Eng. poet. d. 49* not only includes this anti-prelatical section but represents the longest version so far discovered. Two other manuscripts (*Bod. Douce 357* and *B M Sloane 655*), both representing the longer version of the poem, lack any authorial ascription.

Early publication of the poem includes a curtailed version in *Chorus Poetarum*, 1694 (misdated 1674), a collection assembled by Charles Gildon (editions in 1696, 1698 with new title pages), which ascribes the poem to Marvell, and the undated pamphlet including *The Last Instructions* (see introductory note to that poem) in the Free Library of Philadelphia, which seems to antedate the printing of it in the 1697 edition of the *State Poems*. In both the undated pamphlet and the *State Poems*, Marvell's initials appear at the end of the poem. Its appearance in the latter publication is not by itself to be relied on as a guarantee of Marvell's authorship; but the incorporation of the lines from *The Last Instructions* in all versions provides strong presumptive evidence that the poem is indeed Marvell's, particularly when taken in conjunction with its appearance in *Eng. poet. d. 49*.

The title takes its point from a satire written by John Cleveland in 1644 entitled *The Rebel Scot*. Framing the poem is the concept that Cleveland has been elected in the Elysian Fields to do penance for that work by extolling a *loyal* Scot – a device Marvell used earlier in *Tom May's Death* (where Ben Jonson's new judgement of May similarly serves as a kind of retraction). The denunciation of the Anglican clergy is thus voiced by the Royalist poet who had earlier denounced the opposition of the Scottish Presbyterians to Charles I.

Eng. poet. d. 49 provides the copy-text; only departures from it or significant variants are recorded.

title] *as in Sloane 655; others vary slightly, notably the omission of* By Cleveland's Ghost *Douce 357; addition of* Being a Recantation of his Former Satire Entitled The Rebel Scot *1694.*

9 *tumour of his vein* alluding to Cleveland's predilection for 'turgid two-foot words'.

12 *Lethe* the river from which all who entered the underworld drank, the waters cancelling the unhappy memories of their life on earth.

14–15 *As of his satire this had been a part. | Not so brave Douglas . . .* Incorporated in this framework, the lines from *The Last Instructions* now serve as an extension of *The Rebel Scot* and Cleveland's recantation.

15–16 *Not so brave Douglas . . .*] *Douce 357, Sloane 655,* and *1694,* except for minor lapses, accord with *Eng. poet. d. 49,* which has slightly modified the earlier version; for this passage *FL* refers the reader to the text of *The Last Instructions* which precedes it; *1697,* though printing the passage, follows the same version as *FL.*

See the annotations to *The Last Instructions,* pp. 291–2, for these lines.

19 *shady*] yellow *FL, 1697, from The Last Instructions.*

22 *those*] his *FL, 1697, from The Last Instructions.*

27 *the*] that *FL, 1697, from The Last Instructions.*

56 *As one . . . bed*] As one that's warmed himself and went to bed *FL, 1697,* which (except for the substitution of *went* for *gone*) follows *The Last Instructions.*

59–60 *if e'er my verse may claim | That matchless grace to*] if either pencil's fame | Or if my verse can *FL, 1697,* which follows *The Last Instructions.*

63–4 *Skip-saddles Pegasus . . . | Sometimes the Gall'way proves the better nag* These two lines are not in *1694.*
Skip-saddles flighty.
Gall'way a small-sized horse peculiar to southwest Scotland.

67–8 *Curtius brave | . . . closed up the gaping cave* Arrayed in full armour and mounted on his horse, Curtius leaped into a chasm in the Forum, an act which caused it to fill up and symbolized the surrender of arms and strength for the perpetuation of the commonwealth.

70 *hunt of Chevy Chase* recounting the rivalry of Percy and the Douglas against the background of the national quarrel between Scotland and England.

71–2 *Corinthian metal . . . thy colossus frame* The colossal statue of Apollo spanning the port at Rhodes was of bronze, one of the seven wonders of the world. *Sloane 655* adds: 'Shall fix a foot on either neighbouring shore | And join the land that seemed to part before'.

79 *bounder* boundary, as in *The First Anniversary,* l. 281.

79–84 *Will you the Tweed . . .*] not in *Douce 357, Sloane 655.*

92 *Holy Island* Lindisfarne.

93–100 *Nothing but clergy . . .*] *not in 1694.*

96 *Deliver us* echoing the line 'Good Lord deliver us' from the Litany.

97–8 *Never shall Calvin pardoned be for Sales, | For Becket's sake Kent always shall have tails* St Francis de Sales (d. 1622; canonized 1665) tried forceful conversion of the reformed inhabitants around the area of Geneva, even attempting to convert the aged Beza (not Calvin) by bribery.

That Kentishmen had tails was proverbial (see Tilley, K17); Margoliouth connects the allusion with the story of Thomas Becket's having effectively pronounced a curse on the children of Strood after they had cut off his horse's tail.

Douce 357, Sloane 655, FL, 1697 introduce a line between these two: 'Never for Burnet's sake the Lauderdales'. It would be the only instance of a triple rhyme in Marvell's poetry.

99 *Who sermons e'er can pacify and prayers* who can ever reconcile sermons with the Book of Common Prayer.

100 *to the joined stools reconcile the chairs* 'Joined stools' were used in Scottish churches.

    chairs episcopal seats.

    There is punning in the next fifteen lines on ecclesiastical terms: sees–seas; aisles–isles, surcingle–zone.

101–8 *Though kingdoms join . . .*] *not in Douce 357, Sloane 655*; ll. 101–4 only are in *1694*, which then omits ll. 105–238.

102 *mitre* bishop's headdress.

103 *Rogation-week* the week in which Ascension Day falls, devoted to prayers and fasting.

111 *surcingle* a girdle used to tie a cassock.

115–16 *like Mah'met tear the moon, | And slip one half into his sleeve as soon* Asked to confirm his mission by cleaving the moon in two, Mahomet summoned it; after making seven circuits, the moon came to the prophet, entered his right sleeve and came out the left; it next entered his collar, descended to his skirt and then split in sunder.

115–236] *not in 1697.*

117 *Hocus* short for Hocus Pocus, the name assumed by a juggler in the time of James I who used a sham formula to hide his tricks; the term became generic for a conjuror. Cf. Cleveland's own use of the allusion in *The Rebel Scot*, ll. 25–6.

119–20 *had bishops come, | Pharaoh at first would have sent Israel home* based on Ex. vii and imitating Cleveland's most popular lines: 'Had Cain been Scot, God would have changed his doom, | Not forced him wander, but confined him home' (ll. 63–4).

126 *runnet* variant of rennet, an activating agent used in making cheese; used metaphorically to suggest a bawd.

132 *to be by clergy saved* an ironic play on the notion of 'benefit of clergy' or 'to be saved by the book' – with enough 'Clerkship' or ability to read 'to save them from Hanging' (*The Rehearsal Transpros'd*, Smith, p. 4).

135–6 *like Lot's wife . . . pillars too of salt* When Lot and his family were escaping the destruction of Sodom and Gomorrah, 'his wife looked back from behind him, and she became a pillar of salt' (Gen. xix 26).

138 *A bishopric . . . a great Sine-cure* *beneficium sine cure*, a benefice without cure of souls.

142 *their curates, text* It is the curates who assume the task of preaching.

143–4 *No bishop? . . . no king, no people, no* 'No bishop, no king', a declaration of James I.

146 *Aaron cast calves, but Moses them calcines* When Aaron, Moses' brother and assistant, cast the image of the golden calf, Moses 'burnt it in the fire and ground it to powder and strawed it upon the water' (Ex. xxxii 20).

147–80] *not in FL.*

149 *That power alone can loose this spell that ties* a typical Marvellian inversion – that power that binds alone can loose this spell.

152 *Fish and flesh bishops are your ambigue* echoing the proverb (Tilley, F319) 'Neither flesh nor fish'.
  ambigue an entertainment where the main dishes and dessert are served at the same time.

154 *when in commendam* beneficed; '*dare in commendam*' to give in trust, used especially of a benefice.

156 *These Templar Lords exceed the Templar Knights* these spiritual lords exceed those who were members of the medieval religious and military order founded to protect the Holy Sepulchre in Jerusalem; they came to be noted not only for their wealth, but also for their hard drinking and other vices as well.

157 *baron-prelate* lord bishop.

158 *Leviathan . . . and behemóth* in Milton's phrase 'Leviathan / Hugest of living creatures' and 'Behemoth biggest born of earth' (*PL* VII, 412, 471); the former term was used metaphorically of the Devil, and the two beasts commonly linked.

161 *flamen* heathen priest, as used by Geoffrey of Monmouth and subsequently in an English context.

162 *foúr* dissyllabic as in *The Nymph Complaining*, l. 70, and *Upon Appleton House*, l. 323.

164 *Arius stands at th' Athanasian Creed* Arius, a heretic (who denied that Christ was consubstantial with God); the Athanasian Creed was a part of the Book of Common Prayer.

169 *Seth's pillars* Knowing of the coming destruction of the world by fire and water, the descendants of Seth preserved the knowledge that had been acquired on pillars of brick and of stone, so that if the former were destroyed, the latter would endure. The topical allusion, as Margoliouth notes, is probably to Seth Ward, Bishop of Salisbury, who directed much energy to the persecution of dissenters.

171 *Gilbert's tiles* alluding to the Sheldonian Theatre (see l. 180) constructed at Oxford at the expense of the Archbishop, Gilbert Sheldon.

tiles] *Eng. poet. d. 49*; toils *Douce 357*; smiles *Sloane 655*.

175 *Abbot missed bucks, but Sheldon ne'er missed doe* George Abbot, Archbishop of Canterbury (d. 1633) accidentally killed a gamekeeper when shooting; though King James observed that none but a fool or a knave would think the worse of a man for such an incident, the case became a *cause célèbre*.

176 *whiter than his Snow* Margoliouth suggests this refers to Ralph Snow, apparently a member of Archbishop's Sheldon's household.

182 *smutty stories* story refers to a sculpture (or painting) representing a historical subject.

smutty (a) dusky and (b) obscene.

187–8 *apocryphal ... Bel | ... does dragon swell* The apocryphal Bel and the Dragon tells the story (vv. 23–42) of Daniel's putting the Babylonian dragon to death without sword or staff by throwing a ball made of hair, pitch, and fat into its throat, an act which so enraged the people Daniel was forthwith cast into a den of lions.

These lines are not in *FL*. Douce 357 here inserts (188. 1–8) an English version of the epigram *Bludius et Corona* (see p. 213). Though both versions of the epigram may be Marvell's, they deal with a notorious incident of May 1671, and would thus be of later composition than *The Loyal Scot*.

189–90 *that Scotch two-headed man | With single body* Drummond of Hawthornden describes the freakish creature born in Glasgow during the reign of James IV: 'sitting they seemed two men to such who saw not the parts beneath, and standing it could not be discerned to which of the two bulks above, the thighs and legs did appertain. They had differing passions and diverse wills, often chiding others for disorder in their behaviour and actions, after much deliberation embracing that unto which they both consented.' 'By the king's direction', they were carefully brought up and instructed in music (see l. 202) and foreign languages (*The History of Scotland*, 1655, p. 134).

195–6 *But now ... perks up cheek by jowl*] not in *Douce 357*.

197 *Parnassus* the two-headed (δικόρυφος) mountain, one peak sacred to Apollo, the other to Dionysus.

205 *moot* plead their case.

208 *jus divinum* divine right.

211 *like chemists fixing mercury* like alchemists solidifying mercury by adding another substance.

215–18 *'Tis necessary . . . is indifferent*] the order of these lines varies in the other texts; two lines – 'to conform necessary, or be shent, / But to reform is all indifferent' – are added in *FL, Douce 357, Sloane 655*; ll. 217–18 *not in Douce 357, Sloane 655.*

219 *rebabel Paul's* For other allusive uses of the story of the Tower of Babel, see *The Character of Holland*, l. 21 and *Upon Appleton House*, l. 24.

221 *Lambeth* Archbishop of Canterbury, from the site of his palace in London.

230 *postern* See Cleveland's use of the term, cited in notes to *The Last Instructions*, l. 497.

232 *Phlegeton* the fiery river in Hades.

237–8 *such a bias strong . . . ne'er had missed the mark* The diction is taken from the game of bowls.

249–50 *a shibboleth – / Where a mistaken accent causes death* 'Then said [Jephthah] unto [the Ephraimite], say now, shibboleth: and he said sibboleth: for he could not frame to pronounce it right. Then they took him, and slew him at the passages of Jordan: and there fell at that time of the Ephraimites, forty and two thousand' (Judges xii 6).

253 *with a female spite* Cf. the use of the same phrase in *To . . . Mr Richard Lovelace*, l. 43.
   men] *1694, FL, 1697, Douce 357; man Eng. poet. d. 49, Sloane 655.*

264 *'tis all but cross and pile* *cross*, from the side of a coin carrying its impress, gave rise to the proverb (Tilley, C835)
   cross and pile heads or tails.

272 *comb-case* a comb with no honey.

280 *The hare's head against the goose giblets set* proverbial (Tilley, H161) for tit for tat, explicated in the reading, 'My fault against my recantation set' *1694, 1697.*

INSCRIBENDA LUPARAE

These six distichs on the Louvre, first published in the Folio, apparently were written in 1671 or 1672 in response to Louis XIV's offer of a prize for the best verses celebrating the completing of its façade, a situation which explains the several versions. (See E. E. Duncan-Jones, *TLS*, 26 April 1957, p. 257).

2 *Escuriale ingens uritur* In June 1671, the Escorial caught fire and burned for ten days.

11 *geminae Jani portae* The gates of the temple of Janus were closed in time of peace and open in time of war. See also Marvell's use of the allusion in *In Legationem Domini Oliveri St John*, l. 10.

ON MR MILTON'S 'PARADISE LOST'

Written probably in the early summer of 1674, Marvell's verses commending *Paradise Lost* appeared as one of two tributes in the second edition of Milton's poem (entered 6 July). (He had earlier included a defense of 'J. M.' in the Second Part of *The Rehearsal Transpros'd* [1673, Smith, pp. 311–13]). In his rhymed tribute Marvell adopts the Miltonic style in the first ten lines and then alludes in the final lines to Milton's strictures against rhyme, thus turning his own example into a compliment. These verses were later reprinted in the Folio with minor variants.

2 *slender book . . . vast design*   The first edition (1667) comprised ten not twelve books.

6 *misdoubting*   having misgivings about.

7 *ruin*   reduce.

9 *So Sampson groped . . .*   alluding to *Samson Agonistes* which had appeared in 1671.

15 *perplexed*   complicated.

18–22 *some less skilful hand . . .*   alluding to Dryden's heroic opera *The Fall of Angels and Men in Innocence* which, although it was licensed 17 April 1674, was not published until 1677. According to John Aubrey, Dryden had asked Milton's permission to put his epic into rhyme and had been given leave 'to tag' his verses (see l. 50).

25 *that*] *Eng. poet. d. 49*; and *1674, F*. This reading points up the allusion to Dryden's having stopped publication of his opera.

33 *treat'st*] *1674*; treats *Eng. poet. d. 49, F.*

36–7 *Thou sing'st with so much gravity and ease; | And above human flight dost soar aloft*   recalling Milton's 'adventurous song, / That with no middle flight intends to soar / . . . while it pursues / Things unattempted yet . . .' (I, 13–16).

39–40 *The bird named from that paradise . . . | So never flags, but always keeps on wing*   Among the several 'fictions' relating to the Birds of Paradise, Francis Willoughby reports (*Ornithology*, 1678, p. 90) that 'they flew perpetually without any intermission, and took no rest but on high in the air'.

43 *Just heaven thee, like Tiresias*   recalling Milton's allusion to certain 'prophets old' – Teresias and Phineus – 'Those other two equalled with me in fate, / So were I equalled with them in renown' (III, 33–4).

45 *mightst*] *1674, Eng. poet. d. 49*; might *F.*

46 *With tinkling rhyme*   alluding to Milton's comments on the 'jingling sound of like endings' in his prefatory remarks on 'The Verse' of *Paradise Lost*.

thine] *Eng. poet. d. 49*; thy *1674, F.*

47 *Town-Bayes* Dryden, who had been glanced at in the Duke of Buckingham's farcical comedy *The Rehearsal* (1672) in the character of Bayes.

49 *bushy points* tagged or tasselled laces used for attaching the hose to the doublet.

50 *tag* supply rhyme to prose or blank verse.

51 *I too, transported by the mode, offend* alluding to Milton's comment ('The Verse') on 'some famous modern poets, carried away by custom'.

52 *must commend* because of the exigency of his rhyme.

54 *In number, weight, and measure* echoing Wisdom xi 20, 'thou hast ordered all things in measure, and number, and weight'.

ILLUSTRISSIMO VIRO DOMINO LANCELOTO JOSEPHO DE MANIBAN

The hyperbolical tone of this verse letter emphasizes a mocking intent. The identity of the recipient and the date of composition are unknown; Margoliouth, following Legouis ('Marvell's Maniban,' *RES* II (1926), 328–35), would date it circa 1676.

7 *Bellerophonteas ... tabellas* Bellerophon was himself the bearer to the king of Lycia of 'deadly characters' intended to cause his own death.

8 *spiritus intus agit* a Virgilian reminiscence – 'spiritus intus alit ... mens agitat' (*Aen.* VI, 726–7).

15 *cautus aruspex* a priest who derived omens from observing all aspects of a sacrifice, including the entrails of the victim.

19–24 *Distribuit ...* He interprets the influence of the zodiacal signs and of the various constellations.

32 *Sibylla* The celebrated Cumaean sibyl recorded her prophecies on leaves which the wind frequently disturbed, thus confusing their sense. See *Upon Appleton House*, l. 577 for another Marvellian usage.

42–4 *Naupliada credam te Palamede ...* Palamedes, the ingenious son of Nauplius, was credited with the addition to the Greek alphabet of variously specified letters after observing the flight of cranes and with having regulated the year by the sun and the twelve months by the moon.

    English title 'To That Renowned Man ...' The term 'graphologist' did not come into use until the nineteenth century.

APPENDIX I

AD REGEM CAROLUM PARODIA

This *parodia* or countersong in sapphics, a very close adaptation of Horace's *Carmina* I, 2, represents Marvell's earliest published work. It appeared, together with the Greek verses that follow, in a congratulatory volume addressed to King Charles by members of the University of Cambridge on occasion of the birth of the Princess Anne: *Συνωδία sive Musarum Cantabrigiensium Concentus et Congratulatio*. The allusion to the plague (*pestis*), which Marvell uses in place of Horace's harsh snows and hail (*nivis atque dirae | grandines*) gives a *terminus a quo* of November 1636 when the University was forced to suspend its activities, while ll. 41–4 show that the poem was composed before the royal birth on 17 March 1637 since the sex of the child was as yet undetermined. Marvell was then sixteen years of age. Among his fellow contributors were Richard Crashaw, Abraham Cowley, Joseph Beaumont (author of *Psyche*), and Edward King (commemorated in Milton's *Lycidas*).

13 *Chamum* the Cam and the Granta (l. 17) refer to the two streams that form the river in Cambridge.

22 *Turcae* a reference to the pirates of Sallee (Margoliouth), corresponding to Horace's *Medes*.

33 *Erycina nostra* Queen Henrietta Maria.

45–9 *Serus . . . Tollat* These lines show how closely Marvell followed his original, making a change here of only one word – *populo Britanno*: British people.

51 *reparare*] *Cooke +*; reparato *1637*; cf. Horace's *equitare*.

Πρὸς Κάρολον τὸν βασιλέα

Written for the same occasion as *Ad Regem Carolum Parodia*, this is the only surviving example of Marvell's Greek verse.

footnotes Since the Princess Anne was the *fifth* royal child, Marvell added the sidenotes to account for this charge that the number has its hateful aspects, referring first to the Gunpowder Plot (5 November 1605) and then to the Gowrie Conspiracy (5 August 1605).

5 Εἰλείθυια Ilithyia, the Greek goddess of childbirth (Roman Lucina).

DIGNISSIMO SUO AMICO DOCTORI WITTY

These commendatory verses were first published in 1651 in the translation entitled *Popular Errors or The Errors of the People in Matter of Physic* by his friend Robert Witty. For the English verses composed for the same occasion, see p. 62.

2 *Saepia* the cuttle fish which produces a black ink.

3 *preli* an oil or wine press, used here for printing press.

4 *hydra* a nine-headed monster capable of regenerating two heads when one was cut off.
    pressa est] *F*; premitur *1651*, a revision apparently for the sake of the pun.

5   *Anticyris*   the name of two ancient towns noted for their production of 'sharp hellebore' (l. 10).

7   *India*   the West Indies.

10   *Acri*] Cooke +; acci *1651*, F.

11   *olidas libris fumare popinas*   as they are used to light tobacco.

HORTUS

This companion piece to *The Garden* in dactylic hexameters expands on the English poem by adding significant details, specifying, for example, the trees which are to have their names carved on their barks in place of that of a mistress and adding to the classical allusions.

There are several misprints in the Folio printing; *Eng. poet. d. 49* corrects all but two of these and, more importantly, provides a substitute reading for l. 44 which points up the rhetorical structure of the passage.

2   *simplicis herbae*   perhaps the crown of grass awarded to a general who relieved an army under siege; the English poem substitutes oak, the reward for civic achievement.

29   *Neaera, Chloe, Faustina, Corinna*   except for Faustina, stock names used in pastoral and love poetry.

36   *Cytherea*   Venus.

38   *defervescente tyranno*   Sexual love is allayed, symbolized by Cupid's inverted torch (l. 34).

44   *Dum Veneri myrtis Marti dum*] *Eng. poet. d. 49*; Nec Veneris Mavors meminit si F.

52   *candidior*   In contrast to the 'milder' sun of the English.

53   *truci Tauro, stricto pro forcipe Cancri*   actual signs of the zodiac contrasted with the floral signs.

55–6   *apis, mellito intenta labori,* | *Horologo sua pensa thymo signare videtur*   a reminiscence of Horace (IV, 2, 27–9):
apis Mantinae
more modoque
grata carpentis thyma per laborem. . . .
To an English reader, an explicit pun on thyme-time.

ROS

The English counterpart of the poem is on page 102.
17–20   *Qualis inexpertam . . .*   This comparison is omitted from the English, though the effect is rendered by the line in *On a Drop of Dew* 'Trembling lest it grow impure' (l. 16).

26 *toros*] *Cooke* +; thoros *F.*

28 *Tyria veste, vapore Sabae* towns famous for purple dye and myrrh and frankincense.

42 *Hic*] *Eng. poet. d.49*; hinc *F.*

42 *Translation* The translators, though alleging they do not know what the line means, render it as follows: 'Leaving in an instant, it speeds to its goal.' Ll. 33-6 of *On a Drop of Dew* serve to express ll. 39-42.

APPENDIX 2

[BLOOD AND THE CROWN]

This epigram in its two forms may be dated shortly after the attempt made by Colonel Thomas Blood, dressed in clerical garb, to steal the crown from the Tower of London in May 1671. The English version was inserted (sometime after this date) in *The Loyal Scot* in *Bod. Douce 357* (ll. 188. 1-8), and it appears as a separate epigram in the *State Poems*, 1697, attributed to Marvell; there are three other manuscript copies of it (*BM Harleian 7315*, where it is attributed to Marvell in a hand other than the copyist's; *BM Sloane 3413*; and *BM Add. MSS. 18220*). The Latin has been copied in *Bod. Douce 357* and in *BM Sloane 3413* where it is attributed to Marvell. Both versions of the epigram are included in *Eng. poet. d. 49*. The evidence of the manuscripts suggests that the two versions are probably Marvell's.

The copy-text is *Eng. poet. d. 49*; the manuscripts have unimportant variants which have not been recorded.

1 *his rents to have regained* The motive for the theft was that at the Restoration Blood had been deprived of his estates in Ireland.

6 *spared the Keeper's life* Though the Keeper (Edwards) was first bound and then stabbed, the result was not fatal. Two months later, Blood was pardoned by the King and his lands restored.

8 *bishop's cruelty* Cf 'prelate's rage' in *Bermudas* l. 12.

Index of Titles

Index of First Lines

Penguin Critical Anthologies

Pelican Biographies

Penguin Modern Poets

Penguin Modern European Poets